T0150236

DAY HIKES IN THE
Beartooth
Mountains

BILLINGS to RED LODGE to YELLOWSTONE
BOULDER VALLEY • PARADISE VALLEY

Robert Stone

5th EDITION

Day Hike Books, Inc.
RED LODGE, MONTANA

Published by Day Hike Books, Inc.
P.O. Box 865 · Red Lodge, Montana 59068
www.dayhikebooks.com

Distributed by National Book Network
800-462-6420 (direct order) · 800-820-2329 (fax order)

Cover photograph by Roger A. Jenkins
Back photograph by Linda Stone
Layout/maps by Paula Doherty

The author has made every attempt to provide accurate information in this book. However, trail routes and features may change—please use common sense and forethought, and be mindful of your own capabilities. Let this book guide you, but be aware that each hiker assumes responsibility for their own safety. The author and publisher do not assume any responsibility for loss, damage, or injury caused through the use of this book.

Library of Congress Control Number: 2010937194

11 10 9 8 7 6 5 4 3

Cover photo:
Mariane Lake, Beartooth Plateau
(northeast of Kersey Lake, Hike 61)

Back cover photo:
Daisy Pass, Hike 65

ALSO BY ROBERT STONE

West Fork of Rock Creek

Main Fork and Lake Fork of Rock Creek
Meeteetse Trail

Table of Contents

THE HIKES

Beartooth Front
Stillwater • West Rosebud • East Rosebud

West Fork of Rock Creek

Main Fork and Lake Fork of Rock Creek
Meeteetse Trail

Beartooth Plateau • Beartooth Highway

Cooke City Area

Yellowstone National Park
Northeast Entrance

Boulder Valley

Paradise Valley
East Side to the Boulder Valley

Billings

Suggested commercial maps for additional hiking:

U.S. Geological Survey topographic maps

Beartooth Publishing: Beartooth Mountains

Beartooth Publishing: Absaroka Beartooth Wilderness

Rocky Mountain Surveys: Alpine–Mount Maurice

Rocky Mountain Surveys: Mount Douglas–Mount Wood

Rocky Mountain Surveys: Wyoming Beartooths

Rocky Mountain Surveys: Cooke City

U.S. Forest Service: Custer National Forest

Trails Illustrated: Tower/Canyon (Yellowstone)

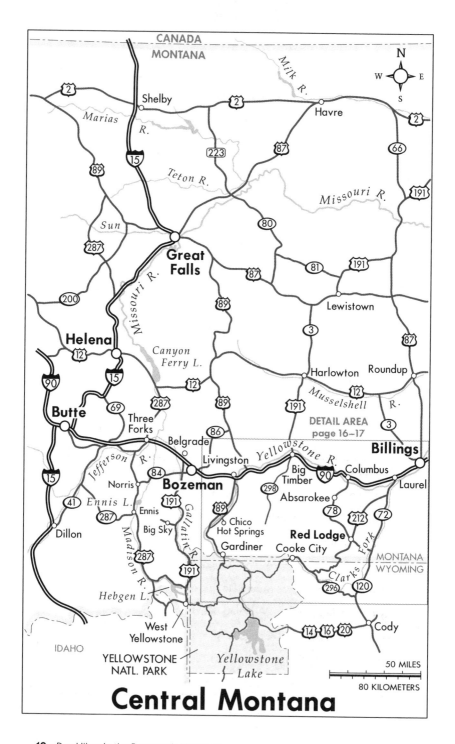

Central Montana

Overview of the Hikes

The rugged Beartooth Mountains are Montana's highest mountain range. This beautiful range of the Rocky Mountains rises dramatically from the plains of southeastern Montana and stretches to the northern reaches of Yellowstone National Park. The three-billion-year-old mountains include the Gallatin, Custer, and Shoshone National Forests. These ancient mountains are among the oldest rocks on earth and lie within a 945,000-acre protected wilderness area. The rugged mountain range contains glaciers, deep canyons, streams, waterfalls, over a thousand lakes, lush forests, panoramic views, abundant wildlife, and the vast Beartooth Plateau. The plateau, shaped by alpine glaciers, is the largest continuous area above 10,000 feet and the largest alpine tundra region in North America.

The Beartooth Highway is the major access road to many of the hikes. This dramatic highway (Highway 212) connects Billings to Red Lodge, heads over the Beartooth Plateau, passes through the communities of Cooke City and Silver Gate, and extends to the northeast entrance of Yellowstone Park. The famous switchbacks start along the east wall of Rock Creek Canyon at 6,000 feet and quickly rise to a top-of-the-world elevation of 10,947 feet. The views are spectacular. The 68-mile highway was originally built in 1936. It has since been designated a National Scenic Byway and heralded as "the most scenic highway in America" by Charles Kuralt of CBS News. The highway is open across the pass, weather permitting, Memorial Day through mid-October.

Now in its fifth edition, *Day Hikes In the Beartooth Mountains* is a comprehensive collection of the area's day hikes within this mountain range and the adjacent foothills and plains. A wide range of scenery and ecosystems accommodates all levels of hiking, from relaxing creek-side strolls to all-day, high-elevation outings. The 123 hikes range from 11,000-foot alpine plateaus and peaks to treks along the Yellowstone River as it begins its journey through the arid plains. The guide now includes hikes around the Billings area, the Boulder Valley, and Paradise Valley.

The trailheads are located within a 120-mile radius of Red Lodge. All hikes can be completed during the day. Many trails, of course, continue for miles, connecting to a network of trails across the mountains. A quick glance at the hikes' statistics and summaries will allow you to choose a hike that is appropriate to your ability and intentions. The map on the next page identifies the overall locations of the hikes. Several other area maps, as well as maps for each hike, provide closer details.

Even though these trails are described as day hikes, many of the trails involve serious backcountry hiking. Reference the hiking statistics for an approximation of difficulty. Times are calculated for continuous hiking. Allow extra time for exploration. Feel free to hike farther than these day hike suggestions, but be sure to carry additional topographic maps. Map sources and references are listed for extending the hikes. Use good judgement about your capabilities.

When hiking in high altitude terrain, be aware that the increased elevation affects your stamina. Weather conditions undoubtedly change throughout the day and seasons. It is imperative to wear warm, layered clothing, especially when hiking up to the plateaus and on the trails accessed from the Beartooth Pass. Snacks, water, extra supplies, and a basic first aid kit are a must. Both black and grizzly bears inhabit the region, so wear a bear bell and hike in a group whenever possible. Some preparation and forethought will help ensure a safe, enjoyable, and memorable hike.

HIKES 1—13 are located along the northeast-facing Beartooth Front, where the mountains meet the rolling foothills and grasslands. These hikes are accessed from Highway 78 between Red Lodge and Columbus. The trails lead into the Stillwater, West Rosebud, East Rosebud, and West Red Lodge Creek drainages, tributaries of the Yellowstone River. Continuing west and south leads into the Boulder Valley and Yellowstone National Park.

HIKES 14—23 are found along the West Fork of Rock Creek. These hikes are a quick drive from Red Lodge and include a variety of beautiful trails, from easy creekside strolls to remote backcountry hikes.

South of Red Lodge, HIKES 24—35 lie along the Main Fork and Lake Fork of Rock Creek. Several of these trails access the 10,000-foot plateaus which flank the Rock Creek Canyon, following creek drainages up the mountains. The Lake Fork is a very scenic and easily accessible area, with trails ranging from easy to moderate. Rugged high-alpine hikes are found at the back end of Rock Creek Canyon or by hiking up to any of the plateaus.

Continuing south on Highway 212 up the Beartooth switchbacks leads to the Beartooth Plateau. HIKES 31—50 are located along this top-of-the-world road that travels over the Beartooth Mountains. Hikes wind across rolling meadows, with far-reaching views across layers and layers of mountains. Many trails lead to lakes tucked into snow-capped mountain cirques. The unique tundra is a landscape like nowhere else on earth. Wear warm clothing for these high-alpine hikes atop the plateau.

After rolling across the alpine tundra, the Beartooth Highway begins to slowly decrease in elevation as it winds down towards the Clarks Fork Valley. The pristine landscape is dominated by dense forests and mountains, punctuated by the distinct Pilot and Index Peaks in the west. HIKES 59—71 are located along this stretch of the highway as it nears the town of Cooke City.

Minutes from Cooke City is the northeast entrance to Yellowstone National Park. HIKES 72—81 are accessed from this road that leads to Tower and the Yellowstone River, exploring the far reaches of the Beartooth Mountains into the Absaroka Range. Highlights include a petrified forest, creekside strolls through Yellowstone's beautiful meadows, and overlooks of the Grand Canyon of the Yellowstone.

Boulder Valley and the adjacent Paradise Valley run through the west end of the Absaroka-Beartooth Wilderness, with access to excellent backcountry trails. From Big Timber, Highway 298 runs south along the main Boulder River, leading to HIKES 82—95. The Boulder drainage lies between the Stillwater drainage and the Beartooth Range (to the east) and Paradise Valley and the Absaroka Range (to the west). HIKES 96—107 are located on the east side of Paradise Valley and head eastward towards the Boulder Valley. Paradise Valley is easily accessed from Highway 89 between Livingston and Yellowstone. A vast network of remote trails in this area interlinks the Absaroka-Beartooth ranges.

At the opposite end of the Beartooth Pass, Highway 212 heads eastward, away from the mountains, to Billings. Montana's largest city lies adjacent to the Yellowstone River in the dry prairie land that gently rolls away from the Beartooth Range. The last section of trails, HIKES 108—123, are located in or near the city, offering some remarkably great trails in the city's natural areas.

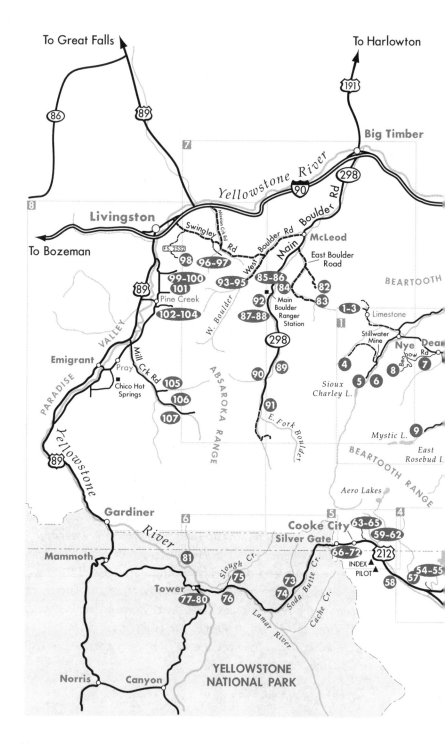

To Great Falls

To Harlowton

86

89

191

7

Yellowstone River

90

298

Big Timber

8

Livingston

Swingley

Mission Crk Rd

Rd

West Boulder Rd

Boulder Rd

Main

Boulder

Rd

McLeod

To Bozeman

F.S. 2532

98

96-97

W. Boulder

93-95

85-86

84

East Boulder
Road

82

BEARTOOTH

89

99-100

101

Pine Creek

102-104

92

87-88

Main
Boulder
Ranger
Station

83

1-3

Limestone

298

Stillwater
Mine

Nye

Dea

Rd

Emigrant

Pray

VALLEY

Mill Crk Rd

PARADISE

Chico Hot
Springs

105

106

107

ABSAROKA
RANGE

90

89

91

E. Fork Boulder

4

5

6

8

7

Sioux
Charley L.

Benbow

BEARTOOTH RANGE

Mystic L.

9

East
Rosebud L

Aero Lakes

89

Yellowstone

Gardiner

River

6

5

4

Cooke City

63-65

59-62

Silver Gate

Mammoth

81

Slough Cr.

75

66-72

212

INDEX
PILOT

58

54-55

57

Tower

77-80

76

73

74

Soda Butte Cr.

Cache Cr.

Lamar River

Norris

Canyon

YELLOWSTONE
NATIONAL PARK

Map of the Hikes

Red Lodge to Yellowstone Park
Billings to Livingston

Master Map

87

3

108-123

Billings

9

Reedpoint

Columbus

Laurel

River

90

RANGE

Yellowstone

78

Stillwater River

420

Absaroka

Cooney
Reservoir

Joliet

Edgar

Fishtail

419 425

Rd

212

72

Fromberg

N

Roscoe

78

Roberts

Red Lodge Cr.

Willow Cr.

Bridger

W ✦ **E**

Luther

12-13

S

10

11

2

23 22 West Fork 19 14

3

Red Lodge

21

20

15 Rd

308

West Fork

16-18

Bear-
creek

Belfry

Clarks

24

Meeteetse Trl

26 25

Lake Fork Rd 28

27

29-32

MONTANA
WYOMING

DETAIL MAPS

34-35 33

37

Glacier L. 38 36

44-53 43 39

40-42

56 Beartooth
Butte and Lake

Beartooth
Highway

1	**1–13:** Beartooth Front
2	**14–23:** West Fork of Rock Creek
3	**24–35:** Main Fork and Lake Fork
4	**36–58:** Beartooth Plateau/Hwy 212
5	**59–71:** Cooke City area
6	**72–81:** NE Yellowstone Park
7	**82–95:** Boulder Valley
8	**96–107:** Paradise Valley/Livingston
9	**108–123:** Billings

296 120

Chief Joseph Highway
Sundance Basin Road

20 MILES

20 KILOMETERS

To Cody

Red Lodge Area

Beartooth Hwy • Hwy 78
Red Lodge to Yellowstone

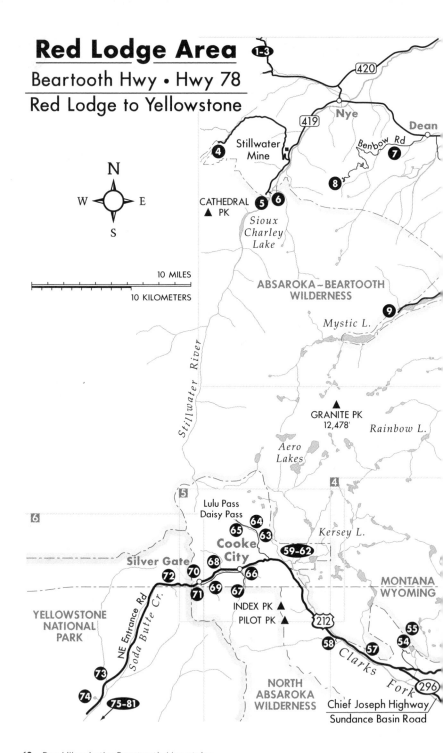

N
W ← ● → E
S

10 MILES
10 KILOMETERS

1-3
420
419 Nye
Benbow Rd Dean
4 Stillwater Mine 7
CATHEDRAL 5 6 8
▲ PK
Sioux Charley Lake

ABSAROKA – BEARTOOTH WILDERNESS
Mystic L. 9

Stillwater River

▲ GRANITE PK
12,478'   Rainbow L.
Aero Lakes
4
5 Kersey L.
Lulu Pass
Daisy Pass 64
65 63
6 Cooke 59-62
Silver Gate 68 City
72 70 66 MONTANA
71 69 WYOMING
67
YELLOWSTONE INDEX PK ▲
NATIONAL PILOT PK ▲ 212 55
PARK 58 54
57
73 Clarks
74 75-81 Fork 296
NORTH
ABSAROKA Chief Joseph Highway
WILDERNESS Sundance Basin Road

NE Entrance Rd
Soda Butte Cr.

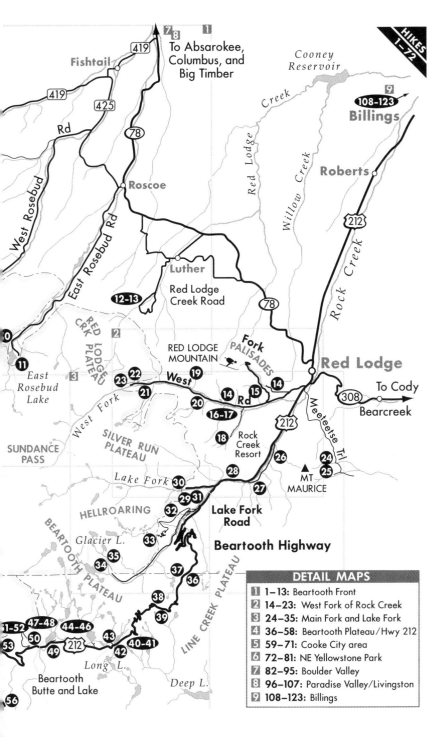

To Absarokee, Columbus, and Big Timber

Fishtail

Cooney Reservoir

419
419
425
78

Rd

West Rosebud

East Rosebud Rd

Roscoe

Red Lodge Creek

Willow Creek

108-123

Billings

Roberts

212

Rock Creek

Luther

Red Lodge Creek Road

12-13

78

RED LODGE CRK PLATEAU

0

11

East Rosebud Lake

2

3

RED LODGE MOUNTAIN

Fork PALISADES

Red Lodge

23
22
21

West

19

14
15
14

20

16-17

308

To Cody

Bearcreek

West Fork

SILVER RUN PLATEAU

18

Rd

212

Meeteetse Trl

SUNDANCE PASS

Lake Fork

30

Rock Creek Resort

26

24
25

MT MAURICE

28

HELLROARING

29 31

32

27

Lake Fork Road

Glacier L.

33

Beartooth Highway

BEARTOOTH PLATEAU

35

34

37

36

38

LINE CREEK PLATEAU

DETAIL MAPS

1–52
47–48
44–46
53
50
49
42
212
43
40–41

39

Long L.

Deep L.

Beartooth Butte and Lake

56

1	**1–13:** Beartooth Front
2	**14–23:** West Fork of Rock Creek
3	**24–35:** Main Fork and Lake Fork
4	**36–58:** Beartooth Plateau/Hwy 212
5	**59–71:** Cooke City area
6	**72–81:** NE Yellowstone Park
7	**82–95:** Boulder Valley
8	**96–107:** Paradise Valley/Livingston
9	**108–123:** Billings

HIKES 1–72

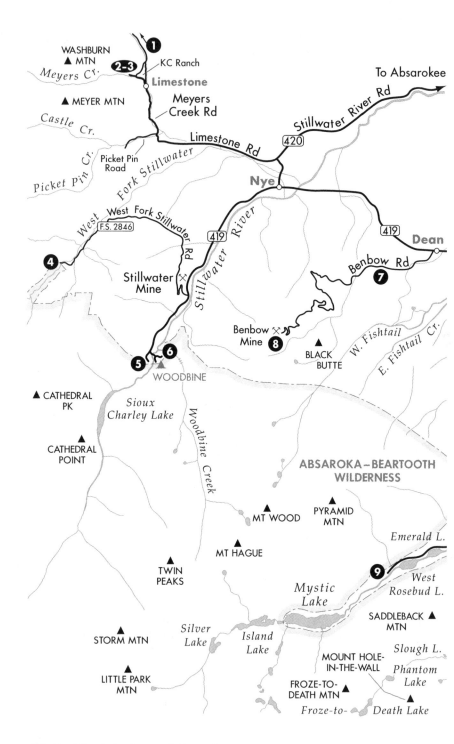

WASHBURN ▲ MTN

2-3 KC Ranch

Meyers Cr.

1

To Absarokee

▲ MEYER MTN

Limestone

Meyers Creek Rd

Castle Cr.

Stillwater River Rd

Limestone Rd

420

Picket Pin Cr.

Picket Pin Road

Nye

Picket Pin

West Fork Stillwater

West

West Fork Stillwater Rd

F.S. 2846

4

Stillwater Mine

419

Stillwater River

419

Dean

Benbow Rd

7

Benbow Mine

8

BLACK BUTTE

W. Fishtail

E. Fishtail Cr.

5 **6**

WOODBINE

▲ CATHEDRAL PK

Sioux Charley Lake

Woodbine Creek

▲ CATHEDRAL POINT

ABSAROKA–BEARTOOTH WILDERNESS

▲ MT WOOD

PYRAMID ▲ MTN

Emerald L.

▲ MT HAGUE

9

West Rosebud L.

▲ TWIN PEAKS

Mystic Lake

SADDLEBACK ▲ MTN

▲ STORM MTN

Silver Lake

Island Lake

MOUNT HOLE-IN-THE-WALL

Slough L.

Phantom Lake

▲ LITTLE PARK MTN

FROZE-TO-DEATH MTN ▲

Froze-to- *Death Lake*

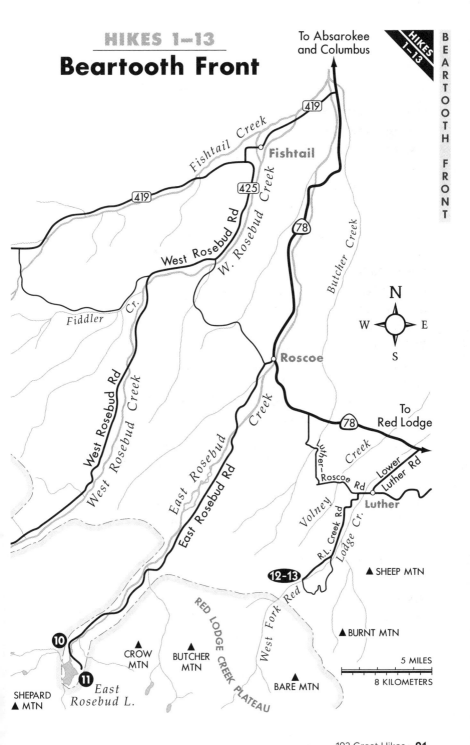

1. Lodgepole Trail to Lower Deer Creek

N.W. STILLWATER WATERSHED

Hiking distance: 6 miles round trip
Hiking time: 3 hours
Elevation gain: 1,150 feet
Maps: U.S.G.S. Sliderock Mountain
Beartooth Publishing: Absaroka Beartooth Wilderness
US Forest Service: Custer National Forest

Summary of hike: Lodgepole Creek, nine miles northwest of Nye, forms on the southern flank of Sugarloaf Mountain at the Custer National Forest boundary. The area, ravished from the Derby Fire in the summer of 2006, is an amazing study in the natural recovery and regeneration of the flora. The Lodgepole Trail climbs strenuously up the canyon along the creek to a 7,100-foot saddle at the Gallatin National Forest boundary. The trail drops down the slope to Lower Deer Creek, where this hike ends. However, the trail crosses the creek and continues west to the Elk Creek Divide and the East Boulder Valley (Hike 82), the next major drainage to the west.

Driving directions: From the north end of Red Lodge, drive 30 miles west on Highway 78 to County Road 419, the Fishtail and Nye turnoff on the left. Turn left (west) on County Road 419 and continue 20.6 miles, passing through Fishtail and Dean, to Nye and the Limestone Road turnoff on the right. Turn right and drive 0.9 miles to a junction with County Road 420. Bear left on Limestone Road, and continue 4.6 miles to a posted road fork with Picket Pin Road. Stay to the right on Meyers Creek Road, and drive 2.4 miles to the Meyers Creek Work Center (en route veering left at the KC Ranch). Turn right, just before the first work center building at the posted Lodgepole Creek turnoff. Continue 2.3 miles on the narrow dirt road to the signed trailhead on the right. Park off the road on the right, just past the

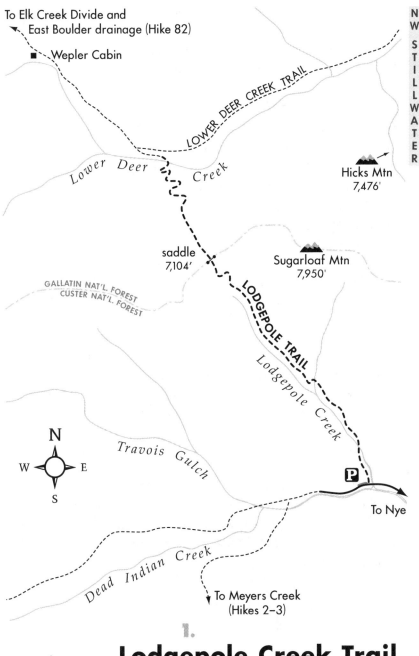

To Elk Creek Divide and
East Boulder drainage (Hike 82)

■ Wepler Cabin

NW STILLWATER

LOWER DEER CREEK TRAIL

Lower Deer Creek

Hicks Mtn
7,476'

saddle
7,104'

Sugarloaf Mtn
7,950'

GALLATIN NAT'L. FOREST
CUSTER NAT'L. FOREST

LODGEPOLE TRAIL

Lodgepole Creek

N
W · E
S

Travois Gulch

P

To Nye

Dead Indian Creek

To Meyers Creek
(Hikes 2–3)

1.

Washburn Mtn
8,455'

Lodgepole Creek Trail
to Lower Deer Creek

trailhead. En route, the road crosses through Lodgepole Creek two times.

From I-90 in Columbus, drive 15 miles south on Highway 78 to Absarokee. Drive through town for 2 miles to County Road 419, the Fishtail and Nye turnoff on the right. Turn right (west) on County Road 419, and follow the directions above.

Hiking directions: Walk north up the slope among aspens and lodgepole pines. At 0.2 miles, rock-hop over Lodgepole Creek. Head up the grassy canyon beneath the rocky ridge of Sugarloaf Mountain. Cross a small tributary draining the southern flank of the mountain. Traverse the east canyon slope above Lodgepole Creek, and steadily climb through open meadows at a moderate grade. Continue uphill through the burned forest from the massive 2006 Derby Fire. Great vistas span across the Stillwater Valley to the towering peaks beyond. The trail reaches the 7,104-foot saddle along the west flank of Sugarloaf Mountain at the Gallatin National Forest boundary. Pass through the forest boundary gate, and cross the grassy saddle to vistas down and across the Lower Deer Creek drainage. Descend the mountain slope on a gently weaving path to Lower Deer Creek. Near the bottom, the trail fades in a meadow. Tree markers and a few stakes mark the path to the creek. This is our turn-around point.

To extend the hike, the trail continues across the creek and continues a mile to Wepler Cabin, a forest service rental cabin, passing the Lower Deer Creek Trail en route. The cabin is located on the west edge of the upper meadow, one hundred feet below the saddle between two prominent rocky peaks. The trail continues westward to the Elk Creek Divide and the East Boulder Valley—Hike 82. ▪

2. Meyers Creek—Pass Creek Trails
N.W. STILLWATER WATERSHED

Hiking distance: 5 miles round trip
Hiking time: 2.5 hours
Elevation gain: 1,100 feet
Maps: U.S.G.S. Meyer Mountain
       Beartooth Publishing: Absaroka Beartooth Wilderness
       US Forest Service: Custer National Forest

Summary of hike: Meyers Creek, nine miles northwest of Nye, tumbles through a scenic landscape with open grasslands, volcanic outcrops and ridges, mixed conifers, and deciduous vegetation. This hike follows the lower end of the Meyers Creek Trail up the scenic canyon. The hike then veers south and climbs up Pass Creek Trail along Pass Creek on the east face of Meyer Mountain. The trails leads to North Pass Creek Spring, a natural spring that fills a trough, and an overlook of the Castle Creek drainage with far-reaching vistas.

Driving directions: From the north end of Red Lodge, drive 30 miles west on Highway 78 to County Road 419, the Fishtail and Nye turnoff on the left. Turn left (west) on County Road 419 and continue 20.6 miles, passing through Fishtail and Dean, to Nye and the Limestone Road turnoff on the right. Turn right and drive 0.9 miles to a junction with County Road 420. Bear left, staying on Limestone Road, and continue 4.6 miles to a posted road fork with Picket Pin Road. Stay to the right on Meyers Creek Road, and drive 2.7 miles to the trailhead parking area at the end of the road. (En route, veer left at the KC Ranch, and pass the Meyers Creek Work Center.)

From I-90 in Columbus, drive 15 miles south on Highway 78 to Absarokee. Drive through town for 2 miles to County Road 419, the Fishtail and Nye turnoff on the right. Turn right (west) on County Road 419, and follow the directions above.

Hiking directions: Walk through the trailhead gate, and follow the two-track road through the open grasslands. At 0.2 miles is a trail split. Stay to the left and continue west along the drainage through groves of young aspen trees to the mouth of the canyon and a trail gate. Pass through the gate and continue on the footpath. Cross over seasonal Meyers Creek, and slowly descend as the canyon narrows. Enter a pine and aspen forest between Washburn Mountain to the north and Meyer Mountain to the south. Pass eroded rock cliffs along the lower slope of Washburn Mountain. Climb to a junction with Pass Creek Trail at 1.6 miles. The Meyers Creek Trail continues straight ahead to Meyers Creek Pass (Hike 3).

For this hike, bear left on the Pass Creek Trail, and weave up the south canyon wall along the east slope of Meyer Mountain. Top the slope and walk through a grassy meadow. Continue up the narrow, forested draw on an easy grade, and pass through a large tree-rimmed meadow. Reenter the forest to North Pass Creek Spring, which flows into a circular trough. Climb 0.3 miles farther to a T-junction near the ridge. The right fork makes a U-bend to the ridge, with southwest views, and descends to Castle Creek. Take the left fork a short distance and veer left. Head down the west-facing slope, descending on a couple of switchbacks. Complete the loop in the upper meadow. Curve right through the meadow, returning to the Meyers Creek Trail. Return to the trailhead to the right (east).

To extend the hike west to Meyers Creek Pass, continue with Hike 3. ▓

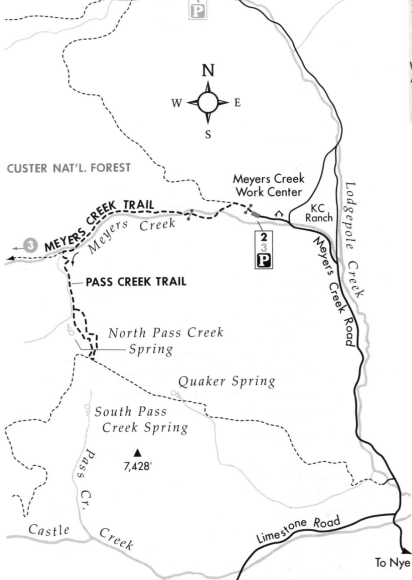

CUSTER NAT'L. FOREST

MEYERS CREEK TRAIL

Meyers Creek

Meyers Creek
Work Center

KC
Ranch

Lodgepole Creek

Meyers Creek Road

PASS CREEK TRAIL

*North Pass Creek
Spring*

Quaker Spring

*South Pass
Creek Spring*

▲
7,428'

Pass Cr.

Castle Creek

Limestone Road

To Nye

2. Meyers Creek–
Pass Creek Trails

3. Meyers Creek Trail to Meyers Creek Pass
N.W. STILLWATER WATERSHED

Hiking distance: 9.2 miles round trip
Hiking time: 5 hours
Elevation gain: 2,450 feet
Maps: U.S.G.S. Meyer Mountain
       Beartooth Publishing: Absaroka Beartooth Wilderness
       US Forest Service: Custer National Forest

Summary of hike: Meyers Creek forms on the upper slopes at Meyers Creek Pass between the Boulder and Stillwater drainages. The creek flows six miles down Meyers Canyon, between Washburn Mountain and Meyer Mountain, to its confluence with Lodgepole Creek. It is a perennial creek, but portions run underground, creating the appearance of an ephemeral stream. This hike parallels Meyers Creek nearly the entire hike. The trail steadily climbs along the waterway to Meyers Creek Pass, which straddles the boundary between the Custer and Gallatin National Forests. From grassy Meyers Creek Pass are sweeping vistas in every direction, including views into the Dry Fork Creek drainage and the East Boulder River Valley. En route, the hike weaves through gorgeous open grasslands, aspen and pine groves, and flower-filled meadows surrounded by mountains.

Driving directions: From the north end of Red Lodge, drive 30 miles west on Highway 78 to County Road 419, the Fishtail and Nye turnoff on the left. Turn left (west) on County Road 419 and continue 20.6 miles, passing through Fishtail and Dean, to Nye and the Limestone Road turnoff on the right. Turn right and drive 0.9 miles to a junction with County Road 420. Bear left, staying on Limestone Road, and continue 4.6 miles to a posted road fork with Picket Pin Road. Stay to the right on Meyers Creek Road, and drive 2.7 miles to the trailhead parking area at the end of the road. (En route, veer left at the KC Ranch, and pass the Meyers Creek Work Center.)

From I-90 in Columbus, drive 15 miles south on Highway 78 to Absarokee. Drive through town for 2 miles to County Road 419, the Fishtail and Nye turnoff on the right. Turn right (west) on County Road 419, and follow the directions above.

Hiking directions: Walk through the trailhead gate and follow the two-track road through the open grasslands. Stay to the left at an unsigned trail split at 0.2 miles, and follow the drainage through groves of young aspen trees. Pass through a trail gate at the mouth of the canyon, and continue on the footpath. Slowly descend as the canyon narrows and enters a pine and aspen forest. Climb to a junction with Pass Creek Trail at 1.6 miles (Hike 2).

For this hike, continue straight ahead, staying on the Meyers Creek Trail between Meyer Mountain to the south (left) and Washburn Mountain to the north (right). Pass a series of small meadows dotted with aspens and pines. Continue west towards Peak 8605, the rounded mountain at the head of the canyon. At 3 miles, begin weaving up the mountain, with views spanning back down the canyon. The path levels out, then drops down into the drainage of the South Fork of Meyers Creek. Head up the flower-laden canyon along the southern base of Peak 8605. Gradually curve right, staying in the meadow surrounded by mountains. Meyers Creek Pass can be seen to the right. Leave the drainage and steadily climb the narrow path to Meyers Creek Pass, a wide, grassy saddle marked with a cairn. From the 8,111-foot pass are 360-degree panoramas. The views include Moccasin Lake and the Dry Fork Creek drainage (Hike 83), the East Boulder River Valley, Morning Star Peak, Boone Mountain, Long Mountain, Meyer Mountain, and Washburn Mountain.

To extend the hike, the trail continues down to Moccasin Lake in the Gallatin National Forest and follows the Dry Fork Creek to the East Boulder River. ▪

N
W   E
S

CUSTER NAT'L. FOREST

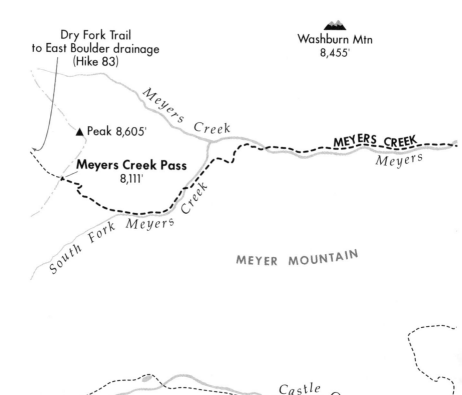

Dry Fork Trail
to East Boulder drainage
(Hike 83)

Washburn Mtn
8,455'

Meyers Creek

▲ Peak 8,605'

Meyers Creek Pass
8,111'

MEYERS CREEK

Meyers

South Fork Meyers Creek

MEYER MOUNTAIN

Castle Creek

3.

Meyers Creek Trail
to Meyers Creek Pass

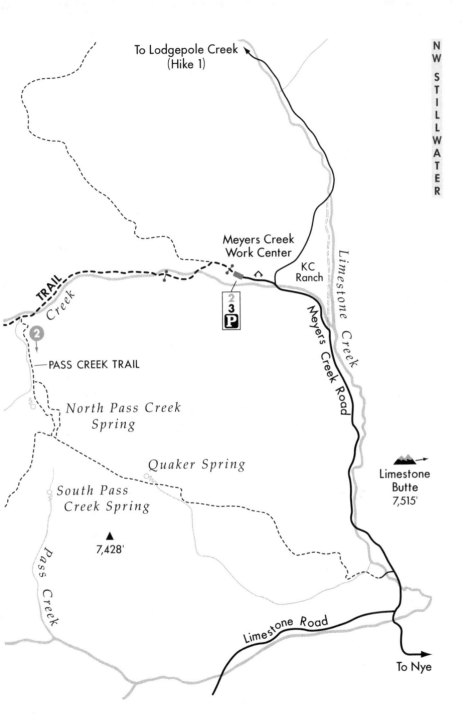

To Lodgepole Creek
(Hike 1)

Meyers Creek
Work Center

KC
Ranch

TRAIL

Creek

Limestone Creek

2
3
P

Meyers Creek Road

PASS CREEK TRAIL

*North Pass Creek
Spring*

Quaker Spring

Limestone Butte
7,515'

*South Pass
Creek Spring*

▲
7,428'

Pass Creek

Limestone Road

To Nye

4. West Fork Stillwater River Trail
WEST FORK STILLWATER DRAINAGE

Hiking distance: 6 miles round trip
Hiking time: 3 hours
Elevation gain: 400 feet
Maps: U.S.G.S. Meyer Mountain, Picket Pin Mountain, and
Tumble Mountain
Rocky Mountain Surveys: Mount Douglas—Mount Wood
US Forest Service: Custer National Forest

Summary of hike: The West Fork of the Stillwater River forms on the southeast slope of Lake Mountain above Lake Plateau at an elevation over 10,000 feet. The river flows 28 miles down the scenic canyon and empties into the Stillwater River near Nye. The West Fork Stillwater Trail parallels the river for 16 miles in the Absaroka-Beartooth Wilderness, then climbs to a series of lakes on the Lake Plateau, between the main Stillwater drainage and the Boulder drainage. This hike follows the lower three miles, all within the wilderness. The trail meanders through a mix of forests and meadows while staying close to the river on an easy grade. Throughout the hike are spectacular vistas. Across the Lake Plateau, connecting trails lead into the East Fork Boulder River drainage (Hike 91).

Driving directions: From the north end of Red Lodge, drive 30 miles west on Highway 78 to County Road 419, the Fishtail and Nye turnoff on the left. Turn left (west) on County Road 419 and continue 26.1 miles, passing through Fishtail, Dean and Nye, to the West Fork Stillwater Road (Forest Service Road 2846) on the right. It is located 0.4 miles past the entrance to the Stillwater Mine. Turn right and drive 8.9 slow-but-scenic miles on the dirt road to the trailhead at the end of the road.

From I-90 in Columbus, drive 15 miles south on Highway 78 to Absarokee. Drive through town for 2 miles to County Road 419, the Fishtail and Nye turnoff on the right. Turn right (west) on County Road 419 and follow the directions above.

Hiking directions: Walk past the trailhead sign and enter the

Absaroka-Beartooth Wilderness. Head southwest through the forest, and pass through a meadow, with views up the canyon and the steep canyon walls. Parallel the West Stillwater River, reaching its banks at a half mile. Continue up the west side of the cascading river. At 1.4 miles, the canyon widens and the river flows wider. Pass the confluence of Saderbalm Creek, which can be seen across the river. Walk through a talus field, following the northwest slope of the canyon above the river. Return to the canyon floor and stroll through a lodgepole pine forest. The path gently climbs the hillside slope and returns to the river several more times. At 3 miles, cross ephemeral Crescent Creek. This is a good turn-around spot.

To extend the hike, continue on an easy uphill grade, staying on the north side of the river. At 4 miles, the deep and steep Tumble Creek drainage, which drains Jasper Lake, can be seen across the river. The trail reaches expansive Breakneck Meadows at 8 miles and eventually leads to Lake Plateau and Wounded Man Lake at 17 miles. ▪

5. Stillwater River Trail to Sioux Charley Lake
MAIN STILLWATER DRAINAGE

Hiking distance: 6 miles round trip
Hiking time: 3 hours
Elevation gain: 600 feet
Maps: U.S.G.S. Cathedral Point
        Beartooth Publishing: Absaroka Beartooth Wilderness
        Rocky Mountain Surveys: Mount Douglas—Mount Wood

Summary of hike: The Stillwater River is a major drainage in the Beartooth Mountains. The river's headwaters begin in an expansive basin high atop the Beartooth Plateau west of Crown Butte and Daisy Pass, just north of Cooke City. The river travels over 70 miles southeast to its confluence with the Yellowstone River at Columbus. This hike follows a dramatic section of the Stillwater River through a narrow, steep-walled canyon at the

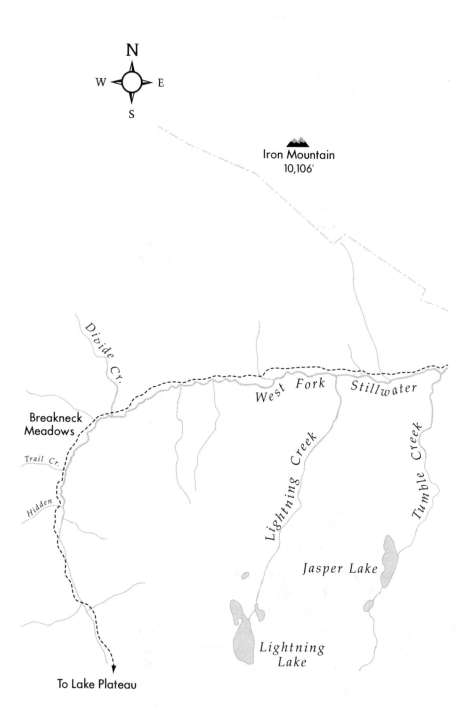

Iron Mountain
10,106'

Divide Cr.

West Fork   Stillwater

Breakneck
Meadows

Trail Cr.

Lightning Creek

Tumble Creek

Hidden

Jasper Lake

Lightning
Lake

To Lake Plateau

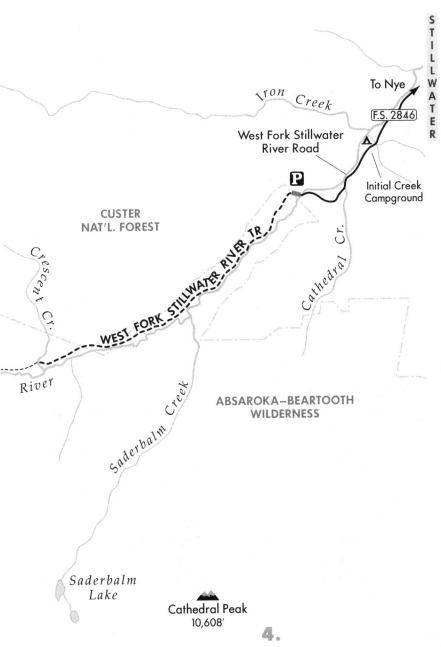

STILLWATER

To Nye

Iron Creek

F.S. 2846

West Fork Stillwater
River Road

Initial Creek
Campground

P

CUSTER
NAT'L. FOREST

WEST FORK STILLWATER RIVER TR.

Crescent Cr.

Cathedral Cr.

River

Saderbalm Creek

ABSAROKA–BEARTOOTH
WILDERNESS

Saderbalm
Lake

Cathedral Peak
10,608'

4.

West Fork
Stillwater River Trail

boundary of the Absaroka-Beartooth Wilderness. The river puts on a spectacular display of waterfalls, cascades, and rapids as it rages down the drainage. The trail emerges into a pristine valley surrounded by majestic mountains. Sioux Charley Lake, a long, slow-moving section of the river, lies nestled in this valley along the eastern base of Cathedral Peak. The trail begins just past the Woodbine Campground at the end of County Road 419.

Driving directions: From the north end of Red Lodge, drive 30 miles west on Highway 78 to County Road 419, the Fishtail and Nye turnoff on the left. Turn left (west) on County Road 419 and continue 28.3 miles, passing through Fishtail, Dean and Nye, to a road fork, located 3 miles past the Stillwater Mine. Take the right fork 0.4 miles to the parking area.

From I-90 in Columbus, drive 15 miles south on Highway 78 to Absarokee. Drive through town for 2 miles to County Road 419, the Fishtail and Nye turnoff on the right. Turn right (west) on County Road 419 and continue 28.3 miles, passing through Fishtail, Dean and Nye, to the road fork. Take the right fork 0.4 miles to the parking area.

Hiking directions: From the far end of the parking area, head south and follow the Stillwater River upstream along its north bank. Within minutes the trail enters a steep-walled, glacially-carved granite gorge with tumbling whitewater. At 0.5 miles, emerge from the canyon into a lush valley meadow. Moderately gain elevation through the valley, and curve north to a rocky knoll. From this overlook are views of the Stillwater drainage and the north end of Sioux Charley Lake. Across the valley to the east, the burn area from the 1988 Storm Creek fire can be detected. Descend through the meadow past aspen groves, and cross a series of streams to Sioux Charley Lake. Return along the same trail.

To hike farther, the trail continues parallel to the Stillwater River for another 23 miles to its headwaters near Lake Abundance Road and Cooke City. From Sioux Charley Lake, it is 8 miles to a junction with the West Fork Stillwater River Trail (Hike 4), which leads up to Lake Plateau. ■

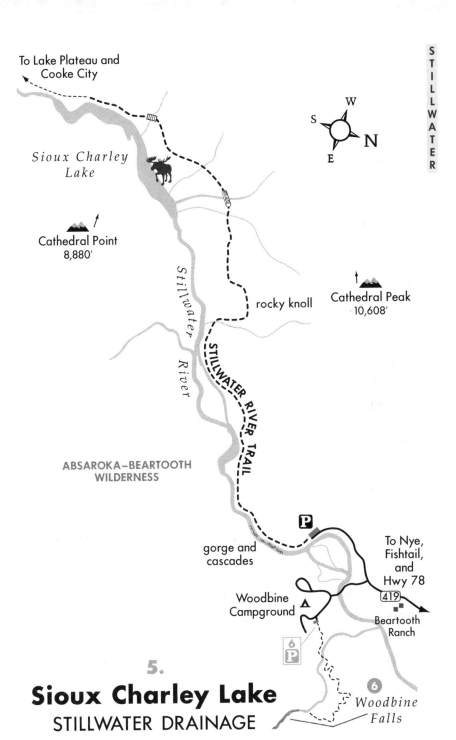

To Lake Plateau and
Cooke City

*Sioux Charley
Lake*

Cathedral Point
8,880'

*Stillwater
River*

rocky knoll

Cathedral Peak
10,608'

STILLWATER RIVER TRAIL

ABSAROKA–BEARTOOTH
WILDERNESS

W
S   N
E

P

gorge and
cascades

To Nye,
Fishtail,
and
Hwy 78
419

Woodbine
Campground

Beartooth
Ranch

6
P

5.

Sioux Charley Lake
STILLWATER DRAINAGE

6
*Woodbine
Falls*

6. Woodbine Falls
MAIN STILLWATER DRAINAGE

Hiking distance: 1.5 miles round trip
Hiking time: 1 hour
Elevation gain: 300 feet
Maps: U.S.G.S. Cathedral Point
        Beartooth Publishing: Absaroka Beartooth Wilderness
        Rocky Mountain Surveys: Mount Douglas—Mount Wood

Summary of hike: Woodbine Falls is a long, stunning free-falling waterfall that plunges down Woodbine Creek, a tributary of the Stillwater River. The creek begins high in the mountains at Twin Peaks and empties into the Stillwater near Woodbine Campground at the end of County Road 419. This trail begins from the campground and climbs 3/4 of a mile to a lookout below the falls, staying close to the frothy, cascading whitewater. The vibrations from the thunderous falls can be felt from the trail.

Driving directions: From the north end of Red Lodge, drive 30 miles west on Highway 78 to County Road 419, the Fishtail and Nye turnoff on the left. Turn left (west) on Road 419 and continue 28.3 miles, passing through Fishtail, Dean and Nye, to a road fork, located 3 miles past the Stillwater Mine. Take the left fork 0.4 miles into Woodbine Campground, bearing left at a junction to the trailhead parking area on the left.

From I-90 in Columbus, drive 15 miles south on Highway 78 to Absarokee. Drive through town for 2 miles to County Road 419, the Fishtail and Nye turnoff on the right. Turn right (west) on County Road 419, and follow the directions above.

Hiking directions: Hike past the trailhead sign to Woodbine Creek. Head upstream to the footbridge. After crossing the bridge, begin a series of gentle switchbacks through the forest, staying close to the raging whitewater of Woodbine Creek. At 0.4 miles, enter the Absaroka-Beartooth Wilderness, and cross small tributaries with lush, mossy alcoves along the mountainside. At 0.75 miles is the Woodbine Falls overlook, corralled by a curved rock wall. This is the turn-around.

Just before reaching the lookout, a steep, unmaintained trail leads to the left up to the brink of the falls. Although the trail is frequently hiked, this portion of the trail has loose rock and gravel. The trail is especially dangerous coming down. Use caution and common sense. ▪

Woodbine Falls

overlook

ABSAROKA–BEARTOOTH WILDERNESS

E
N ✦ S
W

Woodbine Creek

Stillwater River

P

▲ Woodbine Campground

To Nye, Fishtail, and Hwy 78

419 ▪ Beartooth Ranch

6.

Woodbine Falls

STILLWATER DRAINAGE

5 ⤍
To Sioux Charley Lake

5 P

7. Benbow Jeep Road—East Fishtail Creek Trail to Island Lake and Twin Lakes

FISHTAIL CREEK DRAINAGE

Hiking distance: 8 miles round trip
Hiking time: 4 hours
Elevation gain: 800 feet
Maps: U.S.G.S. Beehive and Emerald Lake
Beartooth Publishing: Absaroka Beartooth Wilderness
U.S.F.S. Custer National Forest

Summary of hike: This diverse and scenic hike crosses open meadows, passes through aspen and pine forests, fords streams and creeks, and leads to overlooks of the majestic Beartooth Mountain Range. The trailhead is located by the small town of Dean and heads to East Fishtail Creek, a tributary of the Stillwater River. A loop leads to Island Lake, a scenic 4-acre tarn, and the Twin Lakes, which reside within the West Rosebud Creek system.

Driving directions: From the north end of Red Lodge, drive 30 miles west on Highway 78 to County Road 419, the Fishtail and Nye turnoff on the left. Turn left (west) on County Road 419 and continue 13.9 miles, passing through Fishtail to Benbow Road at the west end of the small town of Dean. Turn left and drive 2.3 miles to the unpaved Forest Service Road 2415 on the left marked "Pole Unit Fuelwood Areas," 0.5 miles past the Custer National Forest sign. Turn left and go 0.1 mile to the parking area on the wide, flat turnout on the right.

Hiking directions: Walk up the jeep road (F.S. 2415) through open forest, reaching the Benbow Jeep Road/East Fishtail Trail #37 sign at a quarter mile. Continue through aspen groves and a young fir forest. At 0.8 miles, cross through a cattle fence and walk across the plateau to a saddle. Descend into the forested drainage to a junction and trail sign at 1.2 miles. Stay on the jeep road, curving to the right and heading uphill to the ridge. The road levels out to a signed trail junction at just under 2 miles. Leave

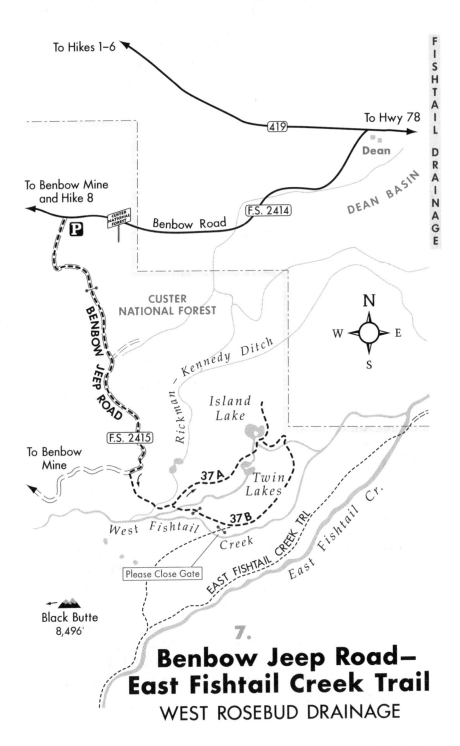

To Hikes 1–6

FISHTAIL DRAINAGE

419

To Hwy 78

Dean

DEAN BASIN

To Benbow Mine
and Hike 8

CUSTER NATIONAL FOREST

P

Benbow Road

F.S. 2414

BENBOW JEEP ROAD

CUSTER NATIONAL FOREST

Kennedy Ditch

Rickman

N
W · E
S

Island Lake

F.S. 2415

To Benbow Mine

37A

Twin Lakes

West Fishtail Creek

37B

EAST FISHTAIL CREEK TRL.

East Fishtail Cr.

Please Close Gate

Black Butte
8,496'

7.
Benbow Jeep Road–
East Fishtail Creek Trail
WEST ROSEBUD DRAINAGE

the road and take the footpath to the left (south), descending to an overlook of the Beartooth Front. Continue downhill to the Rickman–Kennedy Ditch at 2.5 miles. Cross over the log to a trail split, the beginning of the loop.

Begin the loop on the left fork. In a half mile, skirt the west edge of North Twin Lake. Follow a water flume from Twin Lakes to Island Lake, reaching the inlet cascade at Island Lake. After exploring the lake, return to the inlet stream and make a short, steep descent on the main trail along the cascading stream. After crossing, follow the hillside through a ponderosa pine forest. Watch for a "Please Close Gate" sign. (For an extended hike, this detour through the gate crosses West Fishtail Creek to a creekside stroll along East Fishtail Creek.) Back on the main trail, pass through another gate. Ford the creek, completing the loop. Return by retracing your steps. ■

8. Benbow Mine to The Golf Course
FISHTAIL CREEK DRAINAGE

Hiking distance: 6 miles round trip
Hiking time: 3 hours
Elevation gain: 900 feet
Maps: U.S.G.S. Mount Wood
       Beartooth Publishing: Absaroka Beartooth Wilderness
       Rocky Mountain Surveys: Mount Douglas—Mount Wood

Summary of hike: The "Golf Course" is a sprawling 9,200-foot grassy plateau that lies below the north end of the Stillwater Plateau, nearly a mile above the Stillwater Valley. The vistas from this flower-filled subalpine tableland are stunning. The hike begins at Benbow Mine, an abandoned chromite mine dating back to the early 1920s. The mine is named for Thomas Benbow, who homesteaded in Absaroka in 1892 and discovered chrome deposits in 1905. The trail follows an old dirt road that weaves up the mountain, with views of the Fishtail Plateau, Chrome Lake, Black Butte, and Cathedral Peak.

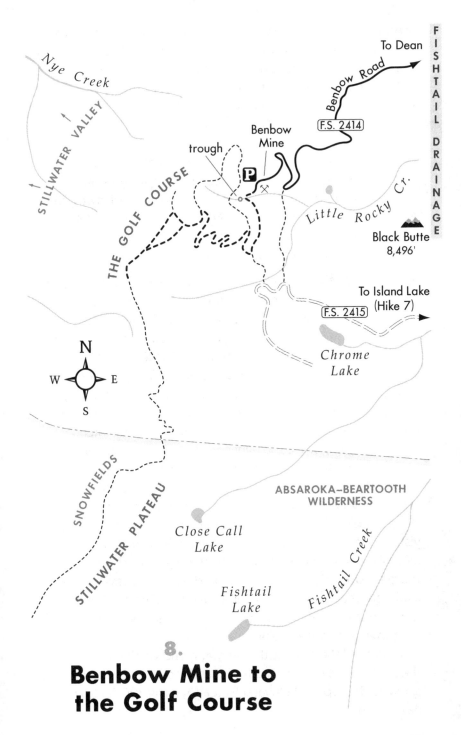

To Dean

To Island Lake (Hike 7)

Nye Creek

STILLWATER VALLEY

Benbow Road

F.S. 2414

FISHTAIL DRAINAGE

trough

Benbow Mine

THE GOLF COURSE

P

Little Rocky Cr.

Black Butte
8,496'

F.S. 2415

Chrome Lake

N
W   E
S

SNOWFIELDS

STILLWATER PLATEAU

Close Call Lake

ABSAROKA–BEARTOOTH WILDERNESS

Fishtail Creek

Fishtail Lake

8.
Benbow Mine to the Golf Course

Driving directions: From the north end of Red Lodge, drive 30 miles west on Highway 78 to County Road 419, the Fishtail and Nye turnoff on the left. Turn left (west) on County Road 419, and continue 13.9 miles, passing through Fishtail to Benbow Road at the west end of the small town of Dean. Turn left and drive 11.6 miles on the unpaved road to the abandoned Benbow Mine, located at the end of the drivable road (Forest Service Road 2414). Park in the wide flat area on the sides of the road. The last 7 miles of the narrow, winding road are bumpy and slow.

From I-90 in Columbus, drive 15 miles south on Highway 78 to Absarokee. Drive through town 2 miles to County Road 419, the Fishtail and Nye turnoff on the right. Turn right (west) on County Road 419, and follow the directions above.

Hiking directions: Head up the steep, narrow jeep road, and cross a stream by a cement water trough. Gently descend to a spectacular view of Black Butte and the Fishtail Plateau. At a half mile is a fork. The left fork leads toward Chrome Lake. Bear right and head uphill. Continue another 0.2 miles to another road split. Take the switchback to the left, and steadily zipper up the forested dirt road on six more switchbacks. Along the way are outstanding vistas of the surrounding mountains and of tree-lined Chrome Lake below. At the seventh and last switchback is a road fork by a cairn. The right fork descends straight ahead.

Go sharply to the left and continue uphill, with great views across the Stillwater Valley nearly a mile below to the west. Make a sweeping curve to the right, and head west to an exposed knoll at the 9,200-foot Golf Course, where sweeping vistas span across the massive Stillwater Plateau. From the summit, take one of a couple paths to the right. Head south across the pine-dotted grassland. Slowly descend, crossing the dramatic landscape and passing survey markers. Drop to the base of the flower-laden plateau, strolling across the back nine. Choose your own turnaround point.

To extend the hike, at the far south end of The Golf Course, the path curves left into the forest and ascends the slope to the snowfields atop the Stillwater Plateau, gaining 800 feet over the next 2 miles. ▩

9. West Rosebud Trail to Mystic Lake
WEST ROSEBUD DRAINAGE

Hiking distance: 7 miles round trip
Hiking time: 3.5 hours
Elevation gain: 1,200 feet
Maps: U.S.G.S. Alpine and Granite Peak
       Beartooth Publishing: Absaroka Beartooth Wilderness
       Rocky Mountain Surveys: Alpine-Cooke City

Summary of hike: Mystic Lake is the largest lake in the Beartooths, covering more than 430 acres. It is a natural lake with a hydro-electric dam at the east end. The hike to Mystic Lake follows the West Rosebud Trail uphill for 1,200 feet. The hike offers spectacular views of the West Rosebud Valley. From the top are beautiful views of Mystic Lake, West Rosebud Canyon, and the surrounding mountain peaks.

Driving directions: From the north end of Red Lodge, drive 30 miles west on Highway 78 to County Road 419, the Fishtail and Nye turnoff on the left. Turn left (west) on County Road 419, and continue 4.3 miles to West Rosebud Road (425) on the left, just after Fishtail. Turn left and drive 6.4 miles to a road split. Take the left fork, staying on West Rosebud Road, and drive 14 miles to the trailhead parking area at the end of the road.

From I-90 in Columbus, drive 17 miles south on Highway 78 to County Road 419, two miles past Absarokee. Turn right (west) on County Road 419, and follow the directions above.

Hiking directions: From the parking area, continue up the road past the power plant and a few houses to the trailhead sign. Cross the wooden bridge over the railroad tracks to the footpath. The trail heads upstream along West Rosebud Creek. At 0.75 miles, cross a 40-foot wooden footbridge to the south side of the creek. A short distance after crossing, enter the Absaroka-Beartooth Wilderness and continue uphill. Zigzag up several switchbacks through rock fields as you near the top. Cross over the ridge to views of Mystic Lake and the dam. Descend to the east shore of the lake and a sandy beach. The trail levels and follows the south shore of the lake to a junction with the Phantom Creek Trail, which leads 10 miles to East Rosebud Lake—Hike 10. This is the turn-around spot. Return along the same trail.

To hike farther, the trail continues west up the main drainage to Island and Silver Lakes, or south past Huckleberry Lake to Granite Peak, Montana's highest peak at 12,799 feet. ■

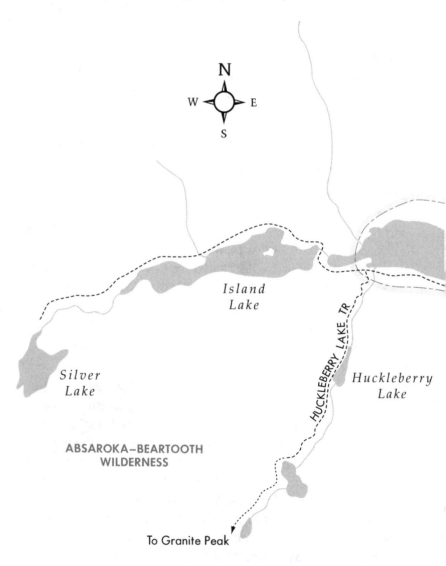

9.
Mystic Lake
WEST ROSEBUD TRAIL

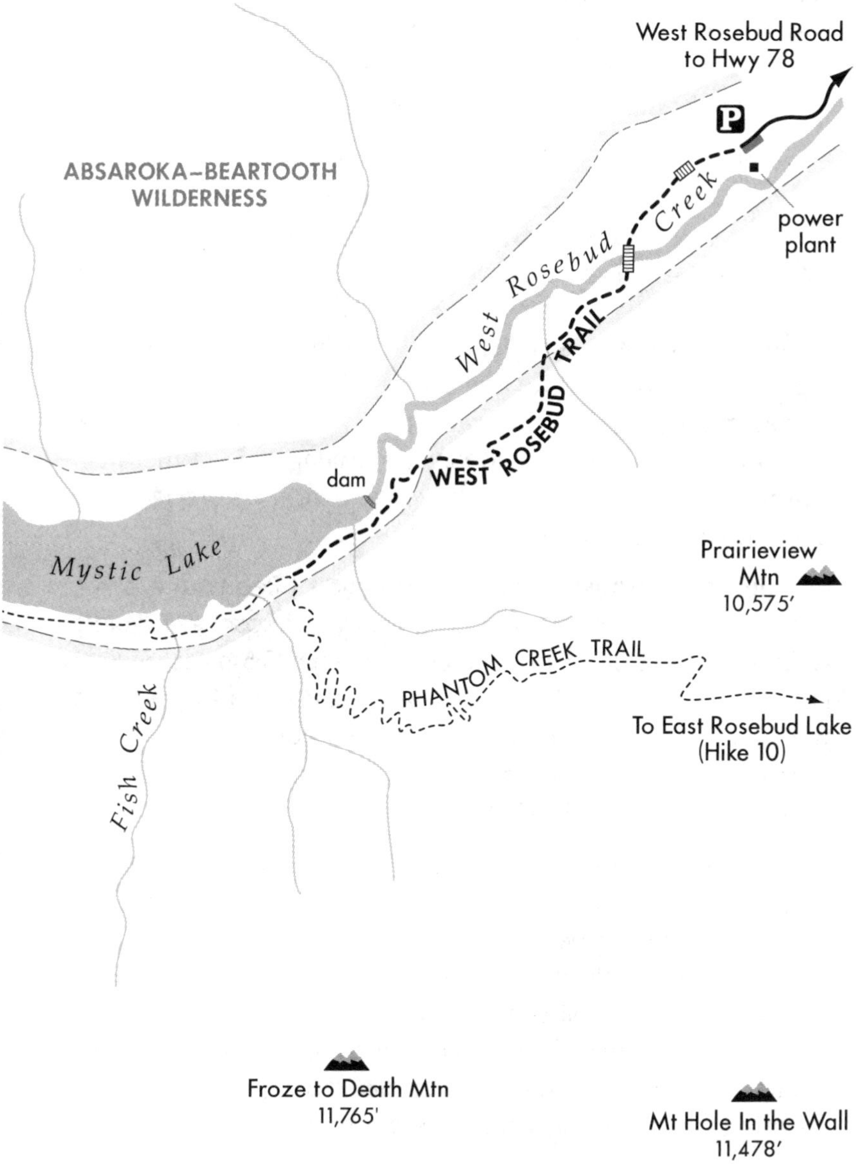

West Rosebud Road
to Hwy 78

P

ABSAROKA–BEARTOOTH
WILDERNESS

West Rosebud Creek

power
plant

WEST ROSEBUD TRAIL

dam

Mystic Lake

Prairieview
Mtn
10,575'

Fish Creek

PHANTOM CREEK TRAIL

To East Rosebud Lake
(Hike 10)

Froze to Death Mtn
11,765'

Mt Hole In the Wall
11,478'

10. Phantom Creek Trail to Slough Lake
EAST ROSEBUD DRAINAGE

Hiking distance: 5 miles round trip
Hiking time: 2.5 hours
Elevation gain: 1,200 feet
Maps: U.S.G.S. Alpine
  Beartooth Publishing: Absaroka Beartooth Wilderness
  Rocky Mountain Surveys: Alpine-Cooke City

Summary of hike: The Phantom Creek Trail is one of two primary routes used to reach 12,799-foot Granite Peak, the highest peak in Montana. (The other route is the Huckleberry Lake Trail from Mystic Lake in the West Rosebud drainage.) This hike takes in the first 2.5 miles of the trail to Slough Lake, paralleling Armstrong Creek. Slough Lake is actually two wide spots of the creek. The 6-acre lake is in a large, glacier-carved meadow surrounded by imposing mountain peaks, including Saddleback Mountain, Froze-to-Death Mountain, Mount Hole-in-the Wall, and Shepard Mountain. Beyond Slough Lake, Armstrong Creek becomes Phantom Creek.

Driving directions: From the north end of Red Lodge, drive 20 miles west on Highway 78 to the town of Roscoe. Turn left (west) on the East Rosebud Road. Continue 13.5 miles on East Rosebud Road to the Phantom Creek trailhead parking area on the right, located 0.4 miles before East Rosebud Lake.

From I-90 in Columbus, drive 27 miles south on Highway 78 to Roscoe, then follow the directions above.

Hiking directions: From the parking area, head west. A series of gradual switchbacks lead quickly into the Absaroka-Beartooth Wilderness, with views south of East Rosebud Lake. The trail hugs the north wall of the canyon above tumbling Armstrong Creek. Continue uphill past two boulder fields and numerous streams. At two miles, the trail begins to level out. As you approach Slough Lake, the canyon opens to a large meadow surrounded by mountains. Follow the north edge of Slough Lake and the meadow. After enjoying the lake and meadow, return along the same route.

The Phantom Creek Trail continues 7.5 miles to Mystic Lake (Hike 9). ■

11. East Rosebud Trail to Elk Lake
EAST ROSEBUD DRAINAGE

Hiking distance: 6 miles round trip
Hiking time: 3 hours
Elevation gain: 500 feet
Maps: U.S.G.S. Alpine
       Beartooth Publishing: Absaroka Beartooth Wilderness
       Rocky Mountain Surveys: Alpine-Cooke City

Summary of hike: The East Rosebud Trail is a popular 26-mile hiking and horsepacking route to Cooke City. The majority of the trail parallels East Rosebud Creek, a major waterway in the Beartooth Mountains. The creek flows through ten lakes. The headwaters begin at Fossil Lake in the high backcountry atop the Beartooth Plateau, then flow southeast to East Rosebud Lake, the lowest lake in the chain. Seventy-six lakes and nine additional streams feed the creek.

The East Rosebud Trail begins at East Rosebud Lake. The 117-acre lake lies at the mouth of the canyon, southwest of the town of Roscoe. This hike takes in the first three miles of the trail, climbing up the canyon to 11-acre Elk Lake. The trail is surrounded by the mountain peaks of Shepard Mountain, Mount Inabnit, and Sylvan Peak. En route, the trail passes a 50-foot waterfall and winds through the burn area from the 1996 fires.

Driving directions: From the north end of Red Lodge, drive 20 miles west on Highway 78 to the town of Roscoe. Turn left (west) on the East Rosebud Road. Continue 14.4 miles on East Rosebud Road to the East Rosebud trailhead parking area at the end of the road on the east side of the lake.

Hiking directions: From the parking area, hike south past the trailhead sign along the east side of East Rosebud Lake. Rock hop across an inlet stream near the south end of the lake. Climb to an overlook of the lake and East Rosebud Creek. Begin a short descent into the majestic canyon, entering the Absaroka-Beartooth Wilderness. Head up canyon along the tumbling whitewater of the creek. At 1.2 miles, a few switchbacks lead past a waterfall. Cross several streams, including a wooden bridge over Snow Creek, where another waterfall can be seen dropping off the cliffs high above. The trail enters the forest, then arrives at Elk Lake. Return along the same route.

Rainbow Lake is another 3 miles farther as the trail continues along East Rosebud Creek. ■

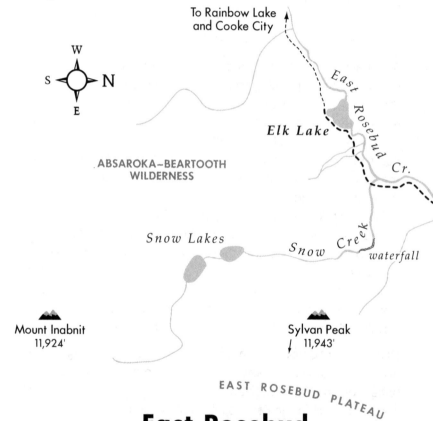

East Rosebud

10. Phantom Creek Trail to Slough Lake
11. East Rosebud Trail to Elk Lake

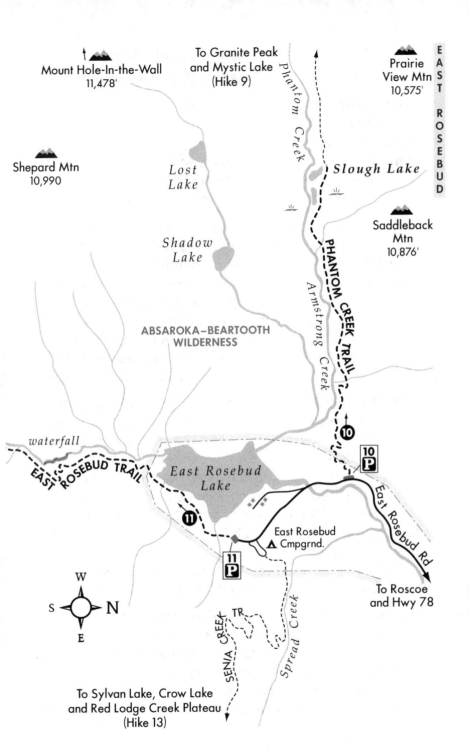

Mount Hole-In-the-Wall
11,478'

To Granite Peak
and Mystic Lake
(Hike 9)

Prairie
View Mtn
10,575'

EAST ROSEBUD

Shepard Mtn
10,990

*Lost
Lake*

Slough Lake

*Shadow
Lake*

Saddleback
Mtn
10,876'

ABSAROKA–BEARTOOTH
WILDERNESS

Phantom Creek

Armstrong Creek

PHANTOM CREEK TRAIL

10

waterfall

EAST ROSEBUD TRAIL

*East Rosebud
Lake*

10
P

East Rosebud
▲ Cmpgrnd.

East Rosebud Rd

11

11
P

To Roscoe
and Hwy 78

W

S — N

E

SENIA CREEK TR

Sparad Creek

To Sylvan Lake, Crow Lake
and Red Lodge Creek Plateau
(Hike 13)

12. West Red Lodge Creek Trail to Absaroka—Beartooth Wilderness

Hiking distance: 2.5 miles round trip
Hiking time: 1.5 hours
Elevation gain: 600 feet
Maps: U.S.G.S. Bare Mountain and Sylvan Peak
Beartooth Publishing: Absaroka Beartooth Wilderness
Rocky Mountain Surveys: Alpine-Mount Maurice

Summary of hike: The West Red Lodge Creek drainage begins atop the 10,000-foot Red Lodge Creek Plateau at the base of Grass Mountain. The narrow canyon is tucked between Butcher Mountain and Bare Mountain and descends to the base of Sheep Mountain, just south of Luther. This hike follows the easy, lower portion of the trail in the foothills along West Red Lodge Creek. The trail leads to the mouth of the narrow rock canyon and a log bridge at the Absaroka-Beartooth Wilderness boundary. For a longer hike, Hike 13 continues steeply up to the alpine plateau.

Driving directions: From Red Lodge, drive 12.7 miles northwest on Highway 78 to the Lower Luther Road, the second Luther turnoff between mile markers 12 and 13. Turn left (southwest) and drive 2.4 miles to a T-junction in the town of Luther. Turn right on the Luther/Roscoe Road, and go 0.5 miles to Red Lodge Creek Road. Turn left and continue 2.6 miles to the signed Custer National Forest boundary and a road split. Take the right fork on Forest Service Road 2141, and drive 1.3 miles to a signed trailhead parking area on the right.

From I-90 in Columbus, drive 34 miles south on Highway 78 to Lower Luther Road. Turn right and follow the directions above.

Hiking directions: Head southwest across the open flat toward the forest. The near-level path parallels West Red Lodge Creek across trickling streams and water ditches to an old road at 0.8 miles. Bear left toward the jagged outcroppings, staying close to the creek. Curve left into the mouth of the canyon drainage. Pass huge mossy boulders to a log bridge and cascading creek at the Absaroka-Beartooth Wilderness boundary. Cross the bridge and continue a short distance up the rock-walled canyon to a second creek crossing that must be waded to cross. This is the turn-around spot. To hike to the top of Red Lodge Creek Plateau, continue with the next hike. ■

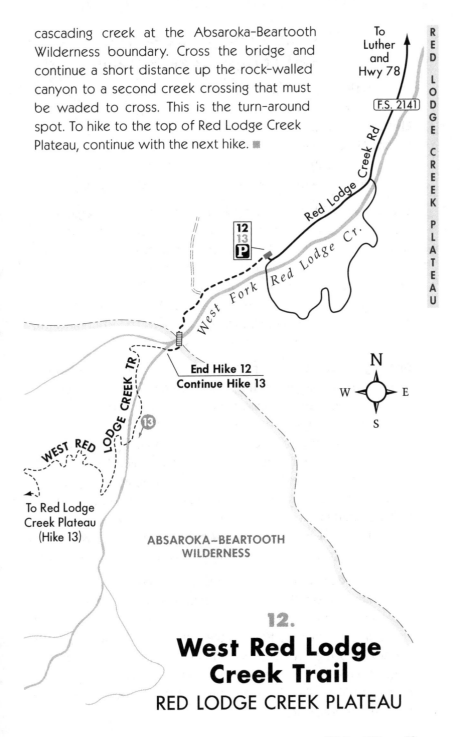

To Luther and Hwy 78

F.S. 2141

Red Lodge Creek Rd

Red Lodge Cr.

12
13
P

West Fork Red Lodge Creek

End Hike 12
Continue Hike 13

WEST RED LODGE CREEK TR.

13

WEST RED

To Red Lodge Creek Plateau (Hike 13)

N
W   E
S

ABSAROKA–BEARTOOTH WILDERNESS

12.
West Red Lodge Creek Trail
RED LODGE CREEK PLATEAU

13. West Red Lodge Creek Trail to Red Lodge Creek Plateau

Hiking distance: 14 miles round trip (or 12-mile shuttle)
Hiking time: 8 hours
Elevation gain: 4,000 feet
Maps: U.S.G.S. Bare Mountain and Sylvan Peak
Beartooth Publishing: Absaroka Beartooth Wilderness
Rocky Mountain Surveys: Alpine-Mount Maurice

Summary of hike: The West Red Lodge Creek Trail begins near the town of Luther and climbs to the Red Lodge Creek Plateau and Crow Lake. It is a full-day, strenuous hike to this 10,000-foot alpine plateau. At the vast windswept summit are wide-ranging, unobstructed vistas of Sylvan Peak, Bare Mountain, and the Silver Run Plateau. This route can also be hiked as a 12-mile, one-way shuttle with the Senia Creek Trail (Hike 22). Bring warm clothing and be prepared for changes in weather.

Driving directions: From Red Lodge, drive 12.7 miles northwest on Highway 78 to the Lower Luther Road, the second Luther turnoff between mile markers 12 and 13. Turn left (southwest) and drive 2.4 miles to a T-junction in the town of Luther. Turn right on the Luther/Roscoe Road, and go 0.5 miles to Red Lodge Creek Road. Turn left and continue 2.6 miles to the signed Custer National Forest boundary and a road split. Take the right fork on Forest Service Road 2141, and drive 1.3 miles to a signed trailhead parking area on the right.

From I-90 in Columbus, drive 34 miles south on Highway 78 to Lower Luther Road. Turn right and follow the directions above.

Hiking directions: Head southwest across the open flat toward the forest. The near-level path parallels West Red Lodge Creek across trickling streams and water ditches to an old road at 0.8 miles. Bear left toward the jagged outcroppings, staying close to the creek. Curve left into the mouth of the canyon drainage. Pass huge mossy boulders to a log bridge and the cascading West Red Lodge Creek at the Absaroka-Beartooth Wilderness boundary.

From the bridge, continue along the south side of the creek up the narrow canyon. Pass towering rock walls and jagged spires. Wade across the creek, and follow the cascading stream to a small meadow with vistas of the surrounding peaks. Curve left on a horseshoe bend and return to the creek. Carefully wade across the creek again and head up canyon. At 3 miles, wade across to the west side of the creek. Follow the creek 0.6 miles to another horseshoe right bend. Begin the steep ascent of the mountain up numerous switchbacks for the next two miles. Near the top, the path breaks out onto the rocky plateau. Follow the cairns southwest to incredible views of the jagged rock walls of Sylvan Peak. Descend towards the cliffs across the rolling hills of the alpine plateau. This is the turn-around spot.

To hike farther, the main trail continues southwest for 2 miles to Crow Lake. Past Crow Lake, the trail continues west to Sylvan Lake and descends into the East Rosebud drainage. Or to the left (southeast), a faint trail descends across the open tundra, reaching the Senia Creek Trail—Hike 22—at a prominent 4-foot cairn above West Red Lodge Creek. ■

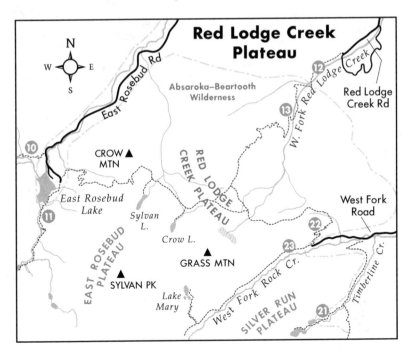

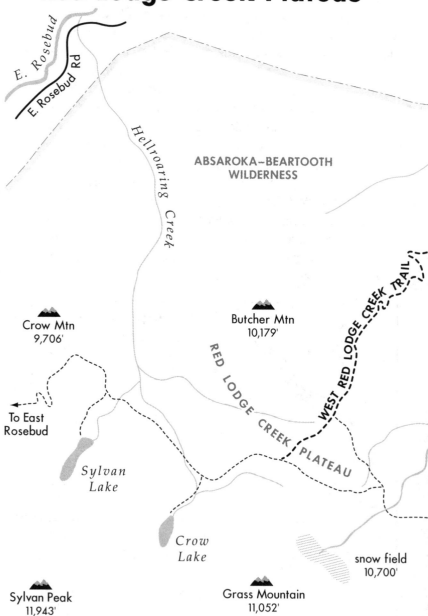

13.
West Red Lodge Creek Trail to
Red Lodge Creek Plateau

E. Rosebud

E. Rosebud Rd

Hellroaring Creek

**ABSAROKA–BEARTOOTH
WILDERNESS**

Crow Mtn
9,706'

Butcher Mtn
10,179'

RED LODGE CREEK PLATEAU

WEST RED LODGE CREEK TRAIL

To East
Rosebud

Sylvan
Lake

Crow
Lake

snow field
10,700'

Sylvan Peak
11,943'

Grass Mountain
11,052'

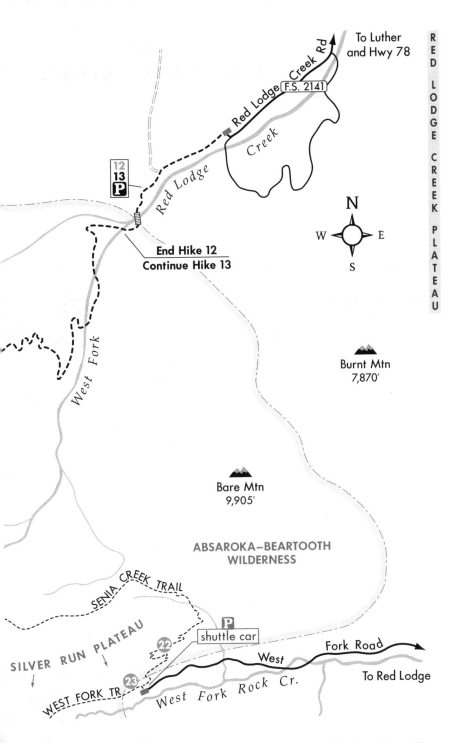

To Luther
and Hwy 78

Red Lodge Creek Rd

F.S. 2141

Creek

Red Lodge

12
13
P

End Hike 12
Continue Hike 13

N
W — E
S

Burnt Mtn
7,870'

West Fork

Bare Mtn
9,905'

ABSAROKA–BEARTOOTH
WILDERNESS

SENIA CREEK TRAIL

SILVER RUN PLATEAU

P
shuttle car

22

23

WEST FORK TR

West Fork Rock Cr.

West

Fork Road

To Red Lodge

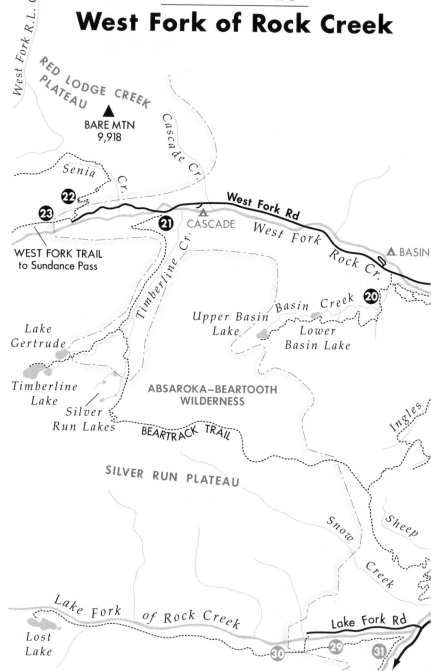

West Fork of Rock Creek

West Fork R.L. Cr.

West Fork

RED LODGE CREEK PLATEAU

▲ BARE MTN 9,918

Senia Cr.

Cascade Cr.

22

23

West Fork Rd

21

▲ CASCADE

West Fork Rock Cr.

▲ BASIN

WEST FORK TRAIL
to Sundance Pass

Timberline Cr.

Basin Creek

20

Upper Basin Lake

Lower Basin Lake

Lake Gertrude

Timberline Lake

Silver Run Lakes

ABSAROKA–BEARTOOTH WILDERNESS

BEARTRACK TRAIL

Ingles

SILVER RUN PLATEAU

Snow Creek

Sheep

Lake Fork of Rock Creek

Lost Lake

Lake Fork Rd

30

29

31

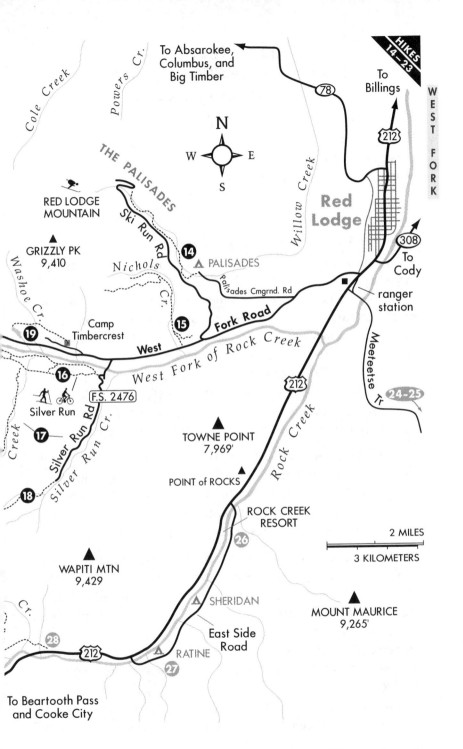

To Absarokee,
Columbus, and
Big Timber

HIKES
14 - 23

To
Billings

78

212

WEST FORK

Cole Creek

Powers Cr.

THE PALISADES

Willow Creek

Red
Lodge

RED LODGE
MOUNTAIN

Ski Run Rd

14

PALISADES

308

To
Cody

GRIZZLY PK
9,410

Nichols Cr.

Palisades Cmgrnd. Rd

Washoe Cr.

15

Fork Road

ranger
station

Camp
Timbercrest

West

West Fork of Rock Creek

19

Meeteetse Tr.

16

F.S. 2476

24-25

Silver Run

Silver Run Rd

Silver Run Cr.

212

Rock Creek

17

TOWNE POINT
7,969'

Creek

18

POINT of ROCKS

ROCK CREEK
RESORT

2 MILES

26

3 KILOMETERS

WAPITI MTN
9,429

SHERIDAN

MOUNT MAURICE
9,265'

28

212

East Side
Road

27

RATINE

To Beartooth Pass
and Cooke City

14. Willow Creek Trail
from Palisades Campground
WEST FORK of ROCK CREEK

Hiking distance: 4 miles round trip
Hiking time: 2 hours
Elevation gain: 1,000 feet
Maps: U.S.G.S. Red Lodge West
Beartooth Publishing: Beartooth Mountains
Rocky Mountain Surveys: Alpine-Mount Maurice

Summary of hike: The Willow Creek Trail is tucked into a narrow draw between Grizzly Peak, home of Red Lodge Mountain ski area, and the Palisades. The Palisades are jagged, weather-sculpted limestone formations originally deposited by an ancient sea. The formation is visible along the eastern face of the Beartooths and is especially prominent at the Meeteetse Spires (Hike 25). This hike weaves through a forested canyon from Palisades Campground to the ski area, following the contours of Willow Creek beneath the limestone and dolomite cliffs. En route, the unmaintained trail passes an old cabin and an abandoned mine, crossing Willow Creek numerous times.

Driving directions: From the south end of Red Lodge, turn west on West Fork Road, which heads to Red Lodge Mountain Resort. At 1.1 mile, turn right on the signed Palisades Campground Road. Drive 1.8 miles on the unpaved road to the far end of the campground. Park in the spaces on the right by the restrooms.

Hiking directions: Walk past the restrooms to the unsigned trailhead on the right by the log railing. Head up the forested path between Willow Creek and the limestone Palisades. Cross the gravel-covered path over the creek. A short distance ahead is a trail fork. Detour 20 yards to the right to a downfall log crossing of Willow Creek by an old abandoned mine. Return to the junction and take the main trail up the canyon, crossing over a culvert to the east side of the creek. Closely follow the creek through the lush riparian terrain as the canyon narrows. At 0.6 miles, cross the creek on a wooden bridge, passing steep rock

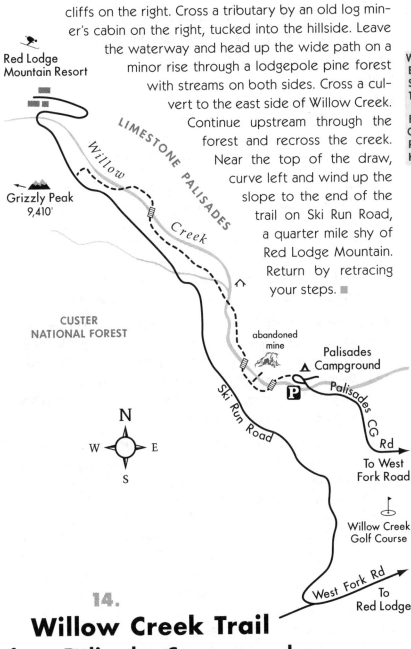

cliffs on the right. Cross a tributary by an old log miner's cabin on the right, tucked into the hillside. Leave the waterway and head up the wide path on a minor rise through a lodgepole pine forest with streams on both sides. Cross a culvert to the east side of Willow Creek. Continue upstream through the forest and recross the creek. Near the top of the draw, curve left and wind up the slope to the end of the trail on Ski Run Road, a quarter mile shy of Red Lodge Mountain. Return by retracing your steps. ▪

Red Lodge
Mountain Resort

WEST FORK

LIMESTONE PALISADES

Willow

Creek

Grizzly Peak
9,410'

CUSTER
NATIONAL FOREST

abandoned
mine

Palisades
▲ Campground

P

Palisades CG
Rd

To West
Fork Road

Ski Run Road

N
W — ⊕ — E
S

Willow Creek
Golf Course

West Fork Rd
To
Red Lodge

14.

Willow Creek Trail
from Palisades Campground
WEST FORK of ROCK CREEK

15. Nichols Creek Trail
WEST FORK of ROCK CREEK

Hiking distance: 4 miles round trip
Hiking time: 2 hours
Elevation gain: 1,100 feet
Maps: U.S.G.S. Red Lodge West
Beartooth Publishing: Beartooth Mountains
Rocky Mountain Surveys: Alpine-Mount Maurice

Summary of hike: Nichols Creek, a tributary of the West Fork of Rock Creek, flows through a beautiful side drainage from Grizzly Peak. The solitary trail parallels Nichols Creek on a rutted Forest Service road, winding through aspen, fir, and pine groves. The hike leads to a couple of overlooks with vistas of the West Fork Canyon, Rock Creek Canyon, Mount Maurice, the limestone spires, and eastward to the Pryor Mountains.

Driving directions: From the south end of Red Lodge, turn west on West Fork Road, which heads to Red Lodge Mountain Resort. At 2.8 miles, stay straight (left) onto West Fork Road as Ski Run Road curves uphill to the right. Continue 0.3 miles to Forest Service Road 2478, the first turnoff on the right. Turn right and park 40 yards ahead in the pullout on the right.

Hiking directions: Head north on the rough, unpaved road along the east side of Nichols Creek. The trail crosses open meadows with groves of aspens, fir, and rock outcroppings. At 0.2 miles is a side road on the right. This detour follows the hillside 0.4 miles to an overlook of the West Fork Canyon, Rock Creek Valley, Mount Maurice, and the Pryor Mountains. Back on the main trail, rock hop across Nichols Creek to a trail split. The right fork leads 100 yards to a primitive campsite by the creek. The left fork heads up the east-facing hillside, entering a lodgepole pine forest. Continue uphill above Nichols Creek. At 1.4 miles, the trail curves left alongside the creek to a junction. The right fork parallels the creek for a quarter mile and ends in the lush grass and brush. Take the horseshoe left bend and climb steeply up the mountain. At the ridge, bend right to a side path on the left. Take the side path 30 yards to an overlook of the West Fork Canyon at 1.6 miles. This is the turn-around spot.

To hike farther, the trail steeply ascends the mountain through the dense forest for 0.7 miles, ending in a small meadow. ▥

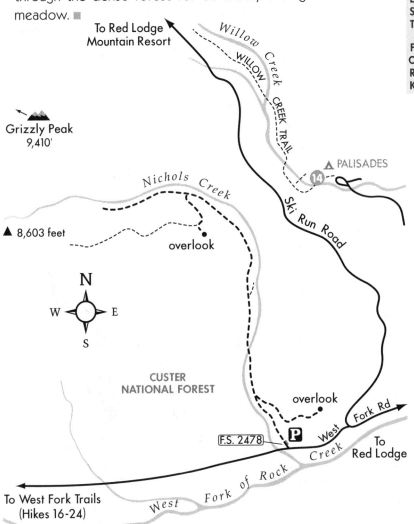

To Red Lodge
Mountain Resort

Willow Creek

WILLOW CREEK TRAIL

▲ PALISADES

14

Grizzly Peak
9,410'

Nichols Creek

Ski Run Road

▲ 8,603 feet

overlook

N

W ◆ E

S

CUSTER
NATIONAL FOREST

overlook

Fork Rd

F.S. 2478

P

West Creek

To
Red Lodge

To West Fork Trails
(Hikes 16-24)

West Fork of Rock Creek

15.
Nichols Creek Trail
WEST FORK of ROCK CREEK

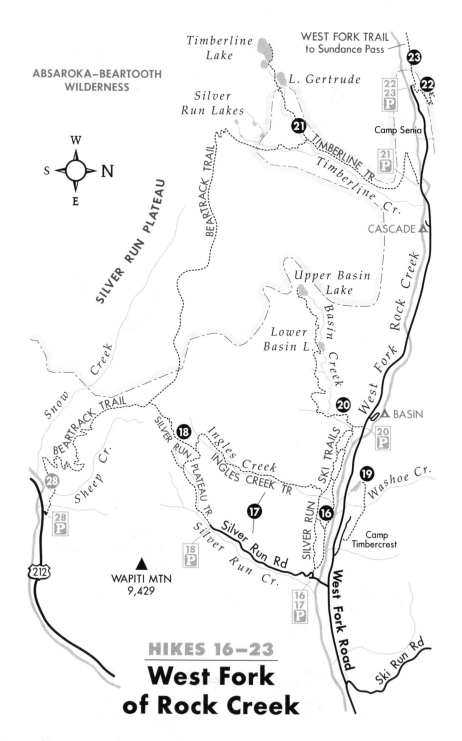

ABSAROKA–BEARTOOTH
WILDERNESS

*Timberline
Lake*

WEST FORK TRAIL
to Sundance Pass

23

*Silver
Run Lakes*

L. Gertrude

22
23
P

22

Camp Senia

21

21
P

W

S ✦ N

E

SILVER RUN PLATEAU

BEARTRACK TRAIL

TIMBERLINE TR.

Timberline Cr.

CASCADE ▲

*Upper Basin
Lake*

West Fork Rock Creek

*Lower
Basin L.*

Basin Creek

Snow Creek

BEARTRACK TRAIL

20

▲ BASIN

20
P

18

Ingles Creek

SKI TRAILS

Sheep Cr.

SILVER RUN PLATEAU TR.

INGLES CREEK TR.

19

Washoe Cr.

28

17

16

SILVER RUN

Camp
Timbercrest

28
P

212

18
P

Silver Run Rd

WAPITI MTN
9,429

Silver Run Cr.

West Fork Road

16
17
P

Ski Run Rd

HIKES 16–23
**West Fork
of Rock Creek**

16. Silver Run Ski Trails
WEST FORK of ROCK CREEK

Hiking distance: 2.4—5 miles round trip
Hiking time: 1—2.5 hours
Elevation gain: 300 feet
Maps: U.S.G.S. Red Lodge West and Bare Mountain
Beartooth Publishing: Beartooth Mountains
Rocky Mountain Surveys: Alpine–Mount Maurice

Summary of hike: The Silver Run Ski Trails are located a few miles west of Red Lodge on the West Fork of Rock Creek. The trails, surrounded by forested mountains, parallel the south side of the cascading creek and form a series of loops. During the winter, they are popular cross-country ski trails. Throughout the snow-free months, the trails are great hiking and mountain biking get-aways close to Red Lodge. The trail also offers access to the Silver Run Plateau (Hikes 17—18).

Driving directions: From the south end of Red Lodge, turn west on West Fork Road, which heads to Red Lodge Mountain Resort. At 2.8 miles, stay straight (left) on West Fork Road as Ski Run Road curves uphill to the right. Continue 1.6 miles to Silver Run Road and turn left. Drive 0.2 miles, crossing the West Fork of Rock Creek, and park in the Silver Run Ski Trails parking area on the left.

Hiking directions: Hike west up the unpaved road, following the "Loop 1—4" sign to a road split. The left road fork heads up Silver Run Creek (Hikes 17—18). Take the right fork onto the trail. Fifty yards ahead is a second fork, which is the beginning of the loop. Bear left on the upper trail through the lodgepole pine forest. At 1.1 mile is a signed trail fork on the right to return on Loop 1, a 2.4-mile hike. Continue on the left to an old wooden hut and a rock stove. Just beyond the hut is a bridge crossing Ingles Creek. After crossing, there is a signed junction with the Ingles Creek Trail (Hike 17). Bear right, staying on the Silver Run Trail to a junction at 2.1 miles. The right fork is the return for Loop 2, a 3-mile hike. For a longer hike, continue left on Loops 3 and 4. Loop 3 is a 4-mile hike and Loop 4 is a 5-mile hike. At the far west end of Loop 4 is a posted junction. The left fork crosses cascading Basin Creek on a footbrige 50 yards ahead and continues 100 yards farther to the Basin Creek Lake Trail (Hike 20). For this hike, veer right, staying on Loop 4 towards the West Fork of Rock Creek. Parallel the West Fork downstream, returning to the trailhead. ▪

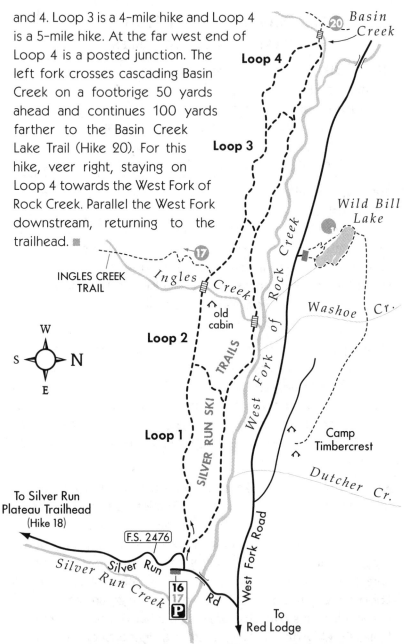

INGLES CREEK TRAIL

Loop 4

Loop 3

Loop 2

Loop 1

Basin Creek

Wild Bill Lake

Washoe Cr.

Camp Timbercrest

Dutcher Cr.

Ingles Creek

old cabin

SILVER RUN SKI TRAILS

West Fork of Rock Creek

W
S ⊕ N
E

To Silver Run Plateau Trailhead (Hike 18)

F.S. 2476

Silver Run Creek

Silver Run Rd

West Fork Road

To Red Lodge

16. **Silver Run Ski Trails**
WEST FORK of ROCK CREEK

17. Ingles Creek—Silver Run Loop
WEST FORK of ROCK CREEK

Hiking distance: 7 miles round trip
Hiking time: 3.5 hours
Elevation gain: 1,600 feet
Maps: U.S.G.S. Red Lodge West, Mount Maurice, Bare Mtn.
      Beartooth Publishing: Beartooth Mountains
      Rocky Mountain Surveys: Alpine-Mount Maurice

Summary of hike: The Ingles Creek drainage is a lush, forested draw between the West Fork of Rock Creek and the Silver Run Plateau. This loop hike begins on the Silver Run Ski Trails, parallel to the West Fork. The trail then climbs up the Ingles Creek drainage, crossing the creek seven times and passing three old cabins. Near the head of the draw, the hike loops east over a ridge and into the Silver Run drainage, returning along the Silver Run Plateau Trail and Silver Run Road (F.S. Road 2476).

Driving directions: From the south end of Red Lodge, turn west on West Fork Road, which heads to Red Lodge Mountain Resort. At 2.8 miles, stay straight (left) on West Fork Road as Ski Run Road curves uphill to the right. Continue 1.6 miles to Silver Run Road and turn left. Drive 0.2 miles, crossing the West Fork of Rock Creek, and park in the Silver Run Ski Trails parking area on the left.

Hiking directions: Head west on the unpaved road to a road fork. Leave the road and begin the loop, bearing right on the signed Silver Run Ski Trails. Follow the blue trail signs for 1.1 mile to a trail split. Stay left on Loop 2 to an old cabin and rock stove by Ingles Creek. Cross the wooden bridge over the creek to a signed junction.

Bear left on the Ingles Creek Trail, leaving the Silver Run Ski Trails, and head up the Ingles Creek drainage on the serpentine path. A half mile up the canyon is the remains of an old miner's cabin. For the next two miles, the trail stays close to the creek and crosses it six times. A half mile after the sixth crossing are the remains of two more cabins on the left. Cross Ingles Creek to the left, and head up the west-facing hillside to a junction on the ridge of the Silver Run drainage—Hike 18—which leads up to Silver Run Plateau. Bear left on the unsigned Silver Run Plateau Trail, and zigzag down into the canyon. Cross a stream and continue downhill to Silver Run Creek. The trail ends at Forest Service Road 2476 (Silver Run Road)—the trailhead to Hike 18. Follow the unpaved road alongside Silver Run Creek for 1.9 miles, completing the loop. ■

18. Silver Run Plateau Trail
from WEST FORK of ROCK CREEK

Hiking distance: 8 miles round trip
Hiking time: 4 hours
Elevation gain: 2,400 feet
Maps: U.S.G.S. Red Lodge West, Mount Maurice, Bare Mtn. and
Black Pyramid Mountain
Beartooth Publishing: Beartooth Mountains
Rocky Mountain Surveys: Alpine-Mount Maurice

Summary of hike: The Silver Run Plateau is a wide open expanse at over 10,000 feet in the Absaroka-Beartooth Wilderness. Atop the massive plateau are dwarfed, windswept trees and grassy alpine meadows. The amazing panoramic vistas include the West Fork drainage down to Red Lodge, the eastern plains, the Lake Fork drainage to the Hellroaring Plateau, and Black Pyramid Mountain. Three trails access the Silver Run Plateau. This hike begins by Silver Run Creek on the north flank of Wapiti Mountain and climbs through a dense conifer forest to the east edge of the plateau. Bring warm clothing and be prepared for changes in weather. (Hikes 22 and 28 offer two other routes up to the Silver Run Plateau.)

Driving directions: From the south end of Red Lodge, turn west on West Fork Road, which heads to Red Lodge Mountain Resort. At 2.8 miles, stay straight (left) on West Fork Road as Ski Run Road curves uphill to the right. Continue 1.6 miles to Silver Run Road and turn left. Drive 0.2 miles, crossing the West Fork of Rock Creek, to the Silver Run Ski Trails parking area on the left. From the parking area, turn right on Forest Service Road 2476, and drive 1.9 miles to the signed trailhead parking area at the end of the road.

Hiking directions: Head west past the trailhead sign along the north side of Silver Run Creek. The trail, an old Forest Service stock road, soon veers away from the creek, winding up the canyon through an open forest. As the trail enters the dense forest, the grade steepens. At one mile is an unsigned trail split. (The left fork ends a half mile up the steep drainage.) Take the right fork and cross a small stream. At 1.2 miles, a switchback to the right leads to an overlook of the forested canyon. Continue uphill to an unsigned junction with the Ingles Creek Trail on the right (Hike 17). Stay left, following the mountain ridge between the Silver Run and Ingles Creek drainages. From the ridge, zigzag up through the forest to the Silver Run Plateau. Near the top, the forest gives way to stunted trees and alpine meadows. The trail reaches the plateau at 3.5 miles. Cairns mark the trail across the plateau to a signed junction with the Beartrack Trail. This is the turn-around spot.

To hike farther, the Beartrack Trail heads west (right) to the Silver Run Lakes (Hike 22), or descends southeast (left) to Highway 212, north of the Lake Fork of Rock Creek (Hike 28). Both routes are popular shuttle hikes. ▪

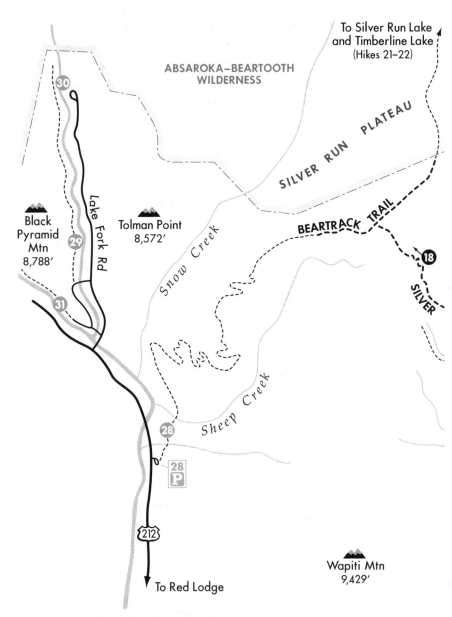

17. Ingles Creek–Silver Run Loop
18. Silver Run Plateau Trail
WEST FORK of ROCK CREEK

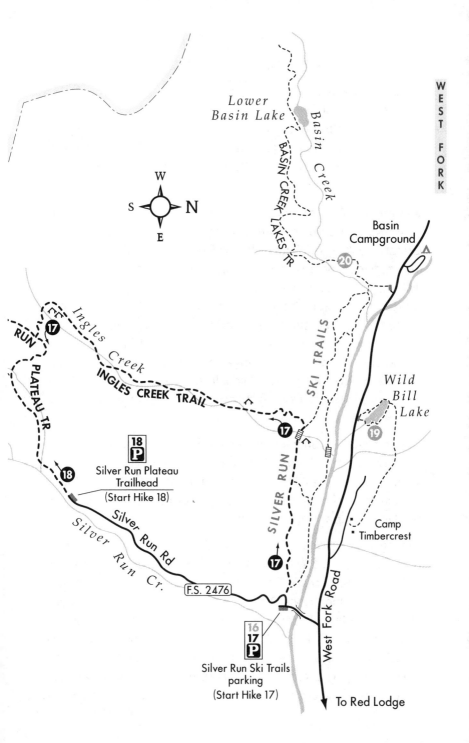

Lower
Basin Lake

Basin Creek

BASIN CREEK LAKES TR

W E S T   F O R K

Basin
Campground

20

W

S → N

E

SKI TRAILS

Wild
Bill
Lake

19

RUN

17

Ingles Creek

PLATEAU TR

INGLES CREEK TRAIL

17

18
P
Silver Run Plateau
Trailhead
(Start Hike 18)

18

SILVER RUN

17

Camp
Timbercrest

Silver Run Rd

Silver Run Cr.

F.S. 2476

17

West Fork Road

16
17
P
Silver Run Ski Trails
parking
(Start Hike 17)

To Red Lodge

19. Wild Bill Lake
WEST FORK of ROCK CREEK

Hiking distance: 0.8 mile loop
Hiking time: 30 minutes
Elevation gain: Level hiking
Maps: U.S.G.S. Red Lodge West
        Beartooth Publishing: Beartooth Mountains
        Rocky Mountain Surveys: Alpine-Mount Maurice

Summary of hike: Wild Bill Lake is a small but charming three-acre lake in the Custer National Forest at the southern base of Grizzly Peak. The lake sits in the West Fork drainage, nestled into a glacial depression and surrounded by mountains. "Wild Bill" Kurtzer created the lake in 1902 by building a dam at the outlet. He stocked the lake and rented boats as a commercial venture. This trail circles the perimeter of the lake. There are two fishing docks with benches extending out into the lake. A picnic area sits among the lodgepole pines on the east side of the lake by the parking lot. Wild Bill Lake, regularly stocked with rainbow and brook trout, is a popular children's fishing area and is wheelchair accessible.

Driving directions: From the south end of Red Lodge, turn west on West Fork Road, which heads to Red Lodge Mountain Resort. At 2.8 miles, stay straight (left) onto West Fork Road as Ski Run Road curves uphill to the right. Continue 3.1 miles to the Wild Bill Lake parking area on the right.

Hiking directions: From the parking lot, walk north past the restrooms up to the bridge that crosses the lake spillway. The trail curves left to a Y-junction. The left fork leads to the peninsula and fishing dock. The right fork continues north, staying close to the lake. The trail narrows to a footpath and meanders along the forested shoreline. Loop around to the west side of the lake, and cross an inlet stream to a trail split. The left fork continues along the lake. The right fork returns to the parking area.

    For a longer walk, take the narrow path that veers off at the northwest end of the lake. The trail gently climbs the hillside, then traverses the slope above Wild Bill Lake, heading east. The path follows the course of the powerlines and crosses Washoe Creek on a log bridge. Pass old wooden wagons, where the trail enters the private land of the Timbercrest Girl Scout Camp. ■

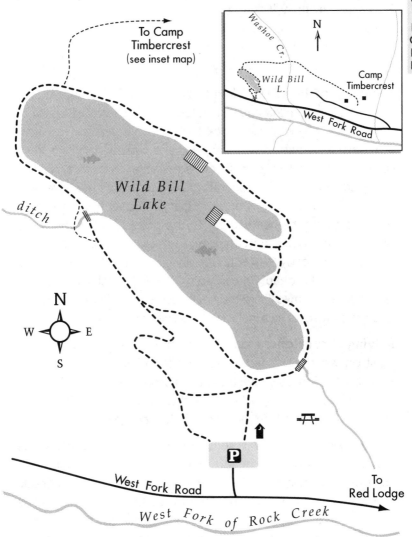

19. **Wild Bill Lake**
WEST FORK of ROCK CREEK

20. Basin Creek Lakes Trail
WEST FORK of ROCK CREEK

Hiking distance: 8 miles round trip
Hiking time: 4 hours
Elevation gain: 2,100 feet
Maps: U.S.G.S. Bare Mountain
Beartooth Publishing: Beartooth Mountains
Rocky Mountain Surveys: Alpine-Mount Maurice

Summary of hike: Upper and Lower Basin Creek Lakes sit below the Silver Run Plateau just outside the Absaroka-Beartooth Wilderness. Lower Basin Creek Lake is a picturesque 2.5-acre tarn partially covered with lily pads and surrounded by forest. Upper Basin Creek Lake, 600 feet above the lower lake, rests at the base of a majestic mountain bowl that fronts the Silver Run Plateau. Snow melting within the glacial cirque fills the 6-acre lake and forms the headwaters of the creek, a tributary of the West Fork of Rock Creek. The trail to the lakes is an old logging road from the early 1900s. It steadily climbs into the Basin Creek valley along the beautiful cascading stream, passing a waterfall less than a half mile from the trailhead. The trail winds through evergreen forests and includes log creek crossings.

Driving directions: From the south end of Red Lodge, turn west on West Fork Road, which heads to Red Lodge Mountain Resort. At 2.8 miles, stay straight (left) onto West Fork Road as Ski Run Road curves uphill to the right. Continue 4.2 miles to the trailhead parking lot on the left. Turn left and park.

Hiking directions: Walk south up the wide trail. At 100 yards is a posted junction on the left with the Silver Run Ski Trails (Hike 16). Continue straight, following the whitewater of Basin Creek. The waterfall is 0.4 miles from the trailhead. As the trail curves to the right, climb some boulders along a spur trail to the left to view Basin Creek Falls, a two-tiered cataract. A short distance after the falls, the trail parallels Basin Creek to a log crossing over the creek. Continue uphill through the dense lodgepole pine forest below the Silver Run Plateau, following the well-

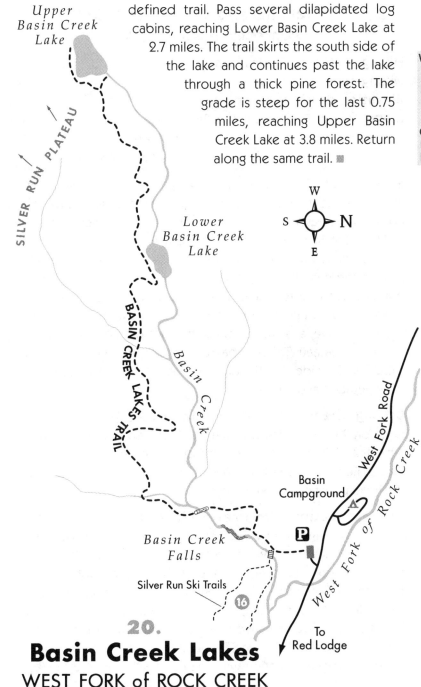

defined trail. Pass several dilapidated log cabins, reaching Lower Basin Creek Lake at 2.7 miles. The trail skirts the south side of the lake and continues past the lake through a thick pine forest. The grade is steep for the last 0.75 miles, reaching Upper Basin Creek Lake at 3.8 miles. Return along the same trail. ▪

Upper Basin Creek Lake

SILVER RUN PLATEAU

Lower Basin Creek Lake

W
S — N
E

BASIN CREEK LAKES TRAIL

Basin Creek

Basin Campground

West Fork Road

West Fork of Rock Creek

P

Basin Creek Falls

Silver Run Ski Trails

16

To Red Lodge

20.
Basin Creek Lakes
WEST FORK of ROCK CREEK

21. Timberline and Gertrude Lakes
WEST FORK of ROCK CREEK

Hiking distance: 9 miles round trip
Hiking time: 4.5 hours
Elevation gain: 2,000 feet
Maps: U.S.G.S. Bare Mountain & Sylvan Peak
Beartooth Publishing: Beartooth Mountains
Rocky Mountain Surveys: Alpine-Mount Maurice

Summary of hike: Timberline Lake sits in a basin below Silver Run Plateau at the base of a gorgeous granite cirque. Towering above the 21-acre lake are snow-capped peaks, including the 12,500-foot Silver Run Peak. Lake Gertrude, a 6-acre tarn just downstream from Timberline Lake, sits in a forested recess a half mile to the east. Both lakes lie within the Absaroka-Beartooth Wilderness and offer excellent trout fishing. The trail begins by the West Fork of Rock Creek and climbs through the Timberline Creek drainage, surrounded on both sides by the 10,000-foot Silver Run Plateau. The hike passes through the burn area from the 2008 Cascade Fire. The burn area has a lush new understory of vegetation and wildflowers.

Driving directions: From the south end of Red Lodge, turn west on West Fork Road, which heads to Red Lodge Mountain Resort. At 2.8 miles, stay straight (left) onto West Fork Road as Ski Run Road curves uphill to the right. Continue 8.4 miles to the trailhead parking area on the left.

Hiking directions: From the parking area, hike southwest past the trailhead sign. Follow the well-maintained, rock-embedded path, with views below of Camp Senia along the West Fork of Rock Creek. The trail is a gradual but steady uphill climb through the fire-burned forest. At just over one mile, enter the Timberline Creek drainage, where the creek can be seen and heard tumbling down canyon. Pass the confluence of the creek from the Silver Run Lakes and Timberline Creek. Cross two tributaries to a signed junction with the Beartrack Trail at 2.7 miles.

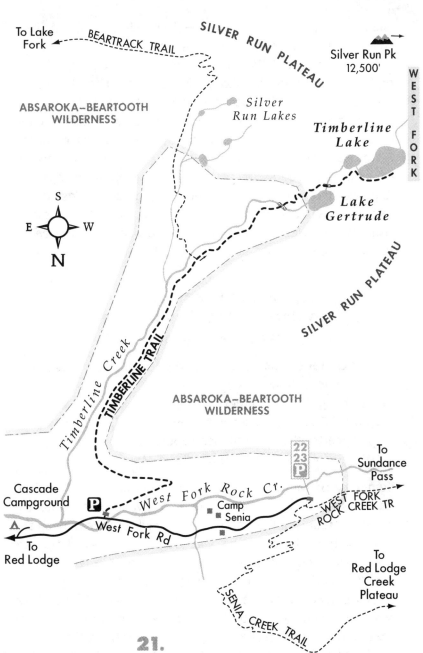

To Lake Fork

BEARTRACK TRAIL

SILVER RUN PLATEAU

Silver Run Pk 12,500'

Silver Run Lakes

Timberline Lake

ABSAROKA-BEARTOOTH WILDERNESS

WEST FORK

Lake Gertrude

S
E ✦ W
N

SILVER RUN PLATEAU

Timberline Creek

TIMBERLINE TRAIL

ABSAROKA-BEARTOOTH WILDERNESS

22 23 P

To Sundance Pass

Cascade Campground

P

West Fork Rock Cr.

Camp Senia

WEST FORK ROCK CREEK TR

West Fork Rd

To Red Lodge

To Red Lodge Creek Plateau

SENIA CREEK TRAIL

21.

Timberline and Gertrude Lakes
WEST FORK of ROCK CREEK

The left fork—the Beartrack Trail—climbs 1.5 miles to the Silver Run Lakes and continues to the Silver Run Plateau.

For this hike, take the fork to the right along the west side of Timberline Creek. Beyond the junction, enter the forest untouched by fire. Wind past a mosaic of trickling streams and memorable views of the surrounding peaks. At 3.8 miles is a log crossing over Timberline Creek. Shortly after crossing, enter the Absaroka–Beartooth Wilderness, and approach the east end of Lake Gertrude. Follow the south side of the lake, crossing more logs over two inlet streams. Continue upstream for less than a half mile to an outlet pond and Timberline Lake at the trail's end. Fisherman trails lead around the lake in a broad cirque of beautiful alpine peaks. Return along the same trail. ▪

22. Senia Creek Trail to Red Lodge Creek Plateau
WEST FORK of ROCK CREEK

Hiking distance: 8.2 miles round trip (or 12-mile shuttle)
Hiking time: 4 hours
Elevation gain: 2,600 feet
Maps: U.S.G.S. Bare Mountain and Sylvan Peak
Beartooth Publishing: Beartooth Mountains
Rocky Mountain Surveys: Alpine-Mount Maurice

Summary of hike: The Senia Creek Trail climbs from West Fork Canyon to Red Lodge Creek Plateau between Grass Mountain and Bare Mountain. The vistas from this high altitude plateau are stunning. The trail crosses the plateau and connects with trails to the east to the East Rosebud drainage and northward down into the West Red Lodge Creek drainage near the town of Luther. This hike switchbacks up the forested southern flank of Bare Mountain, then crosses the alpine plateau and descends 400 feet to tree-lined West Red Lodge Creek, which is fed by snowfields atop the plateau. This hike may be combined with the West Red Lodge Creek Trail (Hike 13) for a 12-mile shuttle hike. Bring warm clothing and be prepared for changes in weather.

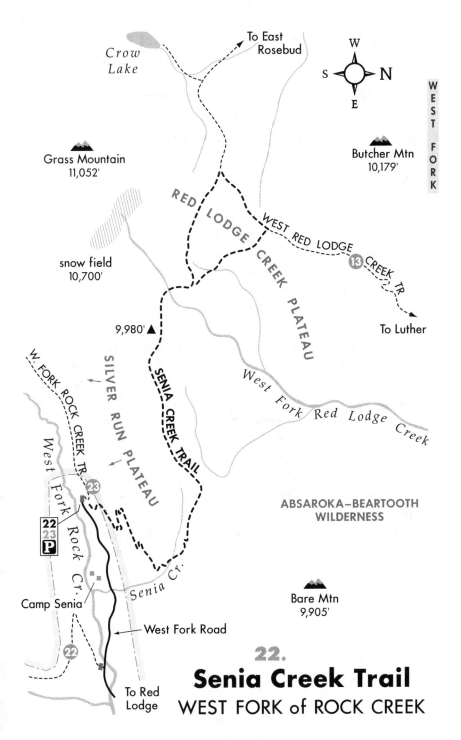

Crow
Lake

To East
Rosebud

W
S — N
E

Grass Mountain
11,052'

Butcher Mtn
10,179'

RED LODGE CREEK PLATEAU

WEST RED LODGE CREEK TR.

13

snow field
10,700'

To Luther

9,980' ▲

SENIA CREEK TRAIL

West Fork Red Lodge Creek

W. FORK ROCK CREEK TR.

SILVER RUN PLATEAU

West Fork Rock Cr.

23

ABSAROKA–BEARTOOTH
WILDERNESS

22
23
P

Senia Cr.

Bare Mtn
9,905'

Camp Senia

West Fork Road

22

To Red
Lodge

22.
Senia Creek Trail
WEST FORK of ROCK CREEK

Driving directions: From the south end of Red Lodge, turn west on West Fork Road, which heads to Red Lodge Mountain Resort. At 2.8 miles, stay straight (left) onto West Fork Road as Ski Run Road curves uphill to the right. Continue 10 miles to the trailhead parking area at the end of the road.

Hiking directions: Walk 70 yards up the posted West Fork Trail to a signed junction with the Senia Creek Trail on the right. Bear right and cross a stream. Traverse the mountainside through the burned area from the 2008 Cascade Fire. Gently gain elevation while views span into the West Fork drainage and of the vertical rock cliffs on the south canyon wall. At a half mile, enter the Absaroka-Beartooth Wilderness. Continue up the north canyon wall to the west ridge of the Senia Creek drainage. Veer left and weave up the side canyon through the forest.

The trail levels out at 2.5 miles as the forest thins near the plateau. Views open up in all directions, from the eastern plains to the Silver Run Plateau. Once you've ascended up to Red Lodge Creek Plateau, the gravel trail is marked with cairns. Cross the plateau, reaching 9,980 feet—the highest point on the trail—at 3.9 miles. Descend 400 feet to the West Red Lodge Creek drainage. The tree-lined, cascading creek is a good spot to take a break and marvel at the views. Return along the same path.

To hike farther, rock hop across the creek and take the path to the right, heading up the hill. Around the bend on the ridge is a four-foot cairn. The clearly defined trail to the left leads 2.7 miles to Crow Lake and 4.2 miles to Sylvan Lake. The faint right fork crosses the open expanse and several meandering streams, connecting with West Red Lodge Creek Trail at the ridge (Hike 13). ▪

23. West Fork Trail to Quinnebaugh Meadows

WEST FORK of ROCK CREEK

Hiking distance and time:

    2.8 miles round trip to Calamity Falls: 1.5 hours

    4.8 miles round trip to Sentinel Falls: 2.5 hours

    8 miles round trip to Quinnebaugh Meadows: 4 hours

    10 miles round trip to Lake Mary: 6 hours

Elevation gain: 900 feet (Quinnebaugh Meadows)

                2,100 feet (Lake Mary)

Maps: U.S.G.S. Sylvan Peak, Bare Mountain

      Beartooth Publishing: Beartooth Mountains

      Rocky Mountain Surveys: Alpine-Mount Maurice

Summary of hike: The West Fork Trail begins at the end of West Fork Road and heads deep into the backcountry. The trail continuously follows the West Fork of Rock Creek along the canyon floor, constricted between Silver Run Plateau and Red Lodge Creek Plateau. The path winds through the forest and open boulder fields while overlooking the creek and the sculpted peaks of Elk and Bowback Mountains. Various trickling brooks flow close to the trail, and the roaring sounds of the West Fork of Rock Creek are always nearby. The hike passes two magnificent waterfalls cutting through rock canyon walls en route to Quinnebaugh Meadows, a lush valley between rugged granite peaks. This trail is part of the 19-mile hike that crosses Sundance Pass and ends at the Lake Fork of Rock Creek (Hike 30), a popular overnight shuttle hike.

Driving directions: From the south end of Red Lodge, turn west on West Fork Road, which heads to Red Lodge Mountain Resort. At 2.8 miles, stay straight (left) onto West Fork Road as Ski Run Road curves uphill to the right. Continue 10 miles to the trailhead at the end of the road.

Hiking directions: Head west from the far end of the parking lot. Follow the creek upstream, passing several boulder fields.

At 1.4 miles, a side path on the left leads to Calamity Falls. The waterfall is not visible from the trail. Listen for the sound of the waterfall, and watch for a side path that leads to the cataract. Returning to the main trail, continue one mile farther to Sentinel Falls. The falls is easy to spot from the trail. Beyond Sentinel Falls, the creek opens up to a beautiful, wide body of slower-moving water. One mile ahead is Quinnebaugh Meadows, a broad meadow with a great view of Whitetail Peak. In the meadow is a

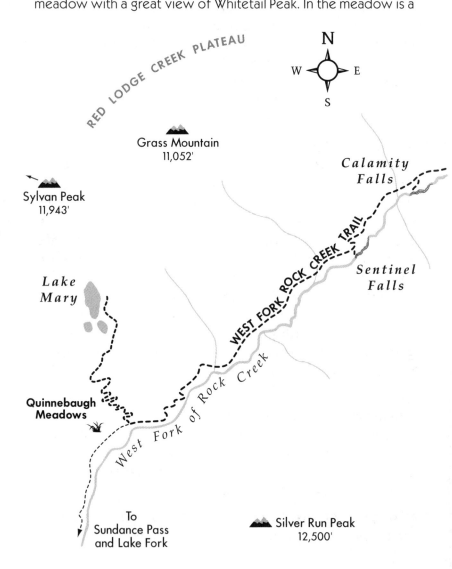

RED LODGE CREEK PLATEAU

N

W ← → E

S

Grass Mountain
11,052'

Calamity
Falls

Sylvan Peak
11,943'

WEST FORK ROCK CREEK TRAIL

Sentinel
Falls

Lake
Mary

West Fork of Rock Creek

Quinnebaugh
Meadows

West Fork of Rock Creek

To
Sundance Pass
and Lake Fork

Silver Run Peak
12,500'

posted trail junction to Lake Mary. This is the turn-around point. Return back down the same trail.

To keep hiking, the right fork steeply climbs one mile to Lake Mary. The left fork (straight ahead) climbs nearly 5 miles up to Sundance Pass.

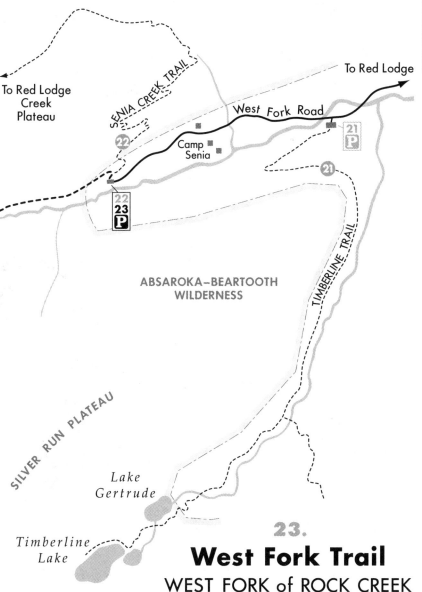

To Red Lodge

To Red Lodge Creek Plateau

SENIA CREEK TRAIL

West Fork Road

Camp Senia

22

22
23
P

21
P

21

TIMBERLINE TRAIL

ABSAROKA–BEARTOOTH WILDERNESS

SILVER RUN PLATEAU

Lake Gertrude

Timberline Lake

23.
West Fork Trail
WEST FORK of ROCK CREEK

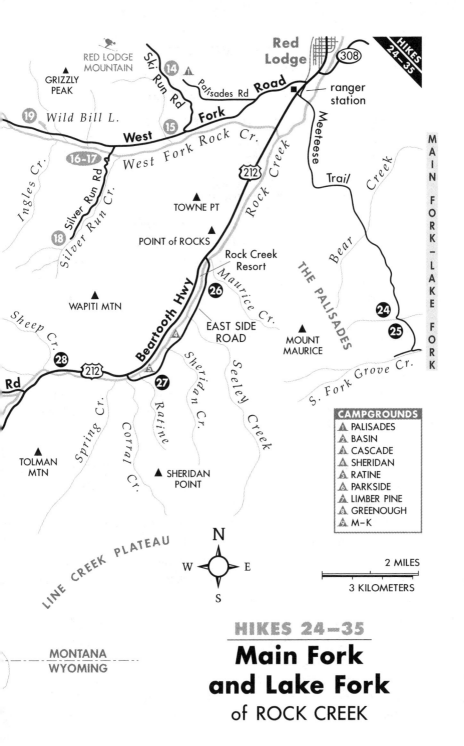

RED LODGE MOUNTAIN

GRIZZLY PEAK

Ski Run Rd

14

Palisades Rd

Red Lodge

308

ranger station

19 Wild Bill L.

West Fork

15

West Fork Rock Cr.

16-17

Silver Run Rd

Ingles Cr.

Silver Run Cr.

18

212

Rock Creek

Meeteese

Trail

Creek

TOWNE PT

POINT of ROCKS

Rock Creek Resort

WAPITI MTN

Beartooth Hwy

26

Maurice Cr.

Bear Creek

THE PALISADES

24

Sheep Cr.

28

212

Rd

EAST SIDE ROAD

MOUNT MAURICE

25

27

Sheridan Cr.

Seeley Creek

S. Fork Grove Cr.

M
A
I
N

F
O
R
K
–
L
A
K
E

F
O
R
K

Spring Cr.

Corral Cr.

Ratine

TOLMAN MTN

SHERIDAN POINT

CAMPGROUNDS
- PALISADES
- BASIN
- CASCADE
- SHERIDAN
- RATINE
- PARKSIDE
- LIMBER PINE
- GREENOUGH
- M–K

LINE CREEK PLATEAU

N
W   E
S

2 MILES

3 KILOMETERS

MONTANA
WYOMING

HIKES 24–35
Main Fork and Lake Fork
of ROCK CREEK

24. The Palisades
North Fork Grove Creek
from MEETEETSE TRAIL

Hiking distance: 2 miles round trip
Hiking time: 1 hour
Elevation gain: 1,000 feet
Maps: U.S.G.S. Tolman Flat
      U.S.F.S. Absaroka Beartooth Wilderness

Summary of hike: The North Fork of Grove Creek begins in the upper reaches of Mount Maurice, south of Red Lodge, and flows through arid Tolman Flat en route to the Clarks Fork of the Yellowstone. The hike follows the creek from the Meeteetse Trail, an old wagon route built by the U.S. Army in 1881 that connected Red Lodge with Clark and Meeteetse, Wyoming. From Red Lodge, the scenic dirt road weaves its way along the eastern face of the Beartooth Mountains.

From the Meeteetse Trail, the short but steep North Fork Grove Creek Trail climbs towards the mountains through an opening in the Meeteetse Spires along the Palisades formation. The spires are the weather-carved crags and pillars that rise dramatically from the jagged limestone cliffs, dominating the landscape. The Palisades, which run for miles along the Beartooth Front, were formed when the sedimentary rocks, originally deposited by an ancient sea, were up-ended by the skyward thrust of the Beartooth Mountains. Golden eagles inhabit the spires and are frequently seen flying above the trail. This area is generally overlooked by hikers, offering quiet solitude and impressive, close-up views of the Palisades. The hike continues up the east slope of Mount Maurice to a hilltop overlook.

Driving directions: From the south end of Red Lodge on Highway 212, turn left on Meeteetse Trail, located 0.1 mile south of West Fork Road and just before the Forest Service ranger station. Drive 6.5 miles on the dirt road to a posted road fork with the North Fork Grove Creek National Forest Access in a forested drainage. At the fork, turn right and park off the road on the left. (En route, the road crosses a bridge over Rock Creek, climbs over the east bench, and weaves along the face of the Beartooths to Tolman Flat.)

Hiking directions: Head 0.1 mile up the forested dirt road to a grassy knoll, surrounded by the colossal Meeteetse Spires. Take the narrow footpath veering off to the left, and drop down to the North Fork of Grove Creek. Rock hop over the creek beneath the jagged, weather-sculpted formations, and head up the south canyon wall. Steeply ascend the narrow canyon between the impressive rock fins and vertical pinnacles. Just beyond the formation, the path levels out and crosses to the north side of the creek. Continue uphill to a grassy flat with sweeping 360-degree views of the North Fork drainage and the forested east face of Mount Maurice. Down canyon is a V-shaped view through the Meeteetse Spires of Tolman Flat (the green irrigated pastureland) and the Pryor Mountains. Follow the ridge on the faded footpath surrounded by mountains, high above the aspen-lined creek. The path fades out on a knoll at the base of a 7,400-foot hilltop. Return by retracing your route. ▪

M E E T E E T S E   T R A I L

25. The Palisades
South Fork Grove Creek
from MEETEETSE TRAIL

Hiking distance: 3.5 miles round trip
Hiking time: 2 hours
Elevation gain: 1,200 feet
Maps: U.S.G.S. Tolman Flat
      U.S.F.S. Wilderness

Summary of hike: The headwaters of South Fork Grove Creek begin in the upper reaches of Mount Maurice. The creek flows down the east slope through Tolman Flat en route to the Clarks Fork of the Yellowstone. The South Fork area was part of the Crow Indian homelands and is considered a sacred place. The Meeteetse Spires contain hard-to-find pictographs and petroglyphs. Tepee rings and ancient stone markers are located in the vicinity. This area was also part of the route used by the Shoshone and Nez Perce tribes to hunt buffalo on the plains of what is now eastern Montana. The 560-acre tract of land is now overseen by the Bureau of Land Management.

This hike starts from the Meeteetse Trail and follows the creek up the lower slopes of Mount Maurice through groves of Douglas fir, limber pine, and aspens. En route, the trail winds through the vertical crags and pillars of the Meeteetse Spires, part of the dramatic Madison limestone formation known as the Palisades. The trail emerges to an amazing overlook of the jagged pinnacles.

Driving directions: From the south end of Red Lodge on Highway 212, turn left on Meeteetse Trail, located 0.1 mile south of West Fork Road and just before the Forest Service ranger station. Drive 7.4 miles on the dirt road to a Y-fork, located 0.9 miles past the posted North Fork Grove Creek national forest access turnoff (Hike 24). The Meeteetse Trail continues on the left fork. Take the right fork, and drive 0.25 miles on the narrow road to the posted parking area on the left.

Hiking directions: Head west on the old dirt road toward the imposing Meeteetse Spires. Parallel the South Fork of Grove Creek into the forested opening between the jagged limestone fins and vertical pinnacles. Stay to the north side of the creek, with eastward vistas across Tolman Flat to the Pryor Mountains. Zigzag up four switchbacks beneath the eroding limestone formations to an overlook with an awesome view of the sawtooth-edged Palisades. Continue uphill into the conifer forest along the north slope of the drainage to a junction with a road/trail on the left—our return route.

Begin the loop to the right, with a sweeping view across the east face of Mount Maurice. Pass pockets of aspen and a log cabin on the left. Enter the Custer National Forest, and stroll through a lodgepole pine forest. Curve left along the back wall of the canyon, passing remnants of an old rock structure by the South Fork of Grove Creek at 1.7 miles. Cross the creek and traverse the hillside, crossing an ephemeral stream, to a T-junction.

The right fork climbs the mountain to the south and forms a loop around a 7,755-foot peak, connecting with the Gold Creek drainage. For this hike, bear left and head down canyon through the lush, old-growth forest. Pass a pair of dilapidated log cabins on the left. Curve left and cross the creek. Climb the grassy slope, completing the loop. Return one mile to the right. ◼

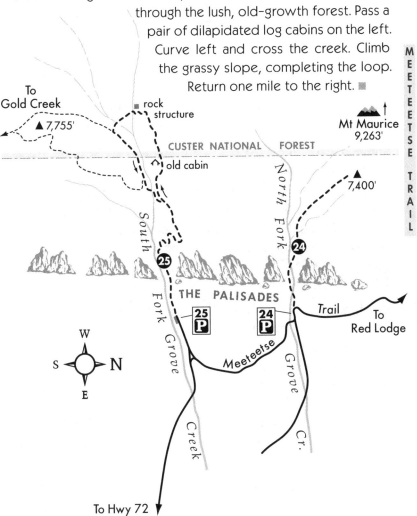

The Palisades
from Meeteetse Trail

HIKE 24: North Fork Grove Creek
HIKE 25: South Fork Grove Creek

26. Maurice Creek Trail to Line Creek Plateau

MAIN FORK of ROCK CREEK

Hiking distance: 9 miles round trip or 13-mile shuttle
Hiking time: 4.5 hours
Elevation gain: 3,200 feet
Maps: U.S.G.S. Mount Maurice
      Beartooth Publishing: Beartooth Mountains
      Rocky Mountain Surveys: Alpine-Mount Maurice

Summary of hike: The Maurice Creek Trail heads up the west flank of Mount Maurice from Rock Creek Canyon. The trail connects Rock Creek Resort, five miles south of Red Lodge, to the Line Creek Plateau. The route parallels but stays high above Maurice Creek, passing the creek's headwaters along the way. The forested path gains 3,200 feet en route to the expansive alpine plateau. The hike can be combined with the Corral Creek Trail (Hike 27) for a one-way, 13-mile shuttle hike.

Driving directions: From downtown Red Lodge, drive 5 miles south on Highway 212 to the first signed East Side Road turnoff on the left (east), between mile markers 64 and 65. Turn left and continue 0.5 miles, crossing Rock Creek, to the signed Maurice Creek Trail on the left, across from Rock Creek Resort. Pull off the road and park.

From Rock Creek Resort, cross the bridge spanning Rock Creek, and walk 30 yards uphill to the East Side Road and the trailhead.

Hiking directions: Walk up the road and pass through a cattle gate. Take the footpath gently uphill to Maurice Creek, the only time that the trail directly meets the creek. Curve right up the hillside, overlooking Rock Creek Resort and the canyon. Switchbacks lead uphill and enter a conifer forest in the Maurice Creek drainage. At 2 miles, the trail reaches a ridge and temporarily levels out. Cross the trickling tributary stream of Seeley Creek at 7,800 feet. This is a good turn-around spot for a short hike. It is the midpoint of the hike in miles and elevation. A short distance ahead, eight switchbacks skirt past the west side of Mount Maurice. The trail finally reaches the northeast edge of the exposed Line Creek Plateau at 4.5 miles, the turn-around point.

To hike farther, follow the faint path through the alpine corridor to the wide expanse of the Line Creek Plateau at 6 miles. There is no visible path across the plateau; widespread cairns mark the route. The hike connects with the Corral Creek Trail (Hike 27) at 9 miles and continues to the Highline Trail Lakes (Hike 36) at the state line. ∎

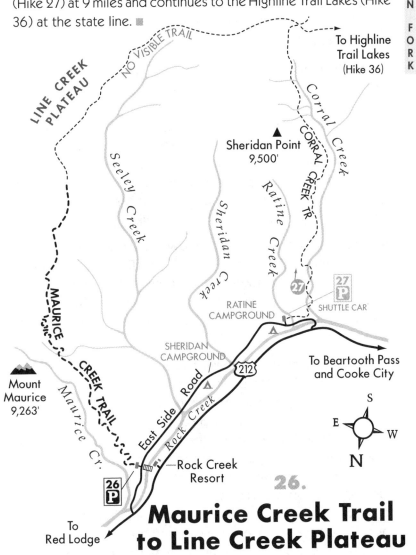

26.
Maurice Creek Trail to Line Creek Plateau

27. Corral Creek Trail
to Line Creek Plateau
MAIN FORK of ROCK CREEK

Hiking distance: 8 miles round trip or 13-mile shuttle
Hiking time: 4 hours
Elevation gain: 3,200 feet
Maps: U.S.G.S. Mount Maurice
        Beartooth Publishing: Beartooth Mountains
        Rocky Mountain Surveys: Alpine-Mount Maurice

Summary of hike: The Corral Creek Trail climbs a narrow mountain drainage from Rock Creek Canyon, near Ratine Campground, to the 9,600-foot Line Creek Plateau. The beautiful but strenuous hike gains more than 3,000 feet up to the plateau. The trail parallels Corral Creek, curving past the west side of Sheridan Point to the headwaters of the creek atop the vast alpine plateau. The well-defined path has five creek crossings in the first mile. The hike can be combined with the Maurice Creek Trail (Hike 26) for a one-way, 13-mile shuttle hike.

Driving directions: From downtown Red Lodge, drive 8 miles south on Highway 212 to the second signed East Side Road turnoff on the left (east), between mile markers 61 and 62. Turn left and continue 0.3 miles, crossing Rock Creek, to the Corral Creek trailhead parking area on the right. It is across from the Ratine Campground.

Hiking directions: Hike past the trailhead sign and cross Ratine Creek. Follow the trail signs past the summer cabins, and head up the canyon between Ratine Creek and Corral Creek. At 0.3 miles, cross over Corral Creek two times by large mossy boulders. Parallel the creek up the west-facing hill. Cross a log bridge over the creek, and continue past cascades and pools, heading up the narrow canyon. At 0.8 miles, cross to the east side and climb up the hillside, leaving the creek. Head steadily up the canyon while curving around the west flank of Sheridan Point. Cross three trickling streams to the top of the canyon. Break out of the forest onto the picturesque meadowlands on the Line Creek Plateau by the Corral Creek headwaters. Cross the trail-less rolling slopes along the rocky drainage to a five-foot rock cairn. Heading right, southwest across the plateau, leads to the Highline Trail Lakes (Hike 31) at the state line. To the left, follow the cairns eastward to the Maurice Creek Trail (Hike 26). There is no visible path across the plateau; widespread cairns mark the route. ■

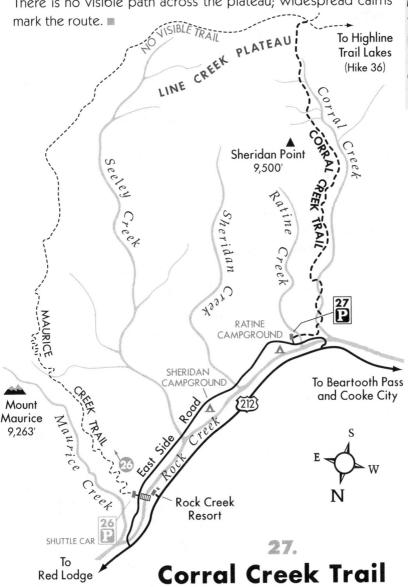

NO VISIBLE TRAIL

LINE CREEK PLATEAU

To Highline
Trail Lakes
(Hike 36)

Corral Creek

Seeley Creek

▲ Sheridan Point
9,500'

CORRAL CREEK TRAIL

Sheridan Creek

Ratine Creek

MAURICE

27
P

RATINE
CAMPGROUND
⛺

CREEK TRAIL

SHERIDAN
CAMPGROUND
⛺

Mount
Maurice
9,263'

East Side Road

26

212

To Beartooth Pass
and Cooke City

Maurice Creek

Rock Creek

S

E ✦ W

N

Rock Creek
Resort

26
P
SHUTTLE CAR

To
Red Lodge

27.
Corral Creek Trail

28. Beartrack Trail to Silver Run Plateau
MAIN FORK of ROCK CREEK

Hiking distance: 8 miles round trip
Hiking time: 4 hours
Elevation gain: 2,900 feet
Maps: U.S.G.S. Mount Maurice and Black Pyramid Mountain
Beartooth Publishing: Beartooth Mountains
Rocky Mountain Surveys: Alpine-Mount Maurice

Summary of hike: The Beartrack Trail (Sheep Creek Trail) climbs nearly 3,000 feet from Rock Creek Canyon to the 10,000-foot Silver Run Plateau. Along the way are great views up and down the Rock Creek Canyon, including the surrounding peaks of Mount Maurice, Tolman Mountain, and Black Pyramid Mountain. The hike begins just west of the burn area from the 2000 Willie Fire. The trail then crosses the windswept alpine plateau and connects with the Silver Run Plateau Trail into the West Fork drainage—Hike 18—an optional 8-mile shuttle hike. Bring warm clothing and be prepared for changes in weather. The hike across the plateau to Timberline Lake (Hike 21) is a popular 17-mile overnight shuttle hike.

Driving directions: From downtown Red Lodge, drive 9.5 miles south on Highway 212 to the turnoff on the right between mile markers 59 and 60. Turn right and park 20 yards ahead by the trailhead sign.

Hiking directions: Cross the meadows towards Wapiti Mountain, then curve left, traversing the foothills towards Tolman Point. Cross a stream, then a footbridge over Sheep Creek, entering the evergreen forest. Continue west to a signed junction. The left fork leads 40 yards to a log crossing at Snow Creek. Take the right fork and begin the ascent, crossing talus slopes and aspen groves. Switchbacks lead very steadily uphill, but the climb is rarely steep. The trail levels out near an 8,800-foot knoll. Head uphill again, breaking out of the trees to the Silver Run Plateau at over 10,000 feet. Follow the cairns across the alpine tundra to a signed junction. The Silver Run Plateau Trail descends northeast into the West Fork of Rock Creek (Hike 18). The left fork continues straight ahead, also descending into the West Fork at the Timberline Lake trailhead (Hike 21). ■

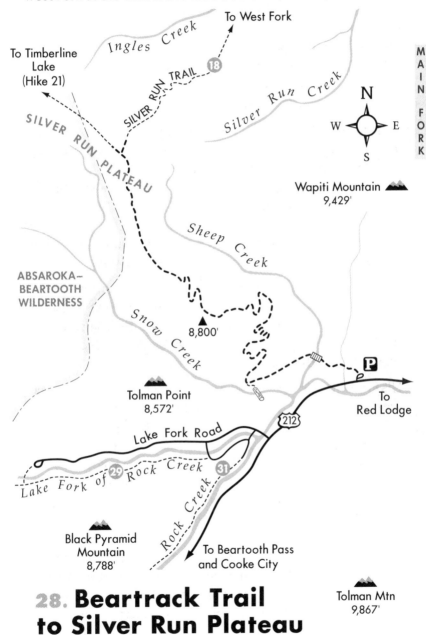

28. Beartrack Trail to Silver Run Plateau

29. Lower Lake Fork Trail
LAKE FORK of ROCK CREEK

Hiking distance: 2.9 miles round trip
Hiking time: 1.5 hours
Elevation gain: 350 feet
Maps: U.S.G.S. Black Pyramid Mountain
       Beartooth Publishing: Beartooth Mountains
       Rocky Mountain Surveys: Alpine-Mount Maurice

Summary of hike: The Lower Lake Fork Trail follows the raging whitewater of the Lake Fork just above its confluence with Rock Creek. The easy, well-defined path stays on the south bank of the creek, passing cascades, pools, and small waterfalls. The trail begins near the Lions Youth Camp in a forest of lodgepole pines and aspen between Black Pyramid Mountain and Tolman Point. Moose are often spotted in the area. During the winter, the Lake Fork Canyon is a popular cross-country ski area.

Driving directions: From Red Lodge, drive 10 miles south on Highway 212 to mile marker 59. Turn right (west) at the signed Lake Fork Road. Drive 0.8 miles to a paved parking pullout on the left. During the snowy months, the Lake Fork Road is usually plowed up to this parking area.

Hiking directions: Descend from either end of the parking area towards the creek. Cross the wooden bridge over the Lake Fork of Rock Creek, and head upstream to the right. The forested path, carpeted with pine needles, follows the watercourse of the cascading Lake Fork. At 1.2 miles, the trail reaches a wooden bridge that crosses the creek to the Lake Fork Trail parking lot. The main trail continues straight ahead to Lost Lake (Hike 30). Return by retracing your steps back to the lower bridge.

To add another half mile to the hike, continue following the creek downstream. At a quarter mile, the trail breaks out of the forest into a meadow, with views of Tolman Point across Rock Creek Canyon. From the meadow, the trail enters the Billings Lions Youth Camp, the turn-around spot. Return along the same route. ■

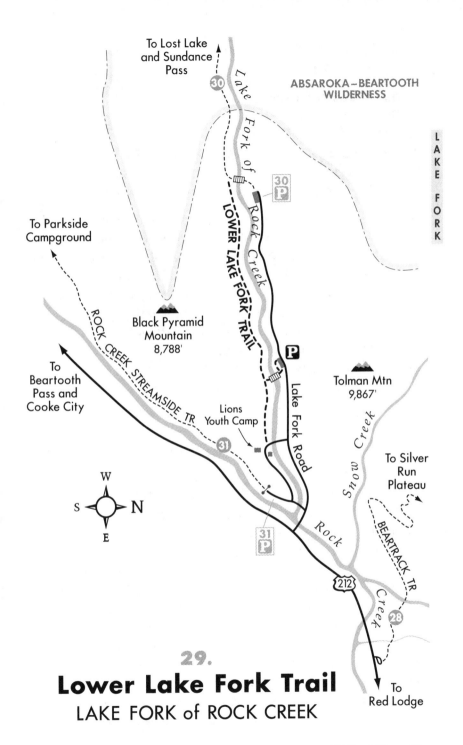

To Lost Lake
and Sundance
Pass

30

Lake Fork of Rock Creek

ABSAROKA–BEARTOOTH
WILDERNESS

30 P

LAKE FORK

LOWER LAKE FORK TRAIL

To Parkside
Campground

ROCK CREEK STREAMSIDE TR

Black Pyramid
Mountain
8,788'

P

To
Beartooth
Pass and
Cooke City

31

Lions
Youth Camp

Lake Fork Road

Tolman Mtn
9,867'

Snow Creek

To Silver
Run
Plateau

W
S — N
E

31 P

Rock

212

BEARTRACK TR

28

Creek

To Red
Lodge

29.
Lower Lake Fork Trail
LAKE FORK of ROCK CREEK

30. Lake Fork Trail to Lost Lake
LAKE FORK of ROCK CREEK

Hiking distance: 10 miles round trip
Hiking time: 5 hours
Elevation gain: 1,350 feet
Maps: U.S.G.S. Black Pyramid Mountain, Silver Run Peak
Beartooth Publishing: Beartooth Mountains
Rocky Mountain Surveys: Alpine-Mount Maurice

Summary of hike: Located south of Red Lodge in Lake Fork Canyon, the Lake Fork Trail follows the beautiful mountain creek through a lodgepole pine forest to a series of lakes. This popular trail follows the Lake Fork of Rock Creek all the way up the canyon to Sundance Pass. Silver Falls, a long, thin waterfall, can be seen flowing down the mountain on the far left near the beginning of the trail. This trail may be combined with the West Fork Trail (Hike 24) for a 19-mile shuttle hike that crosses Sundance Pass between the two canyons. Lake Fork Canyon is a popular cross-country ski area in the winter.

Driving directions: From Red Lodge, drive 10 miles south on Highway 212 to mile marker 59. Turn right (west) at the signed Lake Fork Road. Drive 2 miles to the trailhead parking lot at the end of the road.

Hiking directions: Cross the bridge over Lake Fork and turn right, heading west up canyon. Continue along the gentle, well-defined trail parallel to the creek. At 0.3 miles, the trail enters the Absaroka-Beartooth Wilderness. At one mile is a rocky creekside beach. To the left, Silver Falls can be seen on the north-facing cliffs. The first lake is Broadwater Lake at 3.5 miles, (actually a wide spot along the creek). Lost Lake is at 5 miles, making a 10-mile round trip. The 16-acre lake is a couple hundred yards off the trail on a hill to the left. The entire area is so beautiful that if you choose not to hike all the way up to Lost Lake, the hike will still be a wonderful experience.

Just beyond Lost Lake and before crossing the bridge over the creek is a junction. To the left is Black Canyon Lake. The right fork heads uphill to 9-acre Keyser Brown Lake (1.5 miles farther) and 15-acre September Morn Lake (2.5 miles farther). The 19-mile trail crosses Sundance Pass to the West Fork of Rock Creek (Hike 24), terminating at West Fork Road. ■

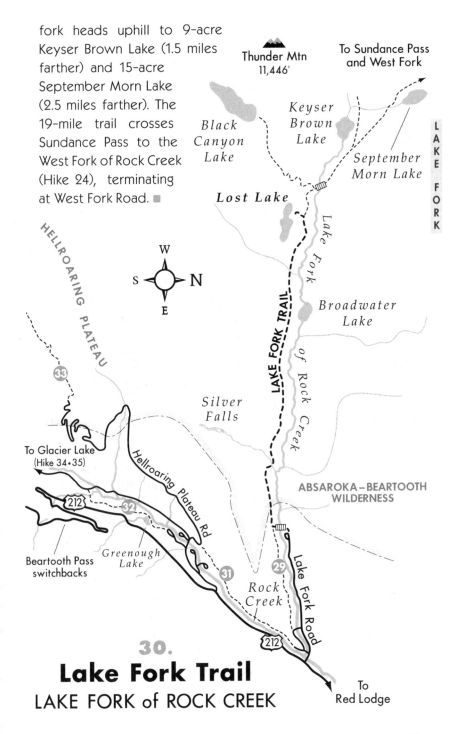

To Sundance Pass and West Fork

Thunder Mtn
11,446'

Keyser Brown Lake

Black Canyon Lake

September Morn Lake

Lost Lake

LAKE FORK

Lake Fork

W
N
S
E

LAKE FORK TRAIL

Broadwater Lake

of Rock Creek

HELLROARING PLATEAU

33

Silver Falls

To Glacier Lake
(Hike 34·35)

ABSAROKA–BEARTOOTH WILDERNESS

Hellroaring Plateau Rd

212

32

Beartooth Pass switchbacks

Greenough Lake

29

Lake Fork Road

31

Rock Creek

212

30.
Lake Fork Trail
LAKE FORK of ROCK CREEK

To
Red Lodge

31. Rock Creek Streamside Trail
MAIN FORK of ROCK CREEK

Hiking distance: 4.4 miles round trip
Hiking time: 2 hours
Elevation gain: 400 feet
Maps: U.S.G.S. Black Pyramid Mountain
        Beartooth Publishing: Beartooth Mountains
        Rocky Mountain Surveys: Alpine-Mount Maurice

Summary of hike: The Rock Creek Streamside Trail follows an unpaved forested road along the cascading whitewater of Rock Creek, the largest tributary of the Clarks Fork River. The road (closed to vehicles) begins in the Lake Fork Canyon and parallels Rock Creek upstream along the base of Black Pyramid Mountain. The creek is easily accessible from the soft, needle-covered road. The trail ends on the Hellroaring Plateau Road near the Greenough and Limber Pine Campgrounds.

Driving directions: From Red Lodge, drive 10 miles south on Highway 212 to mile marker 59. Turn right (west) at the signed Lake Fork Road. Drive over the Rock Creek bridge and turn left. Immediately cross the bridge over Lake Fork, and continue 0.2 miles to boulders blocking the road. Park alongside the road.

Hiking directions: Head southwest up the old road past the large boulders. Enter the pine and aspen forest above the boisterous cascades of Rock Creek. Follow the forested path along the east flank of Black Pyramid Mountain. Various side paths lead down to the edge of Rock Creek. At one mile, the trail climbs up a small hill and out of the forest, giving way to an open area dotted with evergreens. Views of the surrounding mountains stretch up and down the glacier-scoured canyon. The trail veers away from Rock Creek to the unpaved Hellroaring Plateau Road at 2.2 miles. To the right, the gravel road leads up to the plateau (Hike 33). To the left, the road leads to Greenough Lake (Hike 32), Glacier Lake (Hike 34), and Highway 212. ▪

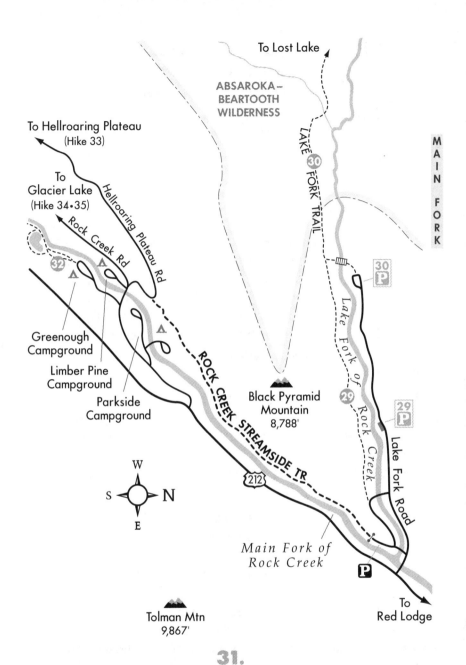

To Lost Lake

ABSAROKA–
BEARTOOTH
WILDERNESS

To Hellroaring Plateau
(Hike 33)

To
Glacier Lake
(Hike 34•35)

Hellroaring Plateau Rd

Rock Creek Rd

32

Greenough
Campground

Limber Pine
Campground

Parkside
Campground

ROCK CREEK STREAMSIDE TR

LAKE FORK TRAIL

30

MAIN FORK

Lake Fork of Rock Creek

30
P

29

29
P

Lake Fork Road

Black Pyramid
Mountain
8,788'

212

W
S — N
E

Main Fork of
Rock Creek

P

Tolman Mtn
9,867'

To
Red Lodge

31.

Rock Creek Streamside Trail
MAIN FORK of ROCK CREEK

32. Parkside National Recreation Trail
from GREENOUGH LAKE
MAIN FORK of ROCK CREEK

Hiking distance: 3 miles round trip
Hiking time: 1.5 hours
Elevation gain: 200 feet
Maps: U.S.G.S. Black Pyramid Mountain
Beartooth Publishing: Beartooth Mountains
Rocky Mountain Surveys: Alpine-Mount Maurice

Summary of hike: The Parkside National Recreation Trail leads to Greenough Lake, a tree-lined, two-acre lake in Rock Creek Canyon. The lake is a popular fishing hole stocked with rainbow trout. A short loop around the lake is a wonderful hike to take with children. Beyond Greenough Lake, the gentle trail parallels Rock Creek, passing through pine forests and open meadows between the Hellroaring Plateau and the switchbacks up to the Beartooth Plateau.

Driving directions: From Red Lodge, take Highway 212 south 11.5 miles to the signed Rock Creek Road turnoff on the right. Turn right (west) and drive 0.8 miles to the Greenough Lake Trail and campground on the left, just after crossing Wyoming Creek. Turn left and go 0.3 miles to the trailhead parking lot at the south end of the campground.

Hiking directions: Walk south past the trailhead sign through a lodgepole pine forest to an unsigned trail split. The left fork follows the old road; the right fork is a footpath along the banks of Rock Creek. At a quarter mile, both trails rejoin at Greenough Lake. Curve right, looping around the west side of the lake. The short loop around the lake heads to the left. The main trail continues straight ahead. At one mile, the trail breaks out of the trees into a large meadow. To the west, switchbacks can be seen winding up the mountainside to the Hellroaring Plateau. To the east are the Highway 212 switchbacks up to the Beartooth Plateau. Walk through the meadow and reenter the forest. At 1.5 miles, cross the wooden footbridge over cascading Quad

Creek to the M-K Trailhead near the M-K Campground. This is the turn-around spot. Return along the same path or follow the gravel road back to the Greenough Lake Campground for a loop hike. ▦

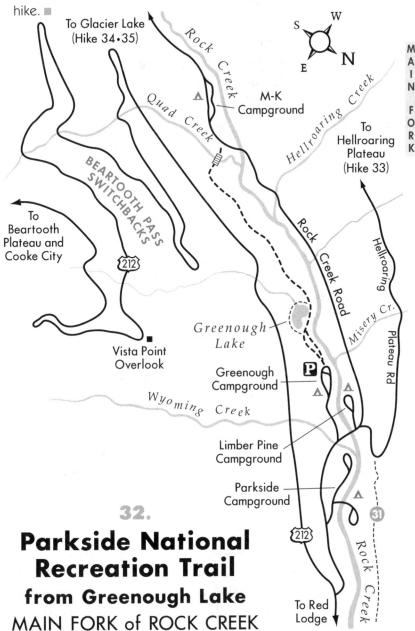

To Glacier Lake
(Hike 34•35)

Rock Creek

Quad Creek

Hellroaring Creek

M-K Campground

BEARTOOTH PASS SWITCHBACKS

To Hellroaring Plateau
(Hike 33)

To Beartooth Plateau and Cooke City

212

Rock Creek Road

Hellroaring

Misery Cr.

Plateau Rd

Vista Point Overlook

Greenough Lake

Greenough Campground

P

Wyoming Creek

Limber Pine Campground

Parkside Campground

31

212

Rock Creek

To Red Lodge

MAIN FORK

32.

Parkside National Recreation Trail
from Greenough Lake
MAIN FORK of ROCK CREEK

33. Hellroaring Plateau
MAIN FORK of ROCK CREEK

Hiking distance: 6 miles round trip
Hiking time: 3 hours to all day
Elevation gain: 600 feet
Maps: U.S.G.S. Black Pyramid and Silver Run Peak
       Beartooth Publishing: Beartooth Mountains
       Rocky Mountain Surveys: Alpine-Mount Maurice

Summary of hike: The Hellroaring Plateau is a vast, top-of-the-world alpine tundra lying above 10,000 feet atop the west wall of Rock Creek Canyon in the Absaroka-Beartooth Wilderness. From the trailhead are great views up Rock Creek Canyon and the Beartooth Highway switchbacks. This hike travels across the 2-mile-long wind-swept, alpine basin filled with a chain of 14 lakes. Many of the lakes offer excellent fishing. Shell fossils are occasionally found atop the grassy plateau. Although the elevation gain of this hike is gradual, at this height the gain feels more substantial. Bring topographic maps and be prepared with warm, protective clothing, as the weather can change abruptly. Accessing the trail requires a rough, slow drive up an old gravel road.

Driving directions: From Red Lodge, take Highway 212 south 11.5 miles to the signed Rock Creek Road turnoff on the right. Turn right (west) and continue 0.9 miles to the Glacier Lake/ Hellroaring Plateau road split. Take the right fork towards Hellroaring Plateau, and continue up a grueling 5.8 miles to the trailhead parking area at road's end. The last 5 miles of the old mining road are steep, rough, winding, and narrow.

Hiking directions: Head west past the trailhead sign and enter the Absaroka-Beartooth Wilderness. The trail—an old mine road—gains elevation gradually along the vast alpine plateau. At one mile, views into the valley basin open to four lower Hellroaring Lakes. Stay on the plateau, continuing to the west as the trail veers left and back to the right. A side trail heads off to the left, leading to an overlook of the Rock Creek drainage.

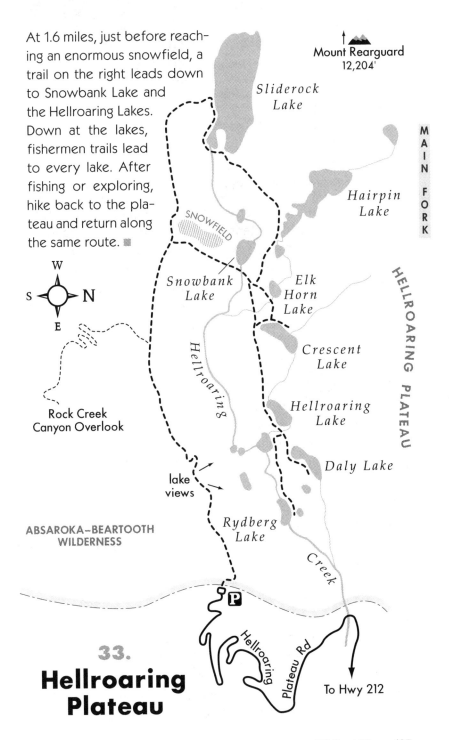

At 1.6 miles, just before reaching an enormous snowfield, a trail on the right leads down to Snowbank Lake and the Hellroaring Lakes. Down at the lakes, fishermen trails lead to every lake. After fishing or exploring, hike back to the plateau and return along the same route. ■

Mount Rearguard
12,204'

Sliderock Lake

MAIN FORK

Hairpin Lake

HELLROARING PLATEAU

W
S ✦ N
E

SNOWFIELD

Snowbank Lake

Elk Horn Lake

Crescent Lake

Rock Creek Canyon Overlook

Hellroaring

Hellroaring Lake

Daly Lake

lake views

ABSAROKA–BEARTOOTH WILDERNESS

Rydberg Lake

Creek

P

33.

Hellroaring Plateau

Hellroaring Plateau Rd

To Hwy 212

34. Glacier Lake
MAIN FORK of ROCK CREEK

Hiking distance: 4 miles round trip
Hiking time: 2.5 hours
Elevation gain: 1,100 feet
Maps: U.S.G.S. Silver Run Peak and Beartooth Butte
　　　Beartooth Publishing: Beartooth Mountains
　　　Rocky Mountain Surveys: Alpine-Mount Maurice

Summary of hike: Glacier Lake, the headwaters of Rock Creek, straddles the Montana-Wyoming border in a deep bowl at 9,691 feet. Surrounded by towering, snow-capped mountains, the 164-acre high-alpine lake is the largest lake in the Rock Creek drainage. The steady climb to Glacier Lake follows the swift, cascading Moon Creek for a half mile, then crosses the creek on a 50-foot-long footbridge. Throughout the hike are stunning views of the high granite cliffs and glacier-carved canyon dotted with old, twisted pines.

Driving directions: From Red Lodge, take Highway 212 south 11.5 miles to the signed Rock Creek Road turnoff, located 0.6 miles south of mile marker 58. Turn right (west) and drive 0.9 miles, crossing Wyoming Creek, to a road fork at the end of the paved road. Bear left and drive 7.8 miles on the bumpy, unpaved road to the parking lot at the end of the road, located at the back of Rock Creek Canyon.

Hiking directions: Walk north towards the vertical rock headwall of the canyon. Follow the cascading watercourse upstream, overlooking the confluence of Rock Creek and Moon Creek. Steadily climb along the east side of Moon Creek through open groves of conifers; pass numerous hillside streams dropping beneath the trail. Zigzag a half mile up the canyon to a footbridge. Cross the bridge over Moon Creek, and begin a continuous series of switchbacks, which minimize the steep grade up the slope. The trail tops out on a 9,800-foot ridge above Glacier Lake. From the ridge is a great view of the massive lake and the surrounding mountains, including 12,350-foot

Mount Rearguard. Descend to the northeastern shoreline by the dam. An angler trail bears right along the northeast side of the lake. After exploring the area, return along the same route.

To hike farther, faint paths lead to both ends of the lake. From the north end of the lake, climb the snowbank to Triangle Lake, and continue north to Sheep Lake and Goat Lake. From the south end of Glacier Lake, cross the cement dam to 11-acre Little Glacier Lake, and continue south to Emerald Lake. ▣

35. Moon Lake
MAIN FORK of ROCK CREEK

Hiking distance: 7 miles round trip
Hiking time: 4 hours
Elevation gain: 1,700 feet
Maps: U.S.G.S. Silver Run Peak
        Beartooth Publishing: Beartooth Mountains
        Rocky Mountain Surveys: Alpine-Mount Maurice

Summary of hike: Moon Lake rests at the base of Spirit Mountain and Mount Rearguard in a giant rock bowl with cliffs angling directly into the water. Sitting in a 10,400-foot valley below the Hellroaring Plateau, the 79-acre high-alpine lake is surrounded by 12,000-foot peaks. It is a magnificent area to explore. The trail begins on the Glacier Lake Trail at the upper end of Rock Creek Canyon, then veers north up the Moon Creek drainage through a jumble of huge boulders. The route to Moon Lake is a backcountry hike and only recommended for seasoned hikers. The unmaintained path fades in and out, and some areas are steep and rocky.

Driving directions: From Red Lodge, take Highway 212 south 11.5 miles to the signed Rock Creek Road turnoff, located 0.6 miles south of mile marker 58. Turn right and drive 0.9 miles, crossing Wyoming Creek, to a road fork at the end of the paved road. Bear left and drive 7.8 miles on the unpaved road to the parking lot at the end of the road, located at the back of Rock Creek Canyon.

Hiking directions: Walk north towards the vertical rock head-wall of the canyon. Follow the cascading watercourse upstream, overlooking the confluence of Rock Creek and Moon Creek. Steadily climb along the east side of Moon Creek through open groves of conifers; pass numerous hillside streams dropping beneath the trail. Zigzag a half mile up the canyon to a 50-foot-long footbridge spanning Moon Creek. Crossing the bridge leads to Glacier Lake (Hike 34).

For this hike, do not cross Moon Creek, but walk past the bridge on the narrow footpath. Follow the watercourse on the east side of the creek, scrambling up the rocky hillside. This section of trail has a steep slope and loose gravel, so exercise extreme caution and use careful footing. Cross a boulder field and a wide tributary stream, steadily gaining elevation. Head for the saddle, using the creek as a guide as the trail fades in and out. Cross the saddle to the open tundra covered with delicate wildflowers and scattered boulders, reaching a pond.

Shelf Lake is over the ridge on the right, tucked between the two narrow, steep cliffs in an enclosed bowl. (The easiest access to Shelf Lake is to climb over the ridge, following the cascading outlet stream from where it merges with Moon Creek.) Cross to the west side of the creek, and follow the rolling meadow along the wide meandering creek. Recross the creek on boulders, and follow the draw to the south end of Moon Lake. Drop down to the lake and explore the eastern shoreline. The north and west shores are at the base of the imposing vertical cliffs. To return, retrace your steps. ◼

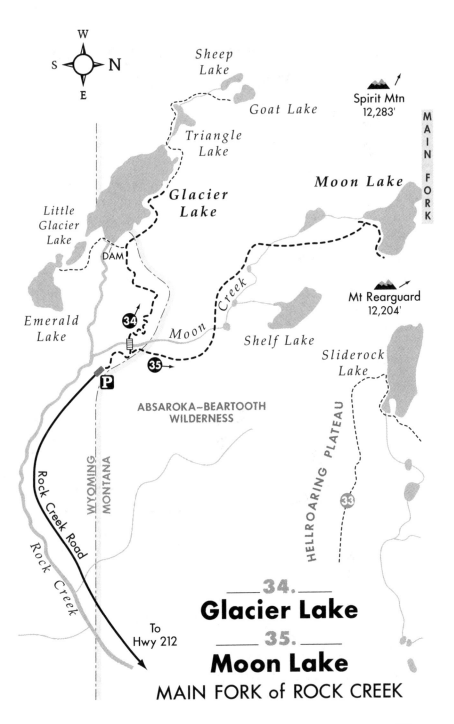

W · N · S · E

Sheep Lake

Goat Lake

Spirit Mtn
12,283'

Triangle Lake

M A I N F O R K

Glacier Lake

Moon Lake

Little Glacier Lake

DAM

Mt Rearguard
12,204'

Emerald Lake

34

Moon Creek

Shelf Lake

35

Sliderock Lake

P

ABSAROKA–BEARTOOTH WILDERNESS

HELLROARING PLATEAU

Rock Creek Road

WYOMING
MONTANA

33

Rock Creek

To
Hwy 212

_____ **34.** _____
Glacier Lake
_____ **35.** _____
Moon Lake
MAIN FORK of ROCK CREEK

Beartooth Highway
Beartooth Plateau

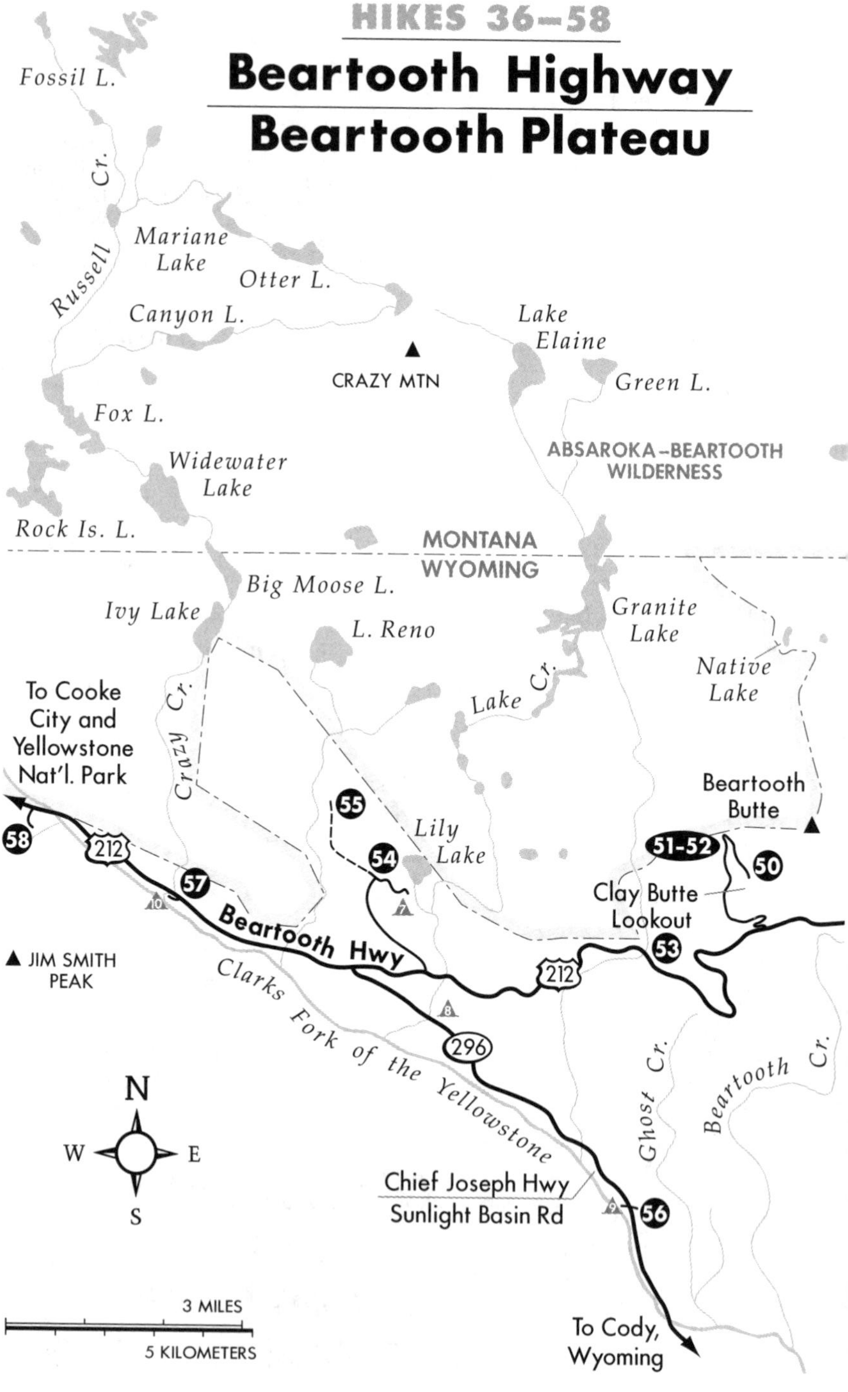

Fossil L.

Russell Cr.

Mariane Lake

Otter L.

Canyon L.

Lake Elaine

▲ CRAZY MTN

Green L.

Fox L.

Widewater Lake

ABSAROKA–BEARTOOTH
WILDERNESS

Rock Is. L.

MONTANA
WYOMING

Big Moose L.

Ivy Lake

L. Reno

Granite Lake

Native Lake

Crazy Cr.

Lake Cr.

To Cooke
City and
Yellowstone
Nat'l. Park

Beartooth
Butte ▲

58

212

57

55

Lily Lake

54

51-52

50

Clay Butte
Lookout

53

▲ JIM SMITH
PEAK

Beartooth Hwy

212

Clarks Fork of the Yellowstone

296

Ghost Cr.

Beartooth Cr.

N

W ✦ E

S

Chief Joseph Hwy
Sunlight Basin Rd

56

3 MILES

5 KILOMETERS

To Cody,
Wyoming

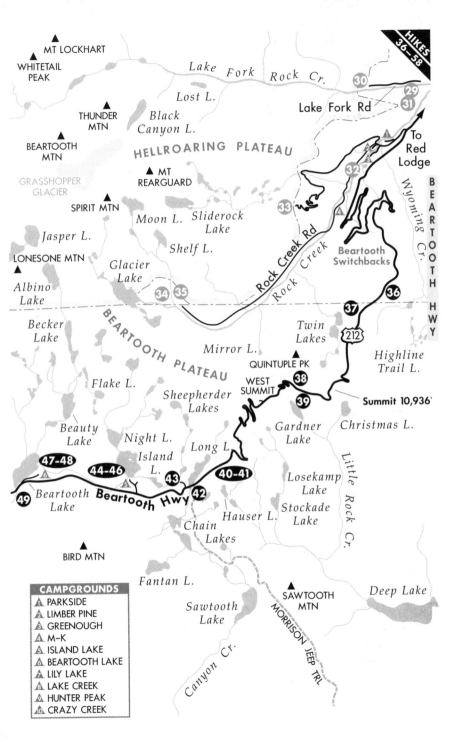

MT LOCKHART ▲

WHITETAIL
PEAK ▲

Lake Fork Rock Cr.

HIKES 36–58

30

29
31

Lost L.

THUNDER
MTN ▲

*Black
Canyon L.*

Lake Fork Rd

To
Red
Lodge

BEARTOOTH
MTN ▲

HELLROARING PLATEAU

32

GRASSHOPPER
GLACIER

▲ MT
REARGUARD

SPIRIT MTN ▲

33

*Moon L. Sliderock
Lake*

Jasper L.

Shelf L.

Beartooth
Switchbacks

B
E
A
R
T
O
O
T
H

LONESOME MTN
▲

*Glacier
Lake*

34 35

36

*Albino
Lake*

BEARTOOTH PLATEAU

Rock Creek Rd

Rock Creek

37

Wyoming Cr.

H
W
Y

*Becker
Lake*

*Twin
Lakes*

212

*Highline
Trail L.*

Mirror L.

QUINTUPLE PK ▲

Flake L.

WEST
SUMMIT

38

Summit 10,936'

39

*Sheepherder
Lakes*

*Gardner
Lake*

Christmas L.

*Beauty
Lake*

Night L.

Long L.

47-48

*Island
L.*

44-46

43

40-41

42

*Losekamp
Lake*

Little Rock Cr.

49

*Beartooth
Lake*

Beartooth Hwy

*Stockade
Lake*

Hauser L.

*Chain
Lakes*

BIRD MTN
▲

Fantan L.

SAWTOOTH
MTN ▲

Deep Lake

CAMPGROUNDS
⛺ PARKSIDE
⛺ LIMBER PINE
⛺ GREENOUGH
⛺ M-K
⛺ ISLAND LAKE
⛺ BEARTOOTH LAKE
⛺ LILY LAKE
⛺ LAKE CREEK
⛺ HUNTER PEAK
⛺ CRAZY CREEK

*Sawtooth
Lake*

MORRISON JEEP TRL

Canyon Cr.

36. Highline Trail Lakes
on LINE CREEK PLATEAU
BEARTOOTH PLATEAU

Hiking distance: 4 miles round trip
Hiking time: 2 hours
Elevation gain: 300 feet
Maps: U.S.G.S. Black Pyramid Mountain and Deep Lake
R.M.S. Alpine-Mount Maurice and Wyoming Beartooths

Summary of hike: The Highline Trail Lakes are a series of ten lakes in an ice-scoured depression on the exposed 10,000-foot alpine plateau. The lakes rest at the south end of Line Creek Plateau near the headwaters of Wyoming Creek. The Highline Creek Trail straddles the Montana-Wyoming state line. This hike begins on an old jeep road, then diverts across the trail-less tundra of the rolling plateau to the series of tiny lakes.

Driving directions: The trailhead is located on Highway 212: 24 miles south from Red Lodge and 40.3 miles east from Cooke City. The trailhead turnoff is a half mile north of the Montana-Wyoming state line. Turn south and drive 0.2 miles to the parking area at the end of the road.

Hiking directions: Head downhill across the exposed alpine tundra toward an unnamed lake. Along the way, pick up the old two-track jeep trail, and follow it down to the west end of the lake. Rock hop over the inlet stream and continue past the lake. Cross another inlet stream, and ascend the hill east of the rock formations and drainage. At the ridge, bear to the right, following the old jeep tracks around another lake. At the southern end of the lake, leave the tracks and head south across the exposed landscape. Descend into the carved depression, exploring the many Highline Trail Lakes, choosing your own route.

To hike farther, head northeast and cross Wyoming Creek towards the distinct Line Creek Plateau. Pick up the jeep trail again above the treeline in the Wyoming Creek drainage. The route follows the immense plateau for 5.5 miles to the Corral Creek

Trail (Hike 27) and Mount Maurice (Hike 26). The trails down into these canyon are marked with cairns but are difficult to detect. Bring topographic maps if heading across the plateau. ■

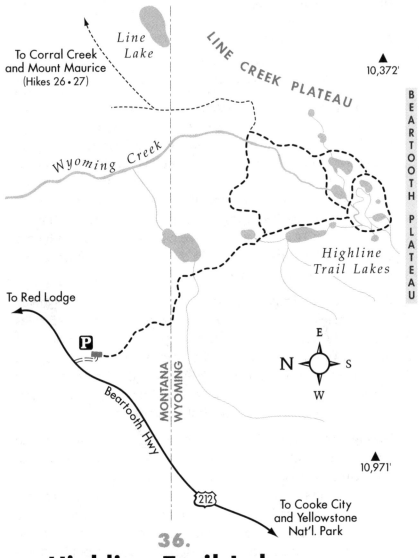

To Corral Creek
and Mount Maurice
(Hikes 26 • 27)

Line Lake

LINE CREEK PLATEAU

▲ 10,372'

B E A R T O O T H   P L A T E A U

Wyoming Creek

Highline Trail Lakes

To Red Lodge

P

Beartooth Hwy

MONTANA
WYOMING

E
N ◆ S
W

▲ 10,971'

212

To Cooke City
and Yellowstone
Nat'l. Park

36.

Highline Trail Lakes
on Line Creek Plateau
BEARTOOTH PLATEAU

37. Twin Lakes
BEARTOOTH PLATEAU

Hiking distance: 4 miles round trip
Hiking time: 2 hours
Elevation gain: 800 feet
Maps: U.S.G.S. Black Pyramid Mountain and Deep Lake
Rocky Mountain Surveys: Wyoming Beartooths

Summary of hike: Twin Lakes are tucked into a gorgeous double cirque at the Montana-Wyoming border. The 9,800-foot lakes sit in a hanging valley above Rock Creek Canyon in the Shoshone National Forest, the first national forest in the United States. The 75-acre lakes rest in glacial depressions below the Twin Lakes headwall. Atop the 10,737-foot headwall is the ski tow used for the Red Lodge International Ski Racing Camp, a training ground for young skiers. The hike crosses the vast tundra of the plateau, carpeted with wild alpine flowers, then drops into a tight glacial-carved valley.

Driving directions: The trailhead is located on Highway 212: 25 miles south from downtown Red Lodge and 39.5 miles east from Cooke City. From Red Lodge, park in the pullout on the right (northwest) side of the road, a quarter mile beyond the winter gate. The pullout is in Wyoming, 0.3 miles south of the Montana border. From Cooke City, the pullout is on the left (northeast), 2.6 miles past the East Summit and ski lift.

Hiking directions: Walk west down the declivitous alpine meadow, parallel to the Montana-Wyoming border. Across the Twin Lakes canyon is the rolling Goat Meadow plateau (Hike 38), and across Rock Creek Canyon are views of Hellroaring Plateau and Mount Rearguard. At 0.7 miles, on the edge of the treeless meadow, is a bird's-eye view of Twin Lakes and the glacial cirque. Head into the ice-scoured bowl from the lower north edge of the meadow for the easiest descent, and head south towards the lakes. An old, faded dirt road winds down the hillside to the tree-lined lakes. A passage through the trees curves around the west side of a rock-lined pond to a T-junction at the north end of the lake. The left fork follows the shoreline to the east end of the lake at the steep, rocky slope. Take the right fork and curve around to the west side of the lake on the forested path. Rock-hop over cascading Chain Creek, the lake's outlet stream and a tributary of Rock Creek. The path leaves the shoreline for a short distance, passing the small rocky division between the two lakes. Meander along the fisherman trails, choosing your own turn-around spot. The south and east sides of the lakes are bordered by steep, rocky walls and are not desirable or advisable for hiking. ■

38. Goat Meadow
BEARTOOTH PLATEAU

Hiking distance: 4.5 mile loop
Hiking time: 2.5 hours
Elevation gain: 600 feet
Maps: U.S.G.S. Deep Lake and Black Pyramid Mountain
Rocky Mountain Surveys: Wyoming Beartooths

Summary of hike: Goat Meadow lies between the East Summit and the West Summit (Beartooth Pass), at over 10,000 feet. To the west are the Quintuple Peaks and Mirror Lake, and to the east are the Twin Lakes (Hike 37). The treeless, alpine meadow sits atop a large peninsula that juts outward 2,500 feet above U-shaped Rock Creek Canyon. A 10,590-foot rounded hill sits in the center of the meadow. This hike loops around the hill on the rim of the rolling meadow, with sweeping vistas of Beartooth Mountain, Mount Rearguard, the pyramid-shaped Bear's Tooth, Twin Lakes, Glacier Lake, Hellroaring Plateau, and the glacier-carved Rock Creek Canyon. This meadow is seldom hiked and does not have a trail, but it is easy to follow because the unobstructed vistas and the canyons act as visual guides. Mountain goats frequent the north end of the meadow. Patches of their hair often linger among the scattered boulders near the rim.

Driving directions: The trailhead turnoff is located on Highway 212: 29 miles south from Red Lodge and 35.5 miles east from Cooke City. From Red Lodge, the dirt road turnoff is located on the right (north), 1.6 miles past the ski lift on the East Summit and 0.2 miles past the Gardner Lake Trailhead (Hike 39). From Cooke City, the turnoff is located on the left, 1.7 miles past the Beartooth Pass (West Summit). Turn on the dirt road and drive 0.2 miles to a wood post at the end of the road.

Hiking directions: Cross the open alpine tundra northeast on the trail-less route toward the saddle on the right. Cross several braids of a tributary stream of Rock Creek. To the left, the Bear's Tooth can be seen poking out between Beartooth Mountain and Mount Rearguard. Cross the saddle by an unnamed lake above Twin Lakes. Curve north and follow the ridge to an overlook of Twin Lakes. Continue up the grassy slope and top the rounded knoll. Descend onto the peninsula, with a view across Rock Creek Canyon to Glacier Lake and the Hellroaring Plateau. At the base of the wide sloping saddle, curve right to the west rim. Follow the rim to the northwest corner of the plateau, straddling the Wyoming-Montana state line by a 4-foot rock cairn. Pass a jumble of rocks atop the 10,256-foot summit. After looping around the tip, return to the saddle and curve right toward the distinct drainage. Traverse the steep slope to the cascading stream. Cross to the west side of the waterway and head upstream. Near the rocky slope, recross the stream and follow the lush east side of the stream. After circling the large knoll, re-enter the first meadow. Stay high to the north, avoiding the wetland and completing the loop. Return to the right. ▪

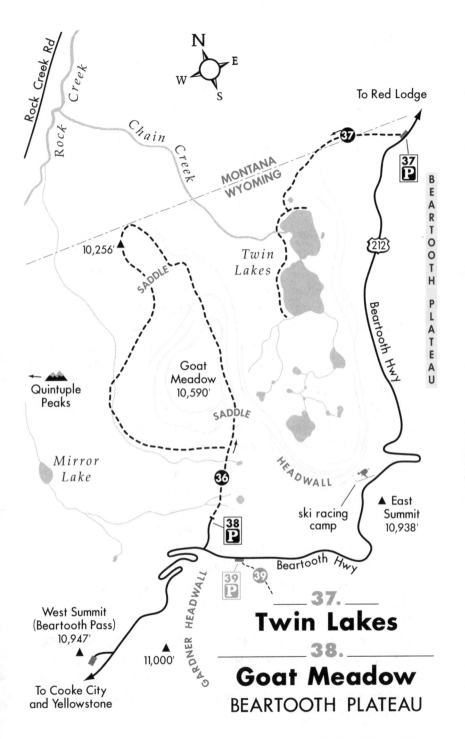

Rock Creek Rd

Rock Creek

Chain Creek

N
W E
S

To Red Lodge

37

37 P

MONTANA
WYOMING

Twin Lakes

10,256'

SADDLE

212

Beartooth Hwy

BEARTOOTH PLATEAU

Goat
Meadow
10,590'

SADDLE

Quintuple
Peaks

Mirror
Lake

HEADWALL

36

East
Summit
10,938'

ski racing
camp

38 P

West Summit
(Beartooth Pass)
10,947'

11,000'

GARDNER HEADWALL

39 P   39

Beartooth Hwy

To Cooke City
and Yellowstone

___ 37. ___
Twin Lakes
___ 38. ___
Goat Meadow
BEARTOOTH PLATEAU

39. Losekamp and Stockade Lakes

from GARDNER LAKE TRAILHEAD

BEARTOOTH PLATEAU

Hiking distance: 8 miles round trip
Hiking time: 4 hours
Elevation gain: 1,150 feet
Maps: U.S.G.S. Deep Lake
 Beartooth Publishing: Beartooth Mountains
 Rocky Mountain Surveys: Wyoming Beartooths

Summary of hike: Gardner Lake is a 24-acre tarn at the base of the Gardner Headwall. From the trailhead is a bird's-eye view of the lake. The trail follows a portion of the Beartooth Loop National Recreation Trail through picturesque meadowlands, carved granite formations, and forested groves. The path leads to Losekamp Lake and Stockade Lake in a sloping meadow at the base of Tibbs Butte. This trail may also be hiked as a 6-mile shuttle to the Hauser Lake trailhead by Long Lake (Hike 40).

Driving directions: The trailhead is located on Highway 212: 29 miles south from Red Lodge and 35.5 miles east from Cooke City. The signed Gardner Lake trailhead is on the south side of the road, 2 miles east of the Beartooth Pass (W. Summit).

Hiking directions: Descend the steep alpine slope along the east side of Gardner Lake. At the south end of the lake, cross a fork of Littlerock Creek, the outlet stream of the lake. Continue across the exposed alpine tundra to a junction at 1.6 miles. Take the right fork, cross the ridge, and descend to the inlet stream at the north tip of Losekamp Lake. The lake rests in a narrow valley between sheer granite formations and the slopes of Tibbs Butte. Cross the stream and follow the west shoreline of Losekamp Lake to a signed junction. The right fork heads west to Hauser Lake and Long Lake at the Beartooth Highway (Hike 40). The left fork continues south, down the draw to Stockade Lake. A lakeside trail follows the west side of the lake. The main trail crosses the inlet stream and heads down the east side of the lake. This is the turn-around spot. ▪

40. Losekamp and Stockade Lakes
from HAUSER LAKE TRAILHEAD
BEARTOOTH PLATEAU

Hiking distance: 6 miles round trip
Hiking time: 3 hours
Elevation gain: 400 feet
Maps: U.S.G.S. Deep Lake
Beartooth Publishing: Beartooth Mountains
Rocky Mountain Surveys: Wyoming Beartooths

Summary of hike: The hike to Losekamp and Stockade Lakes follows a portion of the Beartooth Loop National Recreation Trail. The scenic trail crosses picturesque rocky meadows and subalpine forested knolls to the 9,400-foot high mountain lakes. Both lakes rest in forest-fringed meadows at the base of Tibbs Butte. The trail starts from the Hauser Lake Trailhead and may be hiked as a 6-mile shuttle to Gardner Lake (Hike 39).

Driving directions: The trailhead is located on Highway 212: 36.5 miles south from Red Lodge and 28 miles east from Cooke City. Park along the highway pullout at Long Lake. Across the road to the south is a sign that reads "Hauser Lake Trailhead."

Hiking directions: Start at the Hauser Lake trailhead across the road. Head south, following the cairns for a half mile to the north end of Hauser Lake. Sawtooth Mountain appears above the lake in the southeast horizon. Cross the inlet streams and pass a pond on the exposed alpine tundra. Head uphill through a subalpine forest to 10,600-foot Tibbs Butte Pass, a ridge with dynamic views across the Beartooth Mountains. Descend and cross the rolling wildflower-covered grasslands, a stream, and scattered trees to a signed junction on the west shore of Losekamp Lake. The left fork heads north, uphill to Gardner Lake. The right fork heads south and follows the lake's outlet stream to a creek crossing at Stockade Lake. An angler path to the right follows the west side of the lake. The main trail follows the east side of Stockade Lake. This is the turn-around spot. ■

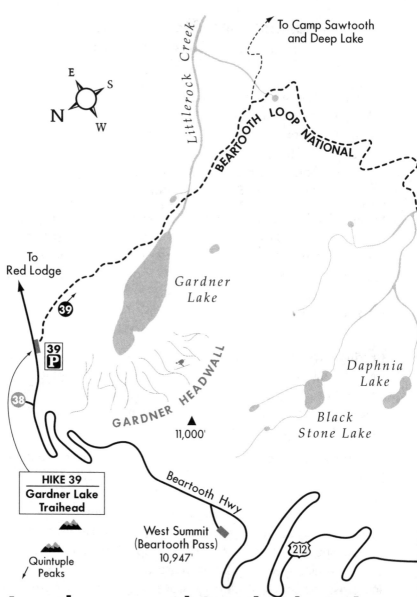

Losekamp and Stockade Lakes

BEARTOOTH PLATEAU

39. from Gardner Lake Trailhead
40. from Hauser Lake Trailhead

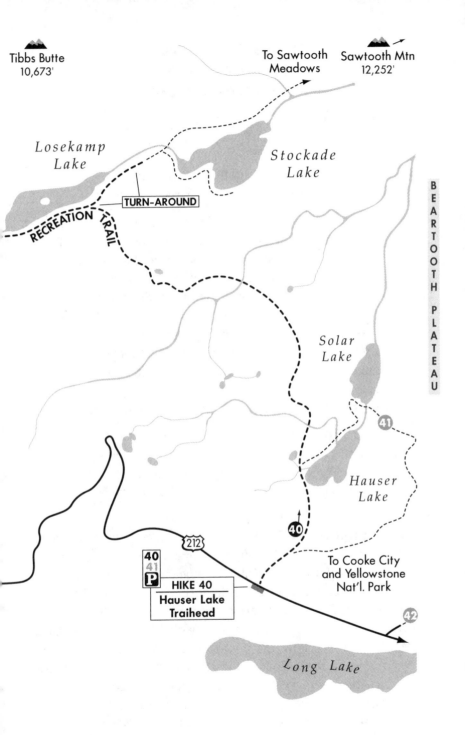

Tibbs Butte
10,673'

To Sawtooth
Meadows

Sawtooth Mtn
12,252'

Losekamp
Lake

Stockade
Lake

TURN-AROUND

RECREATION TRAIL

B E A R T O O T H   P L A T E A U

Solar
Lake

41

Hauser
Lake

40
41
P
HIKE 40
Hauser Lake
Traihead

212

40

To Cooke City
and Yellowstone
Nat'l. Park

42

Long Lake

41. Hauser, Solar, Fort and Rainbow Lakes Loop
BEARTOOTH PLATEAU

Hiking distance: 4 miles round trip
Hiking time: 2 hours
Elevation gain: 300 feet
Maps: U.S.G.S. Deep Lake and Beartooth Butte
Rocky Mountain Surveys: Wyoming Beartooths

Summary of hike: Hauser, Solar, Fort, and Rainbow Lakes rest in the heart of the Beartooth Plateau across the road from Long Lake. The four alpine lakes sit above 9,600 feet in rock-studded meadows amid forested knolls, meandering streams and pools, and abundant wildflowers. Small pines and firs, scattered granite rocks, and alpine tundra surround 18-acre Rainbow Lake, the largest of the four lakes. Throughout the hike are vistas of Beartooth Butte and scalloped Sawtooth Mountain. The hike begins at the Hauser Lake Trailhead on the southwest end of the Beartooth Loop National Recreation Trail (Hikes 39 and 40), then explores the four lakes across the trail-less, open tundra.

Driving directions: The trailhead is located on Highway 212: 36.5 miles south from Red Lodge and 28 miles east from Cooke City. Park along the highway pullout at Long Lake. Across the road to the south is a sign that reads "Hauser Lake Trailhead."

Hiking directions: From the Hauser Lake trailhead, cross the alpine meadow, following the cairns. To the west is a view of Beartooth Butte, the distinct sedimentary rock formation. Descend into a draw dotted with gnarled conifers to the north end of Hauser Lake. The serrated ridge of Sawtooth Mountain rises above the lake. Leave the trail that leads to Losekamp Lake (Hike 40), and follow the east side of Hauser Lake over the open, rolling tundra. Follow the stream flowing out of Hauser Lake to Solar Lake, a half mile ahead. From Solar Lake, cross the inlet stream and head west over the hill to Fort Lake. Fort Lake is not visible until you crest the top of the hill. Walk around Fort

Lake to the right, and head north to Rainbow Lake. Continue north, crossing the meadow back to the trailhead. ▪

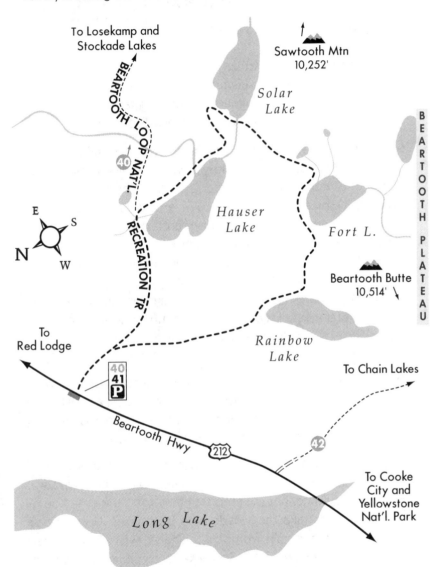

To Losekamp and
Stockade Lakes

Sawtooth Mtn
10,252'

BEARTOOTH LOOP NAT'L.

Solar Lake

40

RECREATION TR.

E
S
N
W

Hauser Lake

BEARTOOTH PLATEAU

Fort L.

Beartooth Butte
10,514'

To
Red Lodge

Rainbow Lake

To Chain Lakes

40
41
P

Beartooth Hwy 212

42

To Cooke
City and
Yellowstone
Nat'l. Park

Long Lake

41. Hauser, Solar, Fort and Rainbow Lakes Loop
BEARTOOTH PLATEAU

42. Upper and Lower Chain Lakes
BEARTOOTH PLATEAU

Hiking distance: 6 miles round trip
Hiking time: 4 hours
Elevation gain: 300 feet
Maps: U.S.G.S. Beartooth Butte
  Beartooth Publishing: Beartooth Mountains
  Rocky Mountain Surveys: Wyoming Beartooths

Summary of hike: Located in the glacial terrain of the Beartooth Plateau, this hike follows a wide but lightly hiked section of the Morrison Jeep Trail through an evergreen forest to open alpine meadows. The meadows are covered in wildflowers and marbled with streams. Upper and Lower Chain Lakes are actually one large, 80-acre lake with a narrow section through the middle. There are beautiful views, including a panoramic overview of Beartooth Butte.

The Morrison Jeep Trail is a rocky, unmaintained road that leads several miles down into the beautiful Box Canyon of the Clarks Fork of the Yellowstone River. It is a popular route for experienced mountain bikers.

Driving directions: The trailhead is located on Highway 212: 35.5 miles south from Red Lodge and 28 miles east from Cooke City. Across the highway from the south end of Long Lake is a jeep trail. Park along the side of the jeep trail.

Hiking directions: Hike along the jeep trail to the bottom of the hill. The stream flows from Long Lake to Upper Chain Lake. You may stay on either the jeep trail that skirts the east side of Chain Lakes, or take the meadow to both lakes. Upper Chain Lake is about one mile from the trailhead, while Lower Chain Lake is just under two miles. Both lakes are visible from the trail. The jeep trail continues past Dollar Lake on the left (2.2 miles) and Duck Lake on the right (3 miles). To return, follow the same trail back.

The Morrison Jeep Trail continues past Sawtooth Mountain and leads 10 miles to the Box Canyon of the Clarks Fork. ■

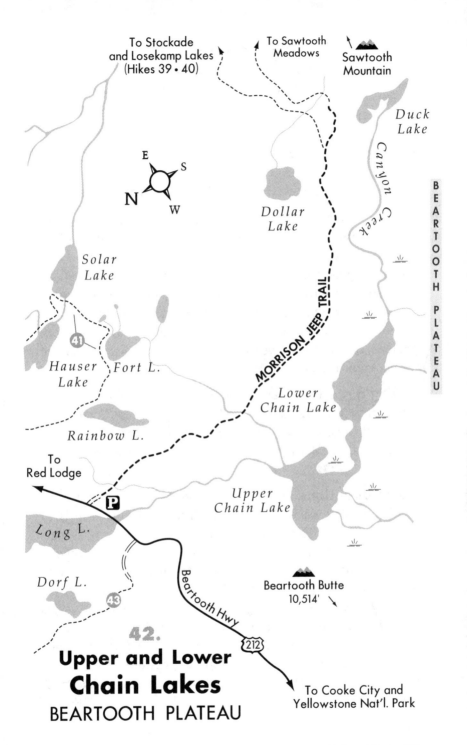

To Stockade
and Losekamp Lakes
(Hikes 39 • 40)

To Sawtooth
Meadows

Sawtooth
Mountain

Duck
Lake

Canyon Creek

BEARTOOTH PLATEAU

E
N S
W

Dollar
Lake

Solar
Lake

MORRISON JEEP TRAIL

41

Hauser
Lake

Fort L.

Lower
Chain Lake

Rainbow L.

To
Red Lodge

P

Upper
Chain Lake

Long L.

Dorf L.

Beartooth Hwy

43

Beartooth Butte
10,514'

42.
**Upper and Lower
Chain Lakes**
BEARTOOTH PLATEAU

212

To Cooke City and
Yellowstone Nat'l. Park

43. Dorf, Sheepherders, Snyder, Promise, and Z Lakes

BEARTOOTH PLATEAU

Hiking distance: 5.5 miles round trip

Hiking time: 3 hours

Elevation gain: 450 feet

Maps: U.S.G.S. Beartooth Butte

Rocky Mountain Surveys: Wyoming Beartooths

Summary of hike: This string of six lakes sits at the eastern base of the Beartooth Plateau in a gorgeous sub-alpine meadow with wildflowers. The hike begins from a short dirt road between Long Lake and Little Bear Lake, but does not follow an actual trail. The route follows Little Bear Creek from lake to lake through open, tree-dotted meadows marbled with small streams and scattered with lichen-covered rocks. Throughout the hike, panoramic views extend across the Beartooth Plateau to the Absaroka Range.

Driving directions: Take Highway 212 to Long Lake: 35.5 miles south from Red Lodge and 28 miles east from Cooke City. Just west of Long Lake is an unimproved road that heads north a short distance. Turn north on this road and park alongside the road.

Hiking directions: Walk north along the unimproved road to its end. You will see Little Bear Creek about 100 yards to the right. Cross the creek using the rocks as stepping stones, and follow the stream uphill. The creek leads to Dorf Lake, a half mile from the trailhead. Parallel Little Bear Creek to Lower and Upper Sheepherder Lakes. From Upper Sheepherder Lake are two hiking options. To the left, about 10 minutes away, is Snyder Lake, sitting above 10,000 feet. Straight ahead, uphill to the north, is Lake Promise and Z Lake, located a half mile past Upper Sheepherder Lake. All of these lakes are beautiful and worth exploring. Return by following the same drainage back downhill. ■

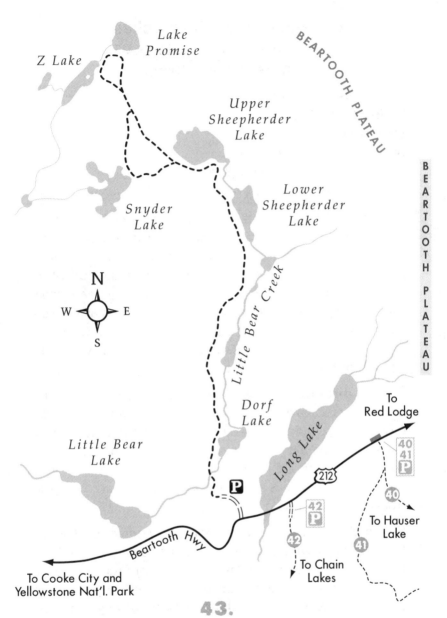

43.
Dorf, Sheepherders, Snyder, Promise, and Z Lakes
BEARTOOTH PLATEAU

44. Island and Night Lakes
BEARTOOTH HIGHLAKES TRAIL
BEARTOOTH HIGHWAY

Hiking distance: 3.4 miles round trip
Hiking time: 2 hours
Elevation gain: 100 feet
Maps: U.S.G.S. Beartooth Butte
  Beartooth Publishing: Beartooth Mountains
  Rocky Mountain Surveys: Wyoming Beartooths

Summary of hike: Located in the high lakes area of the Beartooth Mountains, this extremely scenic hike stays close to the west shores of both Island Lake and Night Lake. The alpine lakes sit at an elevation of 9,500 feet, southwest of the Beartooth Plateau, and are surrounded by snowy peaks. Island Lake encompasses more than 140 acres and contains several islands. Near the trailhead is a crossing of Little Bear Creek. This trail is the beginning of the Beartooth Highlakes Trail, which leads 7 miles northwest to Native Lake.

Driving directions: Take Highway 212 to the Island Lake turnoff: 38 miles south from Red Lodge and 26 miles east from Cooke City. Turn north and continue 0.2 miles to the posted trailhead parking area on the right, by the Island Lake Campground. Turn right and continue 0.2 miles to the lot at the end of the road. A second parking area is near the boat launch, located 0.4 miles from the highway turnoff.

Hiking directions: From the upper parking area near the boat launch, walk down the sloping hill to the south shore of Island Lake. Head west along the lake to Little Bear Creek, the outlet stream that flows into Beartooth Lake. Rock-hop or wade across the creek, depending on the flow, and begin walking north along the shoreline. Stroll along the lake on the level path. Rounded Lonesome Mountain is prominent in the north, just across the state line in Montana. At the north end of Island Lake, parallel

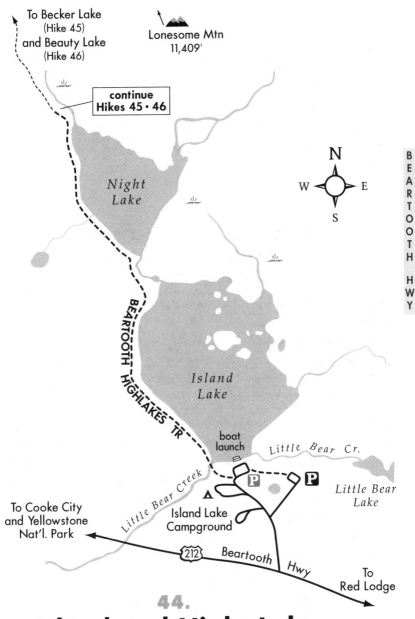

To Becker Lake
(Hike 45)
and Beauty Lake
(Hike 46)

Lonesome Mtn
11,409'

continue
Hikes 45 • 46

*Night
Lake*

N
W E
S

BEARTOOTH HWY

BEARTOOTH HIGHLAKES TR

*Island
Lake*

boat
launch

Little Bear Cr.

Little Bear Creek

P

P

Little Bear
Lake

To Cooke City
and Yellowstone
Nat'l. Park

Island Lake
Campground

212 Beartooth Hwy

To
Red Lodge

44.

Island and Night Lakes
Beartooth Highlakes Trail
BEARTOOTH PLATEAU

the connector creek to Night Lake, which is slightly higher in elevation. Continue north along the west shore of Night Lake to its north end. At 1.7 miles, the trail curves northwest, climbing a small rise away from the lake's inlet stream. This is a good turn-around spot.

To hike farther, trails continue to Becker Lake (Hike 45) and Beauty Lake (Hike 46). The hike to Beauty Lake may also be hiked as a 5-mile shuttle hike to Beartooth Lake. (Reference Hikes 46 and 47.) ▪

45. Island Lake to Becker Lake
BEARTOOTH HIGHLAKES TRAIL
BEARTOOTH HIGHWAY

Hiking distance: 7.5 miles round trip
Hiking time: 4 hours
Elevation gain: 300 feet
Maps: U.S.G.S. Beartooth Butte
Beartooth Publishing: Beartooth Mountains
Rocky Mountain Surveys: Wyoming Beartooths

Summary of hike: Becker Lake is a long, narrow 80-acre lake in Wyoming, just south of the Montana border, at an elevation of nearly 9,700 feet. The scenic, trout-filled lake sits below Albino Lake, which feeds the lake. Pockets of trees and camp sites are scattered around the lake. The trail begins at Island Lake at the base of the Beartooth Plateau. En route, the trail passes a series of interconnecting lakes and ponds.

Driving directions: Take Highway 212 to the Island Lake turn-off: 38 miles south from Red Lodge and 26 miles east from Cooke City. Turn north and continue 0.2 miles to the posted trailhead parking area on the right, by the Island Lake Campground. Turn right and continue 0.2 miles to the lot at the end of the road. A second parking area is near the boat launch, located 0.4 miles from the highway turnoff.

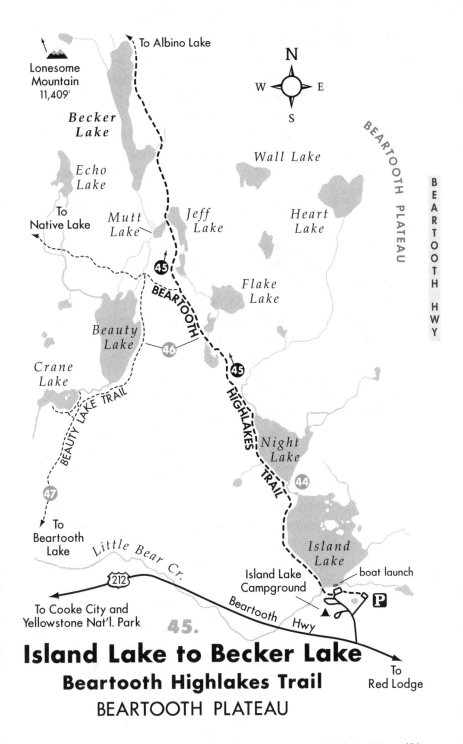

To Albino Lake

N
W ⊹ E
S

Lonesome
Mountain
11,409'

*Becker
Lake*

Wall Lake

BEARTOOTH PLATEAU

BEARTOOTH HWY

*Echo
Lake*

*Heart
Lake*

To
Native Lake

*Mutt
Lake*

*Jeff
Lake*

45

BEARTOOTH

*Flake
Lake*

*Beauty
Lake*

46

45

*Crane
Lake*

HIGHLAKES

BEAUTY LAKE TRAIL

*Night
Lake*

TRAIL

44

47

To
Beartooth
Lake

Little Bear Cr.

*Island
Lake*

boat launch

Island Lake
Campground

212

Beartooth Hwy

P

To Cooke City and
Yellowstone Nat'l. Park

45.

To
Red Lodge

Island Lake to Becker Lake
Beartooth Highlakes Trail
BEARTOOTH PLATEAU

Hiking directions: From the upper parking area near the boat launch, walk down the sloping hill to the south shore of Island Lake. Head west along the lake to Little Bear Creek, the outlet stream that flows into Beartooth Lake. Rock-hop or wade across the creek, depending on the flow, and begin walking north along the shoreline. Stroll along the lake on the level path. Rounded Lonesome Mountain is prominent in the north, just across the state line in Montana. At the north end of Island Lake, parallel the connector creek to Night Lake, which is slightly higher in elevation. Continue north along the west shore of Night Lake to its north end. At 1.7 miles, the trail curves northwest, climbing a small rise away from the lake's inlet stream.

Leave the inlet stream and wind through the forest. Climb a small rise over a ridge to an unnamed lake in a meadow. Lonesome Mountain rises above the trail straight ahead to the northwest. Cross a stream connecting a series of lakes to an unsigned Y-fork at 2.6 miles. The Beartooth Highlakes Trail continues to the left to Beauty Lake (Hike 46) and Native Lake (Hike 48).

Take the right fork and head north, traversing the meadow above Flake Lake. Cross over a rise and descend to Mutt and Jeff Lakes, surrounded by rock cliffs. Cross the stream separating the two lakes, and carefully walk over a boulder field on the west edge of Jeff Lake. Pick up the trail again, and climb the narrow draw between the cliffs to an overlook of Jeff Lake. Top the rise to a view of the south end of Becker Lake. Drop down and cross an inlet stream. Walk through the rolling meadows, slowly descending to the northern end of the lake. This is the turn-around spot.

To hike farther, the trail crosses the unmarked boundary between Wyoming and Montana, then leads to Albino and Jasper Lakes along the east flank of Lonesome Mountain. ■

46. Beauty and Crane Lakes from Island Lake

BEARTOOTH HIGHLAKES TRAIL

BEARTOOTH HIGHWAY

Hiking distance: 7.5 miles round trip or
5-mile shuttle to Beartooth Lake (Hike 47)
Hiking time: 4 hours
Elevation gain: 300 feet
Maps: U.S.G.S. Beartooth Butte
Beartooth Publishing: Beartooth Mountains
Rocky Mountain Surveys: Wyoming Beartooths

Summary of hike: Beauty Lake is a gorgeous high mountain lake that sits in a bowl of forested rock cliffs. Scenic mountains, sloping alpine meadows, pockets of evergreens, and several sandy beaches surround the sinuous 90-acre lake. Crane Lake is a smaller 10-acre lake surrounded by forest that is fed by Beauty Lake. The hike begins at Island Lake just below the Beartooth Plateau. This trail can be combined with Hike 47 for a 5-mile shuttle hike to Beartooth Lake.

Driving directions: Take Highway 212 to the Island Lake turnoff: 38 miles south from Red Lodge and 26 miles east from Cooke City. At the turnoff, turn north and continue 0.2 miles to the posted trailhead parking area on the right, by the Island Lake Campground. Turn right and continue 0.2 miles to the lot at the end of the road. A second parking area is near the boat launch, located 0.4 miles from the highway turnoff.

Hiking directions: From the upper parking area near the boat launch, walk down the sloping hill to the south shore of Island Lake. Head west along the lake to Little Bear Creek, the outlet stream that flows into Beartooth Lake. Rock-hop or wade across the creek, depending on the flow, and begin walking north along the shoreline. Stroll along the lake on the level path. Rounded Lonesome Mountain is prominent in the north, just across the state line in Montana. At the north end of Island Lake, walk parallel to the connector creek to Night Lake, which is slightly higher in elevation. Continue north along the west shore of Night Lake to its north end. At 1.7 miles, the trail curves northwest, climbing a small rise away from the lake's inlet stream.

Leave the inlet stream and wind through the forest. Climb a small rise over a ridge to an unnamed lake in a meadow. Isolated Lonesome Mountain rises above the trail straight ahead to the northwest. Cross the stream connecting a series of lakes to an unsigned Y-fork at 2.6 miles. The right fork heads north to Becker Lake and Jasper Lake (Hike 45). Stay on the Beartooth Highlakes Trail to the left. After meandering through the open forest and meadows, zigzag down into the stream-fed drainage. Beauty Lake can be seen through the trees.

At the base of the short, steep descent is a posted junction at 3 miles. The Beartooth Highlakes Trail continues to the right, passing the north end of Beauty Lake en route to Native Lake. Bear left on the Beauty Lake Trail and head south. Follow the east side of the lake, dropping to the grassy shoreline. Near the south end of the lake, climb the mountain slope and traverse the forested hillside, then return to the lake. Curve to the right and skirt the base of the rounded 9,500-foot knoll bordering the lake's south side. At the outlet stream, leave the lake and follow the cascading stream through the forest. The main trail passes by Crane Lake to Beartooth Lake. A few side paths descend to Crane Lake on the right. Return on the same trail, or continue with Hike 47 for a 5-mile shuttle hike to Beartooth Lake. ▪

47. Beauty and Crane Lakes from Beartooth Lake

BEAUTY LAKE TRAIL
BEARTOOTH HIGHWAY

Hiking distance: 4 miles round trip
5-mile shuttle to Island Lake (Hike 46)
Hiking time: 2 hours
Elevation gain: 520 feet
Maps: U.S.G.S. Beartooth Butte
Beartooth Publishing: Beartooth Mountains
Rocky Mountain Surveys: Wyoming Beartooths

Summary of hike: The Beauty Lake Trail begins at Beartooth Lake where the grandeur of Beartooth Butte towers 1,600 feet above the lake. The 10,514-foot sandstone butte was submerged under an inland sea hundreds of millions of years ago. Clay Butte (Hike 50) and Beartooth Butte are the last remnants of exposed sedimentary rock in the Beartooth Mountains. The trail winds through forests and meadows at an elevation of more than 9,000 feet to Crane Lake and Beauty Lake. Both picturesque, high-mountain lakes have natural rock benches and are surrounded by granite domes, alpine meadows, and conifer groves. This trail can also be hiked as a 5-mile shuttle hike to Island Lake (Hike 46).

Driving directions: Take Highway 212 to the Beartooth Lake Campground turnoff: 41 miles south from Red Lodge and 23 miles east from Cooke City. Turn towards the campground, and drive 0.6 miles to the trailhead road. Turn left and continue 0.1 mile to the trailhead parking area.

Hiking directions: Head north toward Beartooth Lake to a signed junction. The left fork leads to Native Lake (Hike 48). Take the right fork and wade across Little Bear Creek, picking up the trail on the other side. (Early in the season, the water may be dangerously high and crossing is not recommended.) Continue through the pine and spruce forest, passing the east shore of Crane Lake at 1.3 miles. Several spur trails lead down to the shore. The main trail follows the cascading creek upstream to the southern tip of Beauty Lake, then parallels the eastern shore. This is the turn-around spot.

To hike farther, the Beauty Lake Trail intersects the Beartooth Highlakes Trail north of Beauty Lake. The right fork leads to Night Lake and Island Lake, a popular 5-mile shuttle hike (Hike 46). The left fork leads to Native Lake and may be hiked as an 8-mile loop with Hike 48. ■

48. Native Lake
from Beartooth Lake

BEAUTY LAKE TRAILHEAD to BEARTOOTH HIGHLAKES TR.

BEARTOOTH HIGHWAY

Hiking distance: 8 miles round trip
Hiking time: 4 hour
Elevation gain: 900 feet
Maps: U.S.G.S. Beartooth Butte
　　　　Beartooth Publishing: Beartooth Mountains
　　　　Rocky Mountain Surveys: Wyoming Beartooths

Summary of hike: Native Lake rests in a seven-acre bowl at 9,800 feet in the high lakes area of the Beartooths. The lake sits near the northern base of Beartooth Butte, one mile shy of the Montana state line. Meadows, stunted conifers, and snow-capped peaks surround the scenic lake. Native Lake can be reached from three trailheads: the Beartooth Highlakes Trail via Island Lake (Hike 45), the Upper Granite Loop Trail by Clay Butte (Hike 51), and the Beauty Lake Trailhead (this hike). The shortest route begins here by Beartooth Lake at the southern base of Beartooth Butte. The picturesque sedimentary rock formation made of limestone and shale dominates the landscape, which towers 1,600 feet above the lake. The trail crosses open alpine terrain covered with wildflowers while paralleling Beartooth Creek along the east slope of the enormous 3.5-mile-long butte.

Driving directions: Take Highway 212 to the Beartooth Lake Campground turnoff: 41 miles south from Red Lodge and 23 miles east from Cooke City. Turn towards the campground, and drive 0.6 miles to the trailhead road. Turn left and continue 0.1 mile to the trailhead parking area.

Hiking directions: Walk towards Beartooth Lake and a signed trail junction. The right fork leads to Beauty Lake (Hike 47). Head towards the Highlakes Trail, continuing straight ahead on the left fork. (This trail is referred to as F.S. Trail 619.) Wade across Little Bear Creek, and loop around the northeast perimeter of Beartooth Lake. Stay close to the forested hillside on the east edge of a marshy meadow. Cross four consecutive inlet streams. After crossing Beartooth Creek (the fourth stream), curve north, away from Beartooth Lake. Climb the hillside through meadows with stands of evergreens. Traverse the terraced east slope of Beartooth Butte above the creek for two miles. At 2.6 miles, cross the creek and continue north to a signed junction with the Beartooth Highlakes Trail. The right fork drops over the hill into a lake-filled basin and leads to Beauty, Night, and Island Lakes. Bear left and recross the creek to another junction. The left fork heads west to Clay Butte (Hike 51). Continue 0.6 miles on the right fork to Native Lake. Return by retracing your steps.

The trail may be hiked as an 8-mile loop with the Beauty Lake Trail (Hike 47) and the Highlakes Trail. ▪

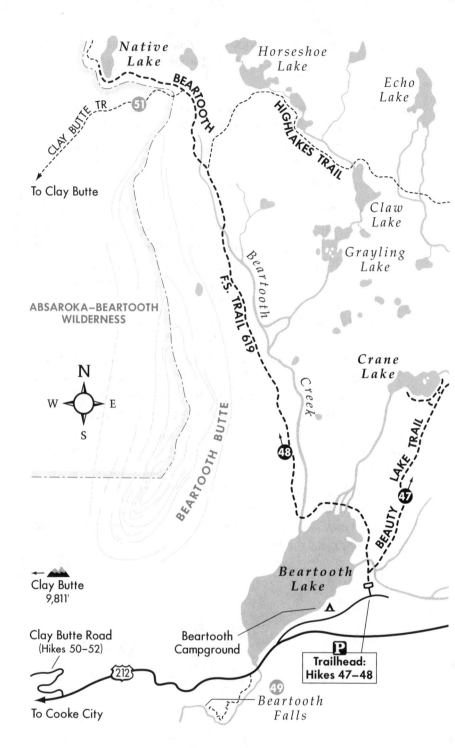

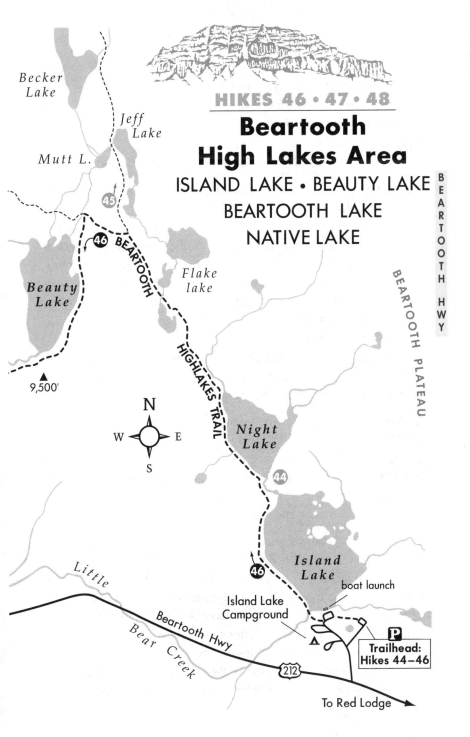

Becker
Lake

Jeff
Lake

Mutt L.

45

46 BEARTOOTH

Flake
lake

Beauty
Lake

▲
9,500'

HIKES 46 • 47 • 48

Beartooth
High Lakes Area
ISLAND LAKE • BEAUTY LAKE
BEARTOOTH LAKE
NATIVE LAKE

BEARTOOTH HWY

BEARTOOTH PLATEAU

HIGHLAKES TRAIL

N
W E
S

Night
Lake

44

46

Island
Lake

boat launch

Island Lake
Campground

P
Trailhead:
Hikes 44–46

Little

Beartooth Hwy

Bear Creek

212

To Red Lodge

49. Beartooth Falls
BEARTOOTH HIGHWAY

Hiking distance: 1 mile round trip
Hiking time: 30 minutes
Elevation gain: 150 feet
Maps: U.S.G.S. Beartooth Butte
   Rocky Mountain Surveys: Wyoming Beartooths

Summary of hike: Just below Beartooth Lake is Beartooth Falls, a spectacular waterfall on Beartooth Creek. The 100-foot cascade plunges over granite rocks with a tremendous volume of water. The short trail to Beartooth Falls is not a designated or maintained trail. It is, however, a hike you will long remember. The trail in this area is vague and there is a short scramble over large boulders to the brink of the falls. The falls can also be spotted from a small pullout along the highway, a quarter mile west of the trailhead.
Caution: Good, stable footing is essential while climbing over the rocks. A small misstep could adversely effect your trip. The trail is not recommended for children.

Driving directions: The trailhead is located on Highway 212: 41.5 miles south from Red Lodge and 22.5 miles east from Cooke City. There are several pullouts on each side of the highway bridge that crosses Beartooth Creek at the south end of Beartooth Lake. The trail starts from the western most pullout, where the highway bends to the west.

Hiking directions: From the parking area, take the narrow trail into the forest towards Beartooth Creek. The trail parallels the creek downstream through the lush, moist groundcover. Within ten minutes, the trail meets boulders on the right and Beartooth Creek on the left. Climb up the boulders to the plateau at the top. The trail is not clearly defined, but all routes lead up to the same area. Once on top, follow a footpath down in the direction of the thunderous sound of Beartooth Falls. There are various viewing points, from the beginning cascades to the lookout atop the falls. The views are guaranteed to give you vertigo. After admiring this powerful display of water, return along the same route. ▪

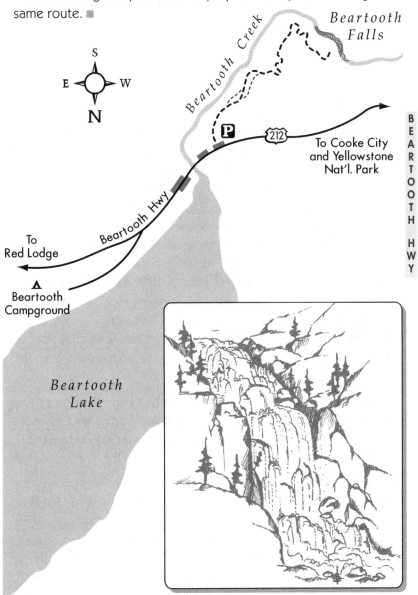

49. **Beartooth Falls**
BEARTOOTH HIGHWAY

50. Clay Butte Overlook
BEARTOOTH HIGHWAY

Hiking distance: 2.5 miles round trip
Hiking time: 1.5 hour
Elevation gain: 300 feet
Maps: U.S.G.S. Muddy Creek and Beartooth Butte
Rocky Mountain Surveys: Wyoming Beartooths

Summary of hike: The Clay Butte Overlook Trail begins at the 9,811-foot Clay Butte Fire Lookout perched on the south tip of the butte. The butte consists of sedimentary rock left by an ancient inland sea. (Clay Butte and Beartooth Butte, directly to the east, lie adjacent to each other.) The trail crosses the expansive alpine plateau, rich with wildflowers, to the north edge of the weathered cliffs, offering a unique view of the backside of Beartooth Butte. The panoramic views are as spectacular as you will find anywhere. The Beartooth Mountains, Beartooth Butte, the Clarks Fork Valley, the twisting highway, and the peaks of the Absaroka Range are all visible from this high mountain overlook. At the lookout tower are interpretive displays of the 1988 Yellowstone Fires, the impact which can be seen from the lookout.

Driving directions: Take Highway 212 to the Clay Butte Fire Lookout turnoff: 43 miles south from Red Lodge and 22 miles east from Cooke City. Turn north at the signed Clay Butte turnoff. Drive 2.6 miles up the winding, gravel road to the fire lookout at the end of the road.

Hiking directions: Before beginning the hike, visit the fire lookout tower with an enclosed observation and interpretive center. After marveling at the grand vistas from the lookout, return to the parking area, and follow the two-track trail across the high, open meadow with panoramic 360-degree views. The alpine meadow is often carpeted with a colorful display of wildflowers. Head gently uphill to a knoll. Due to the high altitude, it is more tiring than it appears. Once at the top of the eroded bald knoll, the path ends at the edge of the limestone cliffs. A few large and distinct cairns mark the route. Follow the cliffs to numerous overlooks on the treeless and seemingly endless expanse. Choose your own turn-around spot. ▪

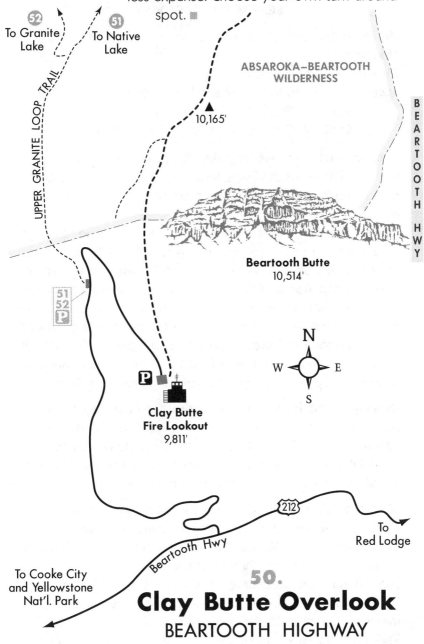

To Granite Lake

To Native Lake

UPPER GRANITE LOOP TRAIL

ABSAROKA–BEARTOOTH WILDERNESS

10,165'

BEARTOOTH HWY

Beartooth Butte
10,514'

51 52 P

N
W · E
S

P
Clay Butte
Fire Lookout
9,811'

212

To Red Lodge

Beartooth Hwy

To Cooke City
and Yellowstone
Nat'l. Park

50.
Clay Butte Overlook
BEARTOOTH HIGHWAY

51. Clay Butte to Native Lake
CLAY BUTTE TRAIL
BEARTOOTH HIGHWAY

Hiking distance: 7.6 miles round trip
Hiking time: 4 hours
Elevation gain: 800 feet
Maps: U.S.G.S. Muddy Creek and Beartooth Butte
Beartooth Publishing: Beartooth Mountains
Rocky Mountain Surveys: Wyoming Beartooths

Summary of hike: Native Lake sits in a deep cirque on the north end of Beartooth Butte, an ancient 3.5-mile-long outcropping of sedimentary rock. Granite erratics—boulders that were transported and deposited by retreating glaciers—are scattered along the butte's northern slope. Three trailheads lead to Native Lake: the Beartooth Highlakes Trail by Island Lake (Hike 46), the Beauty Lake Trail by Beartooth Lake (Hike 48), and the Upper Granite Loop Trail by Clay Butte (this hike). The trail begins at 9,550 feet, just below the Clay Butte Fire Lookout, and crosses expansive alpine meadows with wildflowers and groves of Engelmann spruce, whitebark pine, and subalpine fir. Throughout the hike are fantastic vistas of Pilot and Index Peaks and the snow-capped peaks of the Absaroka and Beartooth Ranges.

Driving directions: Take Highway 212 to the Clay Butte Fire Lookout turnoff: 43 miles south from Red Lodge and 22 miles east from Cooke City. Turn north at the signed Clay Butte turnoff. Drive 1.8 miles up the winding, gravel road to the signed Upper Granite Loop trailhead parking area on the left.

Hiking directions: Follow the footpath past the map kiosk and head down the slope. Cross an open meadow with vast vistas of the Beartooth Plateau, Pilot Peak, and Index Peak. Steadily descend to the north through pockets of mixed evergreens and flower-covered meadows. Cross a series of eight small log bridges over trickling waterways to a signed junction in a meadow at 1.1 mile. The left fork leads to Granite Lake (Hike 52). Take the right fork on the Clay Butte Trail. Continue northeast, gradually ascending the hillside through meadows and forest groves. At 2.5 miles, cross a small stream twice. Head up the draw to a saddle and junction with the Beartooth Highlakes Trail at the north end of Beartooth Butte. (Whenever the trail fades, watch for cairns as a guide.) The right fork returns to Beartooth Lake (Hike 48). Bear left and descend 0.6 miles to Native Lake. The trail continues around the west side of the lake and heads northwest to Green Lake. Return along the same path. ■

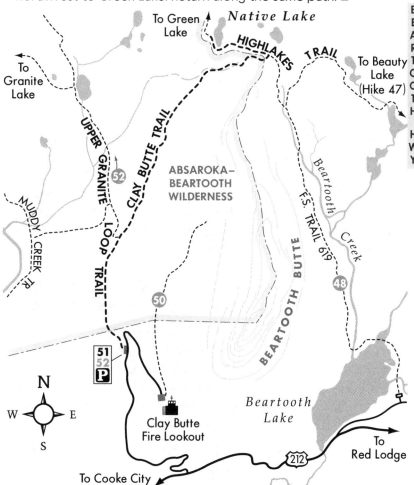

To Green Lake

Native Lake

HIGHLAKES TRAIL

To Beauty Lake (Hike 47)

To Granite Lake

BEARTOOTH HWY

UPPER GRANITE LOOP TRAIL

CLAY BUTTE TRAIL

MUDDY CREEK TR

52

ABSAROKA–
BEARTOOTH
WILDERNESS

Beartooth Creek

F.S. TRAIL 619

BEARTOOTH BUTTE

48

50

51
52
P

N
W — E
S

Clay Butte
Fire Lookout

*Beartooth
Lake*

To
Red Lodge

212

To Cooke City

51. Clay Butte to Native Lake
BEARTOOTH HIGHWAY

52. Granite Lake from Clay Butte

UPPER GRANITE LOOP TRAIL
BEARTOOTH HIGHWAY

Hiking distance: 9 mile loop
Hiking time: 5.5 hours
Elevation gain: 1,500 feet
Maps: U.S.G.S. Muddy Creek
Beartooth Publishing: Beartooth Mountains
Rocky Mountain Surveys: Wyoming Beartooths

Summary of hike: Forested Granite Lake is one of the largest lakes in the Absaroka-Beartooth Wilderness. The lake sits at an elevation of 8,620 feet and encompasses 228 acres, stretching across Montana and Wyoming. The picturesque, tree-lined lake has an irregular shoreline with many peninsulas, small bays, and rocky points jutting out of the water.

This hike begins at Clay Butte, just before the fire lookout, and descends through high mountain meadows rich with wildflowers. Snow-capped peaks frame the trail, including Lonesome Mountain, Pilot Peak, and Index Peak. En route, the trail passes Rush Lake and Elk Lake, small mountain tarns at 9,000 feet. The loop hike returns down the Muddy Creek drainage to a tree-rimmed, boggy meadow covering the valley floor. The climb from Muddy Creek back to the Clay Butte Trail is a very steep climb, gaining 800 feet in 0.8 miles.

Driving directions: Take Highway 212 to the Clay Butte Fire Lookout turnoff: 43 miles south from Red Lodge and 22 miles east from Cooke City. Turn north at the signed Clay Butte turnoff. Drive 1.8 miles up the winding, gravel road to the signed Upper Granite Loop trailhead parking area on the left.

Hiking directions: Follow the footpath past the map kiosk and head down the slope. Cross an open meadow with vast vistas of the Beartooth Plateau, Pilot Peak, and Index Peak. Steadily descend to the north through pockets of mixed evergreens and flower-covered meadows. Cross a series of eight small log

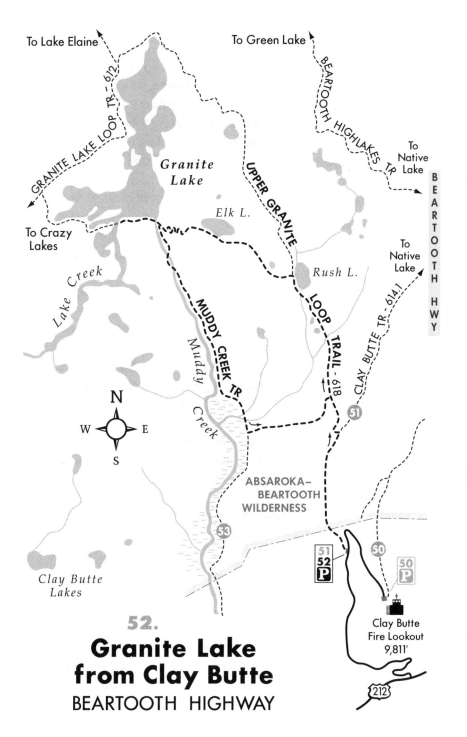

To Lake Elaine

To Green Lake

GRANITE LAKE LOOP TR - 612

BEARTOOTH HIGHLAKES TR

To Native Lake

Granite Lake

UPPER GRANITE

Elk L.

To Crazy Lakes

Rush L.

To Native Lake

BEARTOOTH HWY

Lake Creek

LOOP TRAIL - 618

CLAY BUTTE TR - 614.1

MUDDY CREEK TR

Muddy Creek

N
W ☀ E
S

51

ABSAROKA–
BEARTOOTH
WILDERNESS

53

51
52
P

50

50
P

Clay Butte Lakes

Clay Butte
Fire Lookout
9,811'

52.

Granite Lake
from Clay Butte
BEARTOOTH HIGHWAY

212

bridges over trickling waterways to a signed junction in a meadow at 1.1 mile. The Clay Butte Trail continues straight ahead to the High Lakes (Hike 51). Go left towards posted Granite Lake, and traverse the open slope to another signed junction at 1.4 miles.

Begin the loop straight ahead on the Upper Granite Loop Trail. Walk through the open grasslands, crossing three wide, meandering streams. Pass a lily pad pond and a clear pond on the left. Continue through the pine forest, and cross the inlet stream to Rush Lake, reaching a posted junction high above the lake. The Upper Granite Loop Trail continues straight ahead. Bear left and head west through the forest, passing a wetland meadow and pond on the right. Gently climb, then zigzag downhill. Traverse the hillside to Elk Lake, sitting beneath a vertical rock wall towering 700 feet above the water. Descend to the lake and cross its outlet stream. Follow the south edge of the lake, then climb a small rise and descend again, passing granite monoliths to the south shore of Granite Lake and a junction. The left fork follows the Muddy Creek drainage, our return route.

For now detour straight ahead and follow the southern shoreline. Traverse the hillside above the lake. Descend to Lake Creek, the 40-foot-wide outlet stream of Granite Lake a half mile from the junction. Due to the water volume and depth, fording Lake Creek is dangerous until late in the season.

Return to the junction and head south on the Muddy Creek Trail. Climb the east wall of the creek drainage. Meander on the rock-embedded path among the gorgeous granite walls and boulders. Cross the trickling stream and gently descend along the western slope. Recross the stream and traverse the canyon wall. Follow the narrow, granite-walled canyon downhill, crossing the steam that drains Elk Lake. Continue down through the lodgepole pine forest to a massive wetland meadow formed by Muddy Creek and feeder streams. Skirt the eastern margin of the grassy wetland, attempting to stay dry, and cross a cascading stream. Walk 0.1 mile to a posted junction. The main trail continues straight ahead along Muddy Creek another 2.3 miles to the undeveloped campground by Highway 212 (Hike 53).

To complete this loop, bear left and walk through the tall grass meadow to the treeline, where the distinct trail can be spotted. Begin a very steep 0.8 mile climb, with little relief to ease the grade. Near the top, cairns mark the path through a scenic meadow, completing the loop at the signed junction. Go to the right 0.3 miles to the Clay Butte Trail junction and veer right again, leading 1.1 mile back to the trailhead. ▩

53. Granite Lake from Muddy Creek Trail
UPPER GRANITE LOOP TRAIL
BEARTOOTH HIGHWAY

Hiking distance: 9.5 miles round trip
Hiking time: 5 hours
Elevation gain: 650 feet
Maps: U.S.G.S. Muddy Creek
Beartooth Publishing: Beartooth Mountains
Rocky Mountain Surveys: Wyoming Beartooths

Summary of hike: Aptly named Granite Lake, straddling the Montana-Wyoming border, is surrounded by gorgeous granite knobs and domes. The 228-acre subalpine lake is among the largest lakes in the Absaroka-Beartooth Wilderness. It has an irregular shoreline with numerous inlets and peninsulas. The Muddy Creek Trail begins by the Beartooth Highway and leads nearly 5 miles to the south shore of Granite Lake. The trail parallels Muddy Creek up the scenic canyon through forests of Engelmann spruce and lodgepole pine. The forested valley contains an expansive and scenic meadow (actually a wetland rimmed with trees and granite rock outcrops). The trail follows the east edge of the boggy meadow, which is a wet and muddy event until mid- to late-August, then leads into a narrow, granite-walled canyon.

Driving directions: Take Highway 212 to the unsigned Muddy Creek Road turnoff on the north: 46 miles south from Red Lodge and 19 miles east from Cooke City. The turnoff is located 3.4

miles past the Clay Butte Fire Lookout road. Turn north on Muddy Creek Road, and drive 0.1 mile to a fork. The left fork leads 0.1 mile into the primitive campground. Veer right and go 0.1 mile to the parking area on a knoll above the campground.

Hiking directions: Take the narrow footpath north off the knoll to the Muddy Creek Trail, an extension of the gated road at the north end of the undeveloped campground. Follow the forested hillside path above and parallel to Muddy Creek. Gently descend into a tree-rimmed meadow and a trail sign. Return to the forest and hop over a tributary of Muddy Creek. Pass through another meadow and continue through the forest at an easy grade. Enter the posted Absaroka-Beartooth Wilderness at 0.8 miles. After a few minor dips and rises, the trail reaches the east rim of an expansive wetland formed by Muddy Creek and feeder streams. Skirt the eastern margin of the grassy wetland just inside the forest, reaching a posted junction at 2.3 miles. To the right, the trail leads through the tall grass and climbs severely up to the Clay Butte Trail (Hike 52).

For this hike continue straight ahead to the north, and cross a cascading stream. Continue skirting the edge of the grassy wetland through the lodgepole pine forest. Enter the mouth of the canyon, and gently climb the narrow drainage. Cross the stream that drains Elk Lake, traversing the narrow, granite-walled canyon uphill. Cross trickling Muddy Creek twice, and follow the rock-embedded path among the gorgeous granite walls and boulders. Descend along the east wall of the canyon among spruce, lodgepole pine, and subalpine fir, reaching the south shore of sprawling Granite Lake at just over 4 miles. The right fork leads to Elk Lake and Rush Lake (Hike 52).

Bear left and follow the southern shoreline. Traverse the forested slope above the lake and descend to Lake Creek, the 40-foot wide outlet stream of Granite Lake a half mile from the junction. Due to the water volume and depth, fording Lake Creek is dangerous until late in the season. Return by retracing your steps. ■

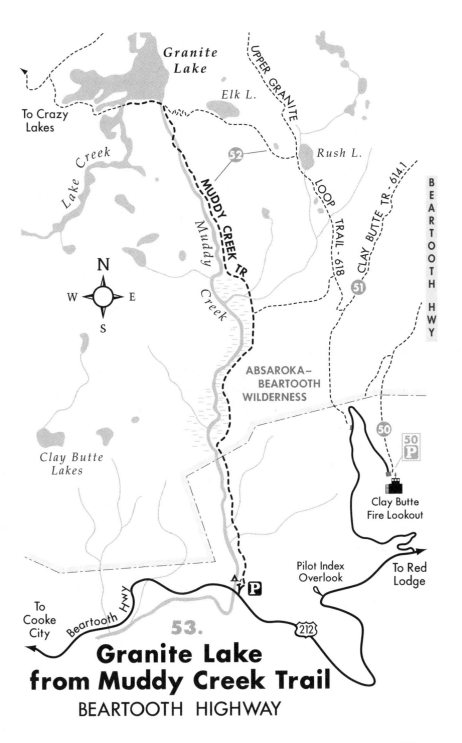

Granite Lake

Elk L.

UPPER GRANITE

To Crazy
Lakes

Lake Creek

52

Rush L.

MUDDY CREEK TR

Muddy Creek

LOOP TRAIL - 618

CLAY BUTTE TR - 614.1

BEARTOOTH HWY

N
W E
S

51

ABSAROKA–
BEARTOOTH
WILDERNESS

Clay Butte
Lakes

50

50
P

Clay Butte
Fire Lookout

Pilot Index
Overlook

To Red
Lodge

To
Cooke
City

Beartooth HWY

53.

212

Granite Lake
from Muddy Creek Trail
BEARTOOTH HIGHWAY

54. Lily Lake
BEARTOOTH HIGHWAY

Hiking distance: 1 mile loop
Hiking time: 30 minutes
Elevation gain: 100 feet
Maps: U.S.G.S. Muddy Creek
       Rocky Mountain Surveys: Wyoming Beartooths

Summary of hike: This beautiful, 40-acre mountain lake sits at 7,670 feet just outside the Absaroka-Beartooth Wilderness. The easy hike utilizes well-worn fisherman paths along the southern portion of Lily Lake, which has an abundance of water lilies and is surrounded by a forest. Some of the best views of Pilot and Index Peak can be seen along Lily Lake Road en route to the lake. The towering peaks are volcanic remnants reaching more than 11,000 feet on the northeast end of the Absaroka Range.

Driving directions: Take Highway 212 to Lily Lake Road: 50 miles south from Red Lodge and 14.5 miles east from Cooke City. The road is 0.4 miles west of the large bridge over Lake Creek and 0.9 miles east of the Chief Joseph Scenic Highway (Wyoming Highway 296). Turn north from Highway 212 onto Lily Lake Road. Drive up the winding road 1.4 miles to the T-junction. Turn right and continue 0.5 miles towards Lily Lake. As you approach the campground, turn right at each of the first two road forks. Park at the end of the road by the campsites.

Hiking directions: Head east and rock-hop across a tributary of Lake Creek. The trail leads through the forest to the shoreline of Lily Lake near a rock outcropping. Take the fisherman trail to the left, which borders the lake along the southwest shore. Continue to the boat launch area. Walk up the gravel road, making a loop back to the parking area on the left. Additional trails continue north of the boat launch for a longer hike. ■

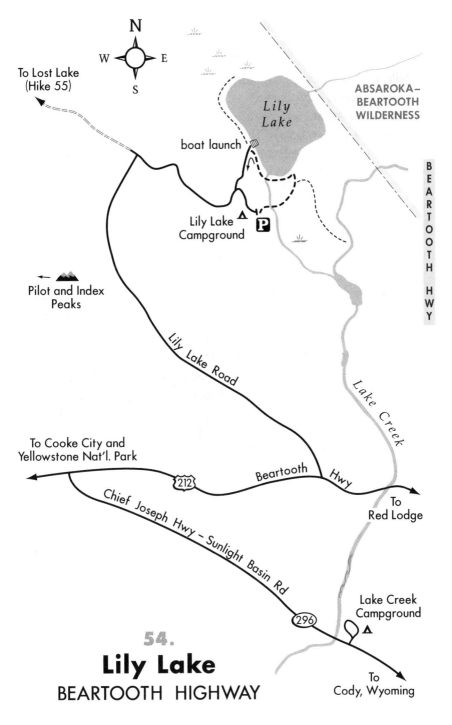

N
W   E
S

To Lost Lake
(Hike 55)

Lily Lake

ABSAROKA–
BEARTOOTH
WILDERNESS

boat launch

Lily Lake
Campground

P

B E A R T O O T H   H W Y

Pilot and Index
Peaks

Lily Lake Road

Lake Creek

To Cooke City and
Yellowstone Nat'l. Park

Beartooth   Hwy

212

To
Red Lodge

Chief Joseph Hwy – Sunlight Basin Rd

296

Lake Creek
Campground

54.
Lily Lake
BEARTOOTH HIGHWAY

To
Cody, Wyoming

55. Lost Lake

BEARTOOTH HIGHWAY

Hiking distance: 4.6 miles round trip
Hiking time: 2.5 hours
Elevation gain: 500 feet
Maps: U.S.G.S. Muddy Creek
        Beartooth Publishing: Beartooth Mountains
        Rocky Mountain Surveys: Wyoming Beartooths

Summary of hike: Lost Lake is a picturesque tarn surrounded by a pine forest and rock cliffs in the Absaroka-Beartooth Wilderness. The 30-acre lake sits at at an elevation of 8,237 feet between Granite Lake and Lake Reno. The hike to the high mountain lake offers excellent views of Pilot Peak and Index Peak. En route, the trail passes a waterfall and parallels Gilbert Creek, the outlet stream of Lost Lake. Fishermen paths skirt the shoreline.

Driving directions: Take Highway 212 to Lily Lake Road: 50 miles south from Red Lodge and 14.5 miles east from Cooke City. The road is 0.4 miles west of the large bridge over Lake Creek and 0.9 miles east of the Chief Joseph Scenic Highway (Wyoming Highway 296). Turn north from Highway 212 onto Lily Lake Road. Drive 1.4 miles up the winding road to the T-junction. To the right is Lily Lake. For Lost Lake, turn left and follow the rough, rocky road 1.4 miles to the road's end. A four-wheel drive vehicle is recommended for this stretch of the road; or park along the road and add the mileage to the hiking distance.

Hiking directions: Head north up the road-turned-trail through a lodgepole pine forest with granite boulders. Pass through meadows and enjoy the prominent vistas of Pilot and Index Peaks directly to the west. Rock hop over Gilbert Creek, the outlet stream from Lake Reno and Lost Lake, to a signed junction at 0.8 miles. The left fork leads 3 miles to Lake Reno, then continues 3 more miles to the Crazy Lakes.

For this hike go to the right, staying on the Lost Lake Trail within the Absaroka-Beartooth Wilderness. Traverse the hillside through a flower-filled meadow, gaining a quick 200 feet in elevation to the wide Lake Reno outlet stream by a waterfall, cascade, and small pools. Cross the creek, using rocks as stepping stones, and continue on the rock-embedded path. Meander through the old forest back to Gilbert Creek, draining from Lost Lake. Veer left along the creek, and head 0.6 miles upstream to the northwest tip of Lost Lake by lily pads at the lake's outlet. Fishermen paths follow the west and north side of the shoreline. ■

Lake Reno

LOST LAKE TRAIL

Lost Lake

To Lake Reno and Crazy Lakes

To Lake Reno

Gilbert Creek

ABSAROKA–
BEARTOOTH
WILDERNESS

Lake Creek

P

N
W   E
S

Lily Lake

54

Lake Creek

Lily Lake Road
to Hwy 212

Lily Lake
Campground

55. **Lost Lake**
BEARTOOTH HIGHWAY

56. Clarks Fork Trail to Beartooth Creek
HIGHWAY 296

Hiking distance: 5 miles round trip
Hiking time: 2.5 hours
Elevation gain: 200 feet
Maps: U.S.G.S. Muddy Creek, Hunter Peak, Windy Mountain
      Rocky Mountain Surveys: Wyoming Beartooths

Summary of hike: The Clarks Fork Trail (also known as the Lewis and Clark Trail) is an extensive pack trail that leads eight miles to the Clarks Fork of the Yellowstone River. There are scenic vistas into the deep river canyon. This hike follows the first 2.5 miles on an easy meandering path to a footbridge over Beartooth Creek, a tributary of the Clarks Fork. The trail crosses through the rolling hills, rocky meadows, and subalpine forested knolls north of the Clarks Fork. The pack trail continues several miles along the Clarks Fork to the Morrison Jeep Trail.

Driving directions: Take Highway 212 to the Chief Joseph Scenic Highway (Wyoming Highway 296): 50.5 miles south from Red Lodge and 14.5 miles east from Cooke City. Drive 4.8 miles southeast on Chief Joseph Scenic Highway to the signed Clarks Fork Trailhead turnoff on the left, directly across from Hunter Peak Campground. Turn left and follow the unpaved road 0.2 miles to the trailhead parking lot.

Hiking directions: Head east on the sandy path past the signed trailhead and cattle gate. Cross a trickling stream and a pond on the right. The near-level trail meanders up and down the rolling hills dotted with evergreens and colorful rock formations. At 0.7 miles, rock hop over Ghost Creek, and pass through an aspen grove in a small draw. Continue across the scenic landscape and cross another stream. Descend into a draw with beautiful rock outcroppings and a young pine forest. The trail reaches Beartooth Creek and a footbridge with trail access gates at 2.5 miles. Return along the same trail.

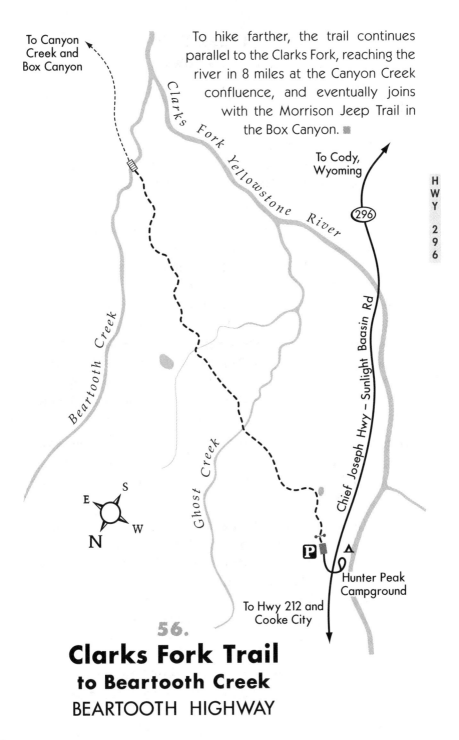

To Canyon Creek and Box Canyon

To hike farther, the trail continues parallel to the Clarks Fork, reaching the river in 8 miles at the Canyon Creek confluence, and eventually joins with the Morrison Jeep Trail in the Box Canyon. ■

Clarks Fork Yellowstone River

To Cody, Wyoming

296

HWY 296

Chief Joseph Hwy – Sunlight Baasin Rd

Beartooth Creek

Ghost Creek

E S
W
N

P

Hunter Peak Campground

To Hwy 212 and Cooke City

56.
Clarks Fork Trail
to Beartooth Creek
BEARTOOTH HIGHWAY

57. Crazy Creek Falls
BEARTOOTH HIGHWAY

Hiking distance: 1 mile round trip
Hiking time: .5 hours
Elevation gain: 150 feet
Maps: U.S.G.S. Jim Smith Peak
Beartooth Publishing: Beartooth Mountains
Rocky Mountain Surveys: Wyoming Beartooths

Summary of hike: Crazy Creek, a tributary of the Clarks Fork of the Yellowstone River, is formed from a string of lakes that includes Fox Lake, Widewater Lake, Big Moose Lake, and Ivy Lake. Crazy Creek Falls, located near the confluence with the Clarks Fork, is a short 15-minute hike, but it is hard not to spend a few hours here. The falls is a massive cascade, plunging over slabs of granite rock. Along the edge of the thunderous cascade are flat, terraced rocks for sunbathing or exploring. Beside the cascades and waterfalls are cold soaking pools and even a bubble-filled "jacuzzi." This natural water park is a favorite spot for those who know about it. The hike follows the first section of the Crazy Lakes Trail, a pack route to Ivy Lake and Crazy Mountain.

Driving directions: The trailhead is located on Highway 212: 53 miles south from Red Lodge and 11 miles east from Cooke City. Pull into the parking turnout on the north, directly across from the Crazy Creek Campground.

Hiking directions: From the parking turnout, follow the Crazy Lakes Trail through a lodgepole pine forest. Within a few minutes, the massive cascade and raw power of Crazy Creek Falls is in full view. At 0.4 miles, watch on the left for a large, flat terrace of rocks. Leave the trail and hike along this terrace toward the sound of the water. This will quickly lead you to the water playground. Use caution, as the rocks can be slick and the water is swift.

To extend the hike, the trail leaves Crazy Creek a short distance ahead and continues 3 miles to Ivy Lake, the outlet of Crazy Creek. ∎

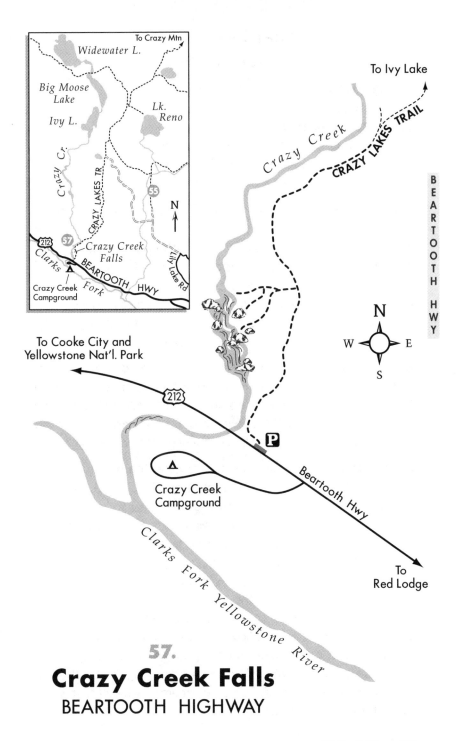

To Crazy Mtn

Widewater L.

Big Moose Lake

Ivy L.

Lk. Reno

Crazy Cr.

CRAZY LAKES TR.

Clarks Fork

BEARTOOTH HWY

Crazy Creek Falls

Crazy Creek Campground

Lily Lake Rd

N

To Ivy Lake

Crazy Creek

CRAZY LAKES TRAIL

B E A R T O O T H H W Y

N
W E
S

To Cooke City and Yellowstone Nat'l. Park

P

Crazy Creek Campground

Beartooth Hwy

To Red Lodge

Clarks Fork Yellowstone River

57.
Crazy Creek Falls
BEARTOOTH HIGHWAY

58. Pilot Creek Trail
BEARTOOTH HIGHWAY

Hiking distance: 5.6 miles round trip
Hiking time: 3 hours
Elevation gain: 800 feet
Maps: U.S.G.S. Jim Smith Peak and Pilot Peak
Beartooth Publishing: Beartooth Mountains
Rocky Mountain Surveys: Wyoming Beartooths

Summary of hike: The Pilot Creek Trail begins at the base of Jim Smith Peak and follows the cliffs overlooking the Pilot Creek drainage. The first 2.8 miles of the hike offer panoramic views of Jim Smith Peak, the snow-capped Beartooth Range, the Clarks Fork valley, and a unique perspective of Pilot Peak directly below its south flank. The entire 7-mile trail crosses high mountain meadows along a forested creek canyon and ends in a steep mountain cirque at the east flank of Republic Peak.

Driving directions: The trailhead is located on Highway 212: 55.4 miles south from Red Lodge and 8.9 miles east from Cooke City. Turn south at the signed Pilot Creek Trailhead turn-off. Drive a quarter mile, curving around the perimeter of the gravel pit, to the signed trailhead parking area on the right.

Hiking directions: Climb up the forested path to a view of Jim Smith Peak on a ridge 150 feet above Pilot Creek. The trail follows the edge of the cliffs overlooking the cascading creek. Across the canyon is the sheer wall of Jim Smith Peak. At 0.6 miles, the path levels out in an open meadow that is teaming with wildflowers and has a magnificent view of Pilot Peak. Cross the meadows and the new-growth forest, staying on the edge of the cliffs. At 1.5 miles, the trail reaches a second meadow with far-reaching views across the Beartooth Plateau. Continue west towards Pilot Peak, following the cliffs above the creek. At the upper end of the meadow, the path enters the canyon and burn area from the 1988 Yellowstone fires along the south flank of Pilot Peak. Descend and cross a stream at 2.8 miles. This is a good turn-around spot.

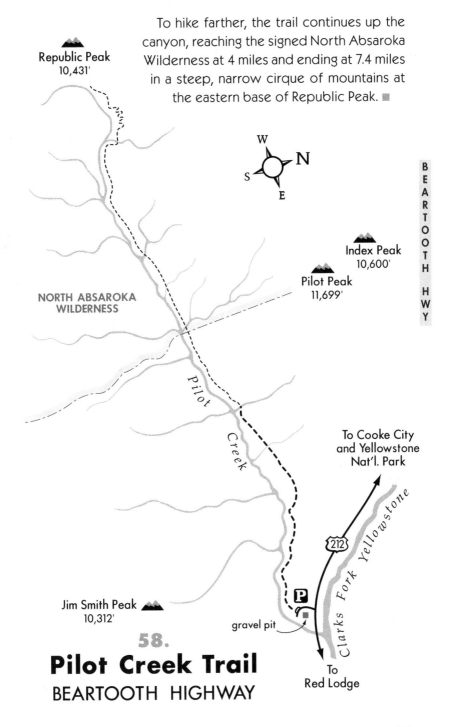

To hike farther, the trail continues up the canyon, reaching the signed North Absaroka Wilderness at 4 miles and ending at 7.4 miles in a steep, narrow cirque of mountains at the eastern base of Republic Peak. ▦

Republic Peak
10,431'

W N S E

Index Peak
10,600'

Pilot Peak
11,699'

NORTH ABSAROKA
WILDERNESS

Pilot Creek

BEARTOOTH HWY

To Cooke City
and Yellowstone
Nat'l. Park

212

Clarks Fork Yellowstone

Jim Smith Peak
10,312'

P

gravel pit

58.
Pilot Creek Trail
BEARTOOTH HIGHWAY

To
Red Lodge

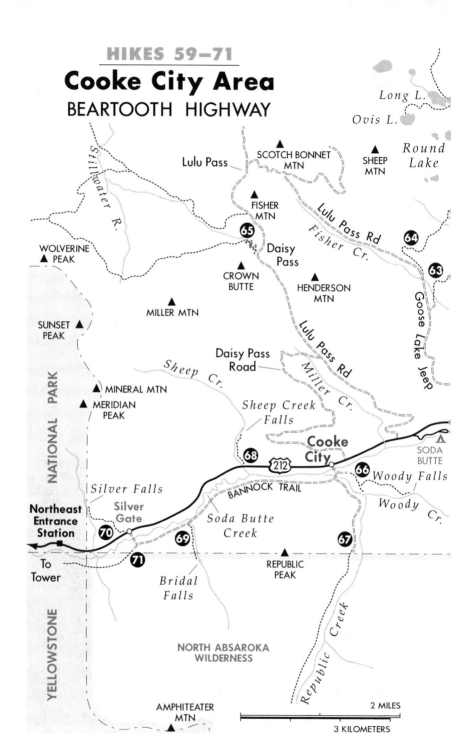

Cooke City Area
BEARTOOTH HIGHWAY

Long L.

Ovis L.

SCOTCH BONNET
MTN

Lulu Pass

SHEEP
MTN

*Round
Lake*

Stillwater R.

Lulu Pass Rd

64

FISHER
MTN

Fisher Cr.

65

Daisy
Pass

63

WOLVERINE
▲ PEAK

CROWN
BUTTE

HENDERSON
MTN

Goose Lake Jeep

MILLER MTN

SUNSET ▲
PEAK

Daisy Pass
Road

Lulu Pass Rd

Sheep Cr.

Miller Cr.

MINERAL MTN

*Sheep Creek
Falls*

▲ MERIDIAN
PEAK

**Cooke
City**

▲
SODA
BUTTE

68

212

66

Woody Falls

Silver Falls

BANNOCK TRAIL

Woody Cr.

**Northeast
Entrance
Station**

Silver
Gate

70

69

*Soda Butte
Creek*

67

To
Tower

71

▲
REPUBLIC
PEAK

*Bridal
Falls*

Republic Creek

NORTH ABSAROKA
WILDERNESS

AMPHITEATER
MTN
▲

2 MILES

3 KILOMETERS

NATIONAL PARK

YELLOWSTONE

ABSAROKA–BEARTOOTH
WILDERNESS

*Sodalite
Lake*

Broadwater R.

Sodalite

Cr.

*Lady of
the Lake*

Aquarius L.

*Broadwater
Lake*

Lady o' Lake Cr.

Curl Lake

Creek

C
O
O
K
E

C
I
T
Y

A
R
E
A

Clarks

Fork

*Kersey
Lake*

Sedge

Clark Fork
Canyon Falls

62

Broadwater R.

Fox L.

Rd

COLTER

212

60

CHIEF JOSEPH

59

Lillis L.

61

Beartooth

Clarks

*Rock Is.
Lake*

Trailhead
Hikes 54–57

Fork

of

the

*Vernon
Lake*

MONTANA
WYOMING

Yellowstone

N

W ✦ E

S

▲ INDEX
PEAK

Fox Cr.

FOX
CREEK

▲ PILOT
PEAK

Highway

To Red Lodge

59. Lillis and Vernon Lakes
COOKE CITY AREA · BEARTOOTH HIGHWAY

Hiking distance: 5.5 miles round trip
Hiking time: 3 hours
Elevation gain: 600 feet
Maps: U.S.G.S. Fossil Lake
        Beartooth Publishing: Beartooth Mountains
        Rocky Mountain Surveys: Cooke City

Summary of hike: Lillis Lake is a small 3-acre tarn with a wet, swampy shoreline. Vernon Lake, just south of Lillis Lake, encompasses 8 acres in a similar wetland. Both backcountry lakes are surrounded by dense forest and mountain peaks, including Pilot and Index Peaks rising prominently in the background. Few people hike to Vernon and Lillis Lakes, so after the Kersey Lake junction, you may not see anyone along the trail. Moose often frequent the meadows. The hike begins by the Clarks Fork Canyon Falls on the Kersey Lake Trail, part of the popular Beaten Path Trail that leads 26 miles to the East Rosebud.

Driving directions: The trailhead is located on Highway 212: 61 miles south from Red Lodge and 3.5 miles east from Cooke City, directly across from Chief Joseph Campground. A trailhead sign on the highway reads "Clarks Fork Trailhead." Turn northeast and park in the parking lot 0.2 miles ahead.

Hiking directions: From the parking area, take the Kersey Lake Trail towards the bridge over the Clarks Fork. The Clarks Fork Canyon Falls is 100 feet downstream from the bridge. After crossing the bridge, a footpath and horse trail parallel each other for over half a mile. Continue 0.5 miles through the shady forest to the Broadwater River Trail junction (Hike 62). Head right and parallel Sedge Creek for 1.2 miles to the posted Vernon Lake trail junction. Climb gently uphill, then head down to a boggy meadow with logs to hop across the wet areas. The path quickly drops down to Lillis Lake. Continue following the northwest shore of Lillis Lake as the trail descends 300 feet through a dense forest to Vernon Lake. The trail ends at the north shore of the lake. Return along the same trail. ■

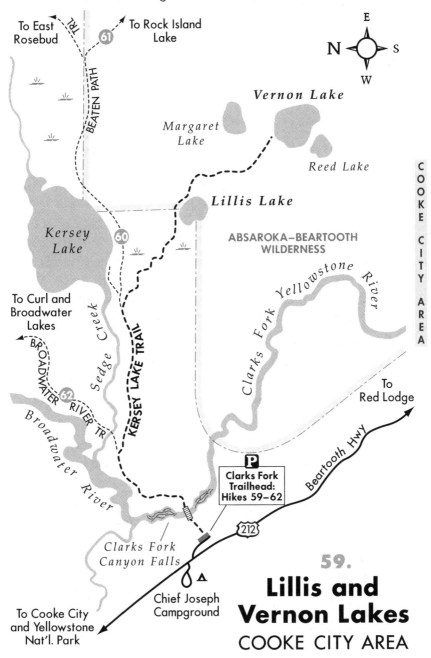

To East Rosebud

To Rock Island Lake

61

BEATEN PATH TRL

Vernon Lake

Margaret Lake

Reed Lake

Lillis Lake

ABSAROKA–BEARTOOTH WILDERNESS

Kersey Lake

60

Clarks Fork Yellowstone River

To Curl and Broadwater Lakes

BROADWATER RIVER TR

62

Sedge Creek

KERSEY LAKE TRAIL

Broadwater River

To Red Lodge

Beartooth Hwy

COOKE CITY AREA

P

Clarks Fork Trailhead: Hikes 59–62

212

Clarks Fork Canyon Falls

▲

Chief Joseph Campground

To Cooke City and Yellowstone Nat'l. Park

59.
Lillis and Vernon Lakes
COOKE CITY AREA

60. Kersey Lake
COOKE CITY AREA · BEARTOOTH HIGHWAY

Hiking distance: 3 miles round trip
Hiking time: 1.5 hours
Elevation gain: 100 feet
Maps: U.S.G.S. Fossil Lake
Beartooth Publishing: Beartooth Mountains
Rocky Mountain Surveys: Cooke City

Summary of hike: The gentle hike to Kersey Lake weaves through lodgepole pine and spruce, following the Broadwater River upstream for the first half mile. The remainder of the trail parallels Sedge Creek, the lake's outlet stream. The 118-acre alpine lake is surrounded by timbered meadows and a rocky shoreline with a couple of cabins. The hike begins from the Clarks Fork Trailhead by a large, grassy picnic area and the Clarks Fork Canyon Falls, which rages through a narrow gorge. This is the trailhead for the Beaten Path Trail, the popular 26-mile traverse through the heart of the Beartooths to the East Rosebud.

Driving directions: The trailhead is located on Highway 212: 61 miles south from Red Lodge and 3.5 miles east from Cooke City, directly across from Chief Joseph Campground. A trailhead sign on the highway reads "Clarks Fork Trailhead." Turn northeast and park in the parking lot 0.2 miles ahead.

Hiking directions: From the trailhead, walk to the bridge crossing the cascading Clarks Fork. A footpath and horse trail parallel each other for over half a mile. At 0.5 miles, pass a trail junction on the left that follows the Broadwater River to Curl and Broadwater Lakes (Hike 62). Stay right on the main trail to Kersey Lake. At 1.2 miles is another trail junction on the right leading to Vernon Lake (Hike 59). Stay left on the main trail. Near Kersey Lake, an anglers' path bears left along the shoreline. Stay on the main trail, which is minutes away from Kersey Lake. After exploring the shoreline, return on the same path.

To hike farther, continue with Hike 61 to Rock Island Lake, 1.5 miles ahead. ■

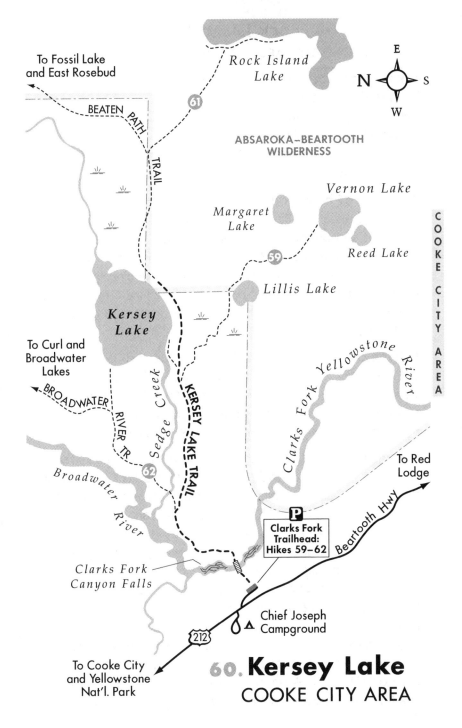

To Fossil Lake
and East Rosebud

*Rock Island
Lake*

N E S W

BEATEN PATH TRAIL

61

**ABSAROKA–BEARTOOTH
WILDERNESS**

Vernon Lake

*Margaret
Lake*

Reed Lake

59

Lillis Lake

*Kersey
Lake*

C O O K E C I T Y A R E A

To Curl and
Broadwater
Lakes

Clarks Fork Yellowstone River

BROADWATER RIVER TR.

Sedge Creek

KERSEY LAKE TRAIL

62

*Broadwater
River*

To Red
Lodge

P
**Clarks Fork
Trailhead:
Hikes 59–62**

Beartooth Hwy

*Clarks Fork
Canyon Falls*

⚲ Chief Joseph
Campground

212

To Cooke City
and Yellowstone
Nat'l. Park

60. **Kersey Lake**
COOKE CITY AREA

61. Rock Island Lake
COOKE CITY AREA · BEARTOOTH HIGHWAY

Hiking distance: 6 miles round trip
Hiking time: 3 hours
Elevation gain: 200 feet
Maps: U.S.G.S. Fossil Lake
Beartooth Publishing: Beartooth Mountains
Rocky Mountain Surveys: Cooke City

Summary of hike: Rock Island Lake is a sprawling 156-acre lake in the Absaroka-Beartooth Wilderness that is stocked with cutthroat and brook trout. The lake sits in a flat, forested terrain at an elevation of 8,177 feet. There are numerous wooded islands and primitive campsites. The well-maintained trail gains little elevation for a relaxing day outing. The hike begins by the Clarks Fork Canyon Falls and a large grassy picnic area on the banks of the Clarks Fork.

Driving directions: The trailhead is located on Highway 212: 61 miles south from Red Lodge and 3.5 miles east from Cooke City, directly across from Chief Joseph Campground. A trailhead sign on the highway reads "Clarks Fork Trailhead." Turn northeast and park in the parking lot 0.2 miles ahead.

Hiking directions: From the north end of the parking area, cross the footbridge over the raging Clarks Fork River. Walk through the shade of a pine and fir forest towards Kersey Lake (Hike 60). A footpath and horse trail parallel each other for over a half mile. At 0.5 miles, pass the junction to the Broadwater River Trail on the left (Hike 62). Parallel Sedge Creek past the signed Vernon Lake junction on the right at 1.2 miles (Hike 59). At the southwest corner of Kersey Lake, an anglers' path bears left along the shoreline. The main trail follows the south side of Kersey Lake, traversing the north-facing slope above the lake.

Beyond Kersey Lake, the trail reenters the dense forest and skirts the south edge of a boggy meadow, reaching a signed junction along the Absaroka-Beartooth Wilderness boundary. The left fork leads to Fossil Lake and the East Rosebud on the

Beaten Path Trail. Take the right fork southeast towards Rock Island Lake. The level path leads 0.7 miles through lodgepole pines to the northwest corner of the lake. Angler paths meander along the shoreline. The southern route crosses talus slopes and the northern route crosses marshy wetlands. ■

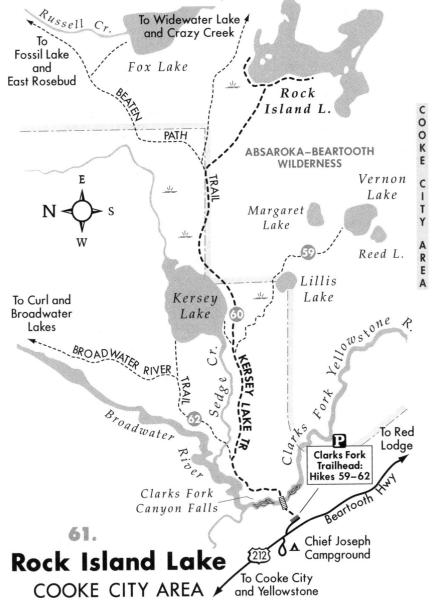

61.
Rock Island Lake
COOKE CITY AREA

62. Broadwater River to Curl Lake
COOKE CITY AREA • BEARTOOTH HIGHWAY

Hiking distance: 6.5 miles round trip
Hiking time: 3.5 hours
Elevation gain: 250 feet
Maps: U.S.G.S. Fossil Lake
Beartooth Publishing: Beartooth Mountains
Rocky Mountain Surveys: Cooke City

Summary of hike: This top-of-the-world hike leads past cascading water, open meadows, and trees to majestic high country lakes, all with relatively little elevation gain. The trail meanders through scenic Broadwater Meadow along the east side of the cascading river to Curl Lake and Broadwater Lake. The lakes are actually one huge 124-acre lake strung together by the Broadwater River, a tributary of the Clarks Fork of the Yellowstone River. A wooded valley with open meadows surrounds the lakes. The trail begins from the Clarks Fork Trailhead and Clarks Fork Canyon Falls, where the thunderous cascade is forced through a narrow gorge.

Driving directions: The trailhead is located on Highway 212: 61 miles south from Red Lodge and 3.5 miles east from Cooke City, directly across from Chief Joseph Campground. A trailhead sign on the highway reads "Clarks Fork Trailhead." Turn northeast and park in the parking lot 0.2 miles ahead.

Hiking directions: From the north end of the parking lot, cross the footbridge near the cascade and waterfall. The Clarks Fork Canyon Falls is 100 feet downstream from the bridge. Continue on the footpath and horse trail, which parallel each other for over half a mile. At 0.5 miles, watch for the Broadwater River Trail junction. The trail to the right leads to Kersey Lake (Hikes 59—61) and East Rosebud.

Take the trail to the left on the Broadwater River Trail. Continue gently uphill another half mile to a second posted trail junction on the left for the Broadwater River Trail. (The right trail leads to Kersey Lake.) Stay on the left trail, following the cascading water

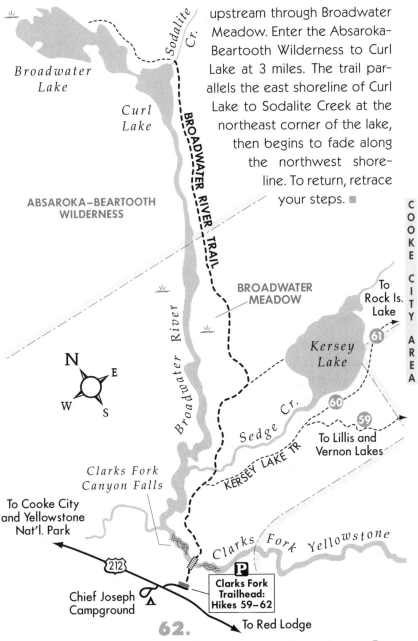

upstream through Broadwater Meadow. Enter the Absaroka-Beartooth Wilderness to Curl Lake at 3 miles. The trail parallels the east shoreline of Curl Lake to Sodalite Creek at the northeast corner of the lake, then begins to fade along the northwest shoreline. To return, retrace your steps. ∎

Broadwater Lake

Curl Lake

Sodalite Cr.

BROADWATER RIVER TRAIL

ABSAROKA–BEARTOOTH WILDERNESS

BROADWATER MEADOW

Broadwater River

N **E** **W** **S**

C O O K E   C I T Y   A R E A

To Rock Is. Lake

61

Kersey Lake

60

59

Sedge Cr.

To Lillis and Vernon Lakes

KERSEY LAKE TR.

Clarks Fork Canyon Falls

To Cooke City and Yellowstone Nat'l. Park

Clarks Fork Yellowstone

212

P

Clarks Fork Trailhead: Hikes 59–62

Chief Joseph Campground

To Red Lodge

62.

Broadwater River to Curl Lake
COOKE CITY AREA

63. Lady of the Lake Trail
COOKE CITY AREA

Hiking distance: 4 miles round trip
Hiking time: 2 hours
Elevation gain: 300 feet
Maps: U.S.G.S. Cooke City
           Beartooth Publishing: Beartooth Mountains
           Rocky Mountain Surveys: Cooke City

Summary of hike: Lady of the Lake sits in a serene, forested bowl surrounded by mountains at 8,800 feet. To the north and south of the 42-acre lake are meadows filled with wildflowers. Lady of the Lake Creek flows through the meadows and joins with the Clarks Fork of the Yellowstone. The forested trail to the lake crosses Fisher Creek, passes several old log cabins, and enters the Absaroka-Beartooth Wilderness. This is the beginning of the hike to Lower and Upper Aero Lakes.

Driving directions: From Cooke City, drive 2 miles east on Highway 212 to the unpaved Goose Lake Jeep Road on the left, just west of the Colter Campground. Turn left and continue 1.9 miles up the road to a road split. Go right 0.1 mile and park along the side of the road. (See inset map.)

Hiking directions: Head up the jeep road, following the trail sign. A short distance ahead, rock hop or wade across Fisher Creek. After crossing, bear to the right, heading uphill to the remnants of an old stone building and several log cabins on the left. Just beyond the cabins is a "Lady of the Lake—1 mile" trail sign. In reality, it is closer to 1.5 miles to the lake. The trail gains elevation for a short distance before leveling off. Continue north through the forest, beginning the long descent to the lake. At 1.6 miles, the trail enters the Absaroka-Beartooth Wilderness. As the trail emerges from the trees, cross a large meadow with trickling brooks to the south end of Lady of the Lake. The trail winds along the west shore and then continues on to Goose Lake and the Aero Lakes. After enjoying the lake and alpine meadows, return to the trailhead on the same path, or make a 5.8-mile loop on the Goose Lake Jeep Road—Hike 64. ■

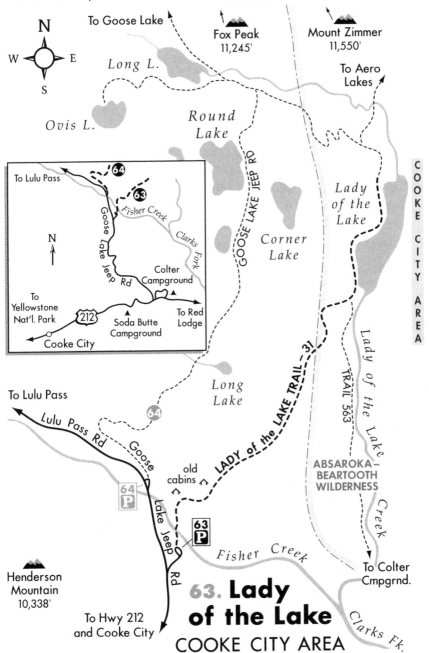

63. **Lady of the Lake**
COOKE CITY AREA

64. Round Lake
COOKE CITY AREA

Hiking distance: 3 miles round trip
Hiking time: 1.5 hours
Elevation gain: 500 feet
Maps: U.S.G.S. Cooke City
      Beartooth Publishing: Beartooth Mountains
      Rocky Mountain Surveys: Cooke City

Summary of hike: Round Lake is a gorgeous 24-acre lake at a high elevation of 9,340 feet. The lake is rimmed with grass and trees. The trail to Round Lake follows the Goose Lake Jeep Road (also used by all-terrain vehicles). The trail crosses through the rolling alpine terrain past conifer forest groves, rock outcroppings, and stream-laden meadows covered in wildflowers.

Driving directions: From Cooke City, drive 2 miles east on Highway 212 to the unpaved Goose Lake Jeep Road on the left, just west of the Colter Campground. Turn left and continue 1.9 miles up the road to a road split. Take the left fork 0.6 miles, crossing a bridge over Fisher Creek, to the signed Lulu Pass/ Goose Lake road split. Park in the pullouts near this junction. (See inset map on page 173.)

Hiking directions: Take the Goose Lake Jeep Road to the right. Henderson, Scotch Bonnet, and Sheep Mountains tower above the trail. Head uphill through the forest on the rocky jeep road for 0.7 miles, where the trail levels out in a meadow. Rock hop over a stream, and continue along the meadow marbled with trickling streams and wildflowers. Follow the small dips and rises past beautiful rock outcroppings, and climb to a saddle overlooking Mud Lake on the left. The rock-lined lake appears more like a shallow pond. Curve around the lake and descend to Round Lake. Mount Zimmer, Mount Fox, and Sheep Mountain rise above the lake. This is the turn-around spot.

To hike farther, the road/trail skirts the east side of Round Lake, continuing past Long and Star Lakes, to Goose Lake at 5.5

miles. For a 5.8-mile loop hike, take the trail east to Lady of the Lake—Hike 63. ▪

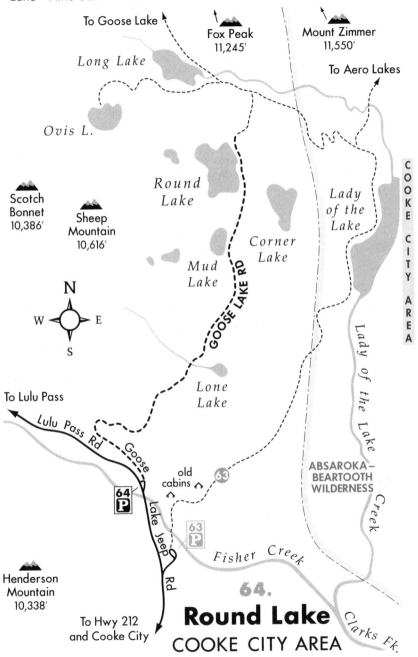

To Goose Lake

Fox Peak
11,245'

Mount Zimmer
11,550'

Long Lake

To Aero Lakes

Ovis L.

*Round
Lake*

*Lady
of the
Lake*

Scotch
Bonnet
10,386'

Sheep
Mountain
10,616'

*Corner
Lake*

GOOSE LAKE RD

*Mud
Lake*

N
W   E
S

Lady of the Lake

*Lone
Lake*

To Lulu Pass

Lulu Pass Rd

Goose

old
cabins

63

**ABSAROKA–
BEARTOOTH
WILDERNESS**

Lake Jeep Rd

64
P

63
P

Fisher Creek

Henderson
Mountain
10,338'

64.
Round Lake
COOKE CITY AREA

To Hwy 212
and Cooke City

Clarks Fk.

C
O
O
K
E

C
I
T
Y

A
R
E
A

65. Daisy Pass
to Wolverine Pass Loop
COOKE CITY AREA

Hiking distance: 8-mile loop
Hiking time: 4.5 hours
Elevation gain: 1,200 feet
Maps: U.S.G.S. Cooke City and Cutoff Mountain
Beartooth Publishing: Beartooth Mountains
Rocky Mountain Surveys: Cooke City

Summary of hike: Daisy Pass and Wolverine Pass lie above 9,000 feet in the Gallatin National Forest just north of Cooke City (back cover photo). Wolverine Pass is on the Absaroka-Beartooth Wilderness boundary and adjacent to Yellowstone National Park. This hike begins atop 9,750-foot Daisy Pass (back cover photo) and crosses several forks of the Stillwater River headwaters. The scenic footpath follows the base of the towering, jagged peaks to Wolverine Pass in a deep saddle between Wolverine Peak and Mount Abundance. Throughout the hike are spectacular top-of-the-world vistas of the surrounding peaks, including Crown Butte, Chimney Rock, Miller Mountain, Sunset Peak, Wolverine Peak, Mount Abundance, and Scotch Bonnet Mountain.

Driving directions: From Cooke City, drive a half mile east on Highway 212 to the unpaved Daisy Pass Road on the left (north). Turn left and go 1.4 miles up the winding bumpy road to a T-junction with a well-graded road. Turn left and continue 2.5 miles to Daisy Pass on a saddle between Crown Butte and Chimney Rock. Park in the pullout on the left.

A second and smoother route is to turn left (north) onto Lulu Pass Road, located 1.4 miles east of Cooke City on Highway 212. Wind up the hill 2 miles to the junction with the Daisy Pass Road. (En route, make a horseshoe left bend at the only road fork.) Continue straight and go 2.5 miles to Daisy Pass on a saddle between Crown Butte and Chimney Rock. Park in the pullout on the left.

Hiking directions: From atop Daisy Pass, zigzag down the rocky slope to the grassy valley and a fork of the trickling Stillwater River headwaters. Skirt the northern base of Crown Butte, with 360-degree vistas of Miller Mountain, Sunset Peak, Wolverine Peak, Wolverine Pass, Mount Abundance, Lake Abundance, and Scotch Bonnet Mountain. Pass through fir groves and drop down a minor draw to the foot of Wolverine Peak. Cross the headwaters of the Stillwater River, and pass the remnants of an old miner's cabin on the right. Continue through meadows and a lava rock garden with awe-inspiring views. As the slope of Wolverine Peak drops into a saddle, watch for an unsigned junction on the right. This is the return route.

For now, continue straight ahead 0.2 miles into the saddle, framed between the towering peaks of Abundance Mountain and Wolverine Peak at the posted Absaroka-Beartooth Wilderness boundary, just north of Yellowstone National Park. From the saddle, the trail continues west along Wolverine Creek and leads into Yellowstone to Slough Creek.

For this hike, return to the unsigned junction and veer left (north). Walk through the flower-laden meadow, parallel to a clear stream at the base of Mount Abundance. Cross another fork of the Stillwater River, and descend through the grasslands surrounded by majestic peaks. Steadily descend to the main Stillwater River, then cross the rippling stream. Walk around a vehicle gate, and begin the gradual but steady climb up to Daisy Pass Road. Along the way, pass through open forests and meadows with incredible vistas. At the top, bear right on Daisy Pass Road and walk south for 0.6 miles, completing the loop at the trailhead. ▩

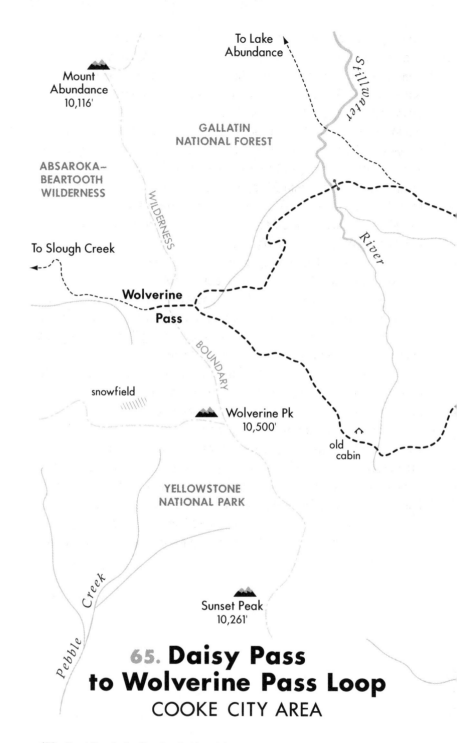

To Lake
Abundance

Stillwater

Mount
Abundance
10,116'

GALLATIN
NATIONAL FOREST

ABSAROKA–
BEARTOOTH
WILDERNESS

WILDERNESS

River

To Slough Creek

Wolverine

Pass

BOUNDARY

snowfield

Wolverine Pk
10,500'

old
cabin

YELLOWSTONE
NATIONAL PARK

Creek

Pebble

Sunset Peak
10,261'

65. **Daisy Pass**
to Wolverine Pass Loop
COOKE CITY AREA

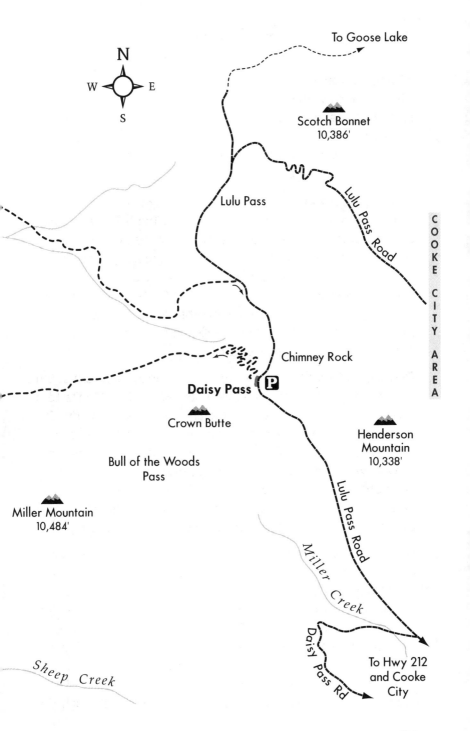

To Goose Lake

Scotch Bonnet
10,386'

Lulu Pass

Lulu Pass Road

COOKE CITY AREA

Chimney Rock

Daisy Pass P

Crown Butte

Henderson
Mountain
10,338'

Bull of the Woods
Pass

Miller Mountain
10,484'

Lulu Pass Road

Miller Creek

Daisy Pass Rd

To Hwy 212
and Cooke
City

Sheep Creek

66. Woody Falls
COOKE CITY AREA

Hiking distance: 3 miles round trip
Hiking time: 2 hours
Elevation gain: 700 feet
Maps: U.S.G.S. Cooke City
              Beartooth Publishing: Beartooth Mountains
              Rocky Mountain Surveys: Cooke City

Summary of hike: Woody Falls is a spectacular 150-foot, three-tiered falls with a pool at the base. The falls is a popular destination for the locals that is located in the heart of downtown Cooke City. Woody Creek forms on the northern slope of Ram Pasture. The creek cascades 2.5 miles west to its confluence with Republic Creek, a tributary of Soda Butte Creek. This hike begins on an old mining road that leads to the Mohawk Mine, then veers off to Woody Falls. In the winter, the trail to the falls is a cross-country ski trail.

Driving directions: From downtown Cooke City, turn south from Highway 212 onto Republic Road, and drive 0.1 mile to a road split. Take the left fork on the unpaved road, and drive 0.2 miles to the loop at the end of the road. Park along the road.

If you do not mind fording a stream and prefer to walk from downtown, a second trailhead is located at the south end of River Street behind the old General Store. At the end of River Street is a buck fence and trail entrance. Walk south on the trail past old log cabins. Wade across the creek to the parking area.

Hiking directions: From the parking area off of Republic Road, walk up the jeep road to the southeast. Within five minutes from the trailhead is a well-defined footpath on the left. This is the trail to Woody Falls. For a short side trip, stay on the jeep road an additional 200 yards, just past a sign reading "Woody Creek Ski Trail." Take the spur trail to the right 100 yards to a beautiful cascade and smaller waterfall.

Return to the main jeep trail and the Woody Falls Trail. The well-worn footpath begins a steady uphill climb through the forest. As the canyon below narrows, the falls can be heard on the right. Spur trails lead to the canyon edge for a variety of commanding over-views of Woody Falls. Return along the same trail. ■

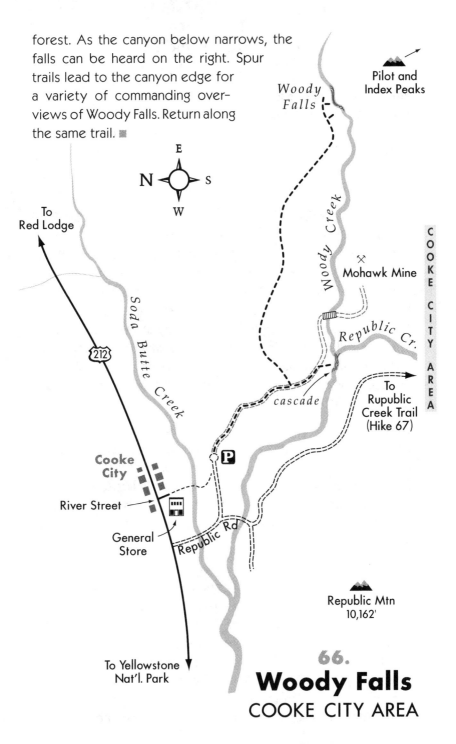

Woody Falls

Pilot and Index Peaks

To Red Lodge

N E S W

Soda Butte Creek

212

Woody Creek

Mohawk Mine

COOKE CITY AREA

Republic Cr.

cascade

To Rupublic Creek Trail (Hike 67)

Cooke City

P

River Street

General Store

Republic Rd

Republic Mtn 10,162'

To Yellowstone Nat'l. Park

66.
Woody Falls
COOKE CITY AREA

67. Republic Creek Trail
COOKE CITY AREA

Hiking distance: 3.2—8.4 miles round trip
Hiking time: 2—5 hours
Elevation gain: 200—1,900 feet (meadow to Republic Pass)
Maps: U.S.G.S. Cooke City and Pilot Peak
Beartooth Publishing: Beartooth Mountains
Trails Illustrated: Tower/Canyon

Summary of hike: Republic Creek forms on the north slope of 10,431-foot Republic Peak. The creek flows over five miles and merges with Soda Butte Creek in Cooke City. The Republic Creek Trail begins at Cooke City and follows a high mountain meadow parallel to the creek. The trail crosses over Republic Pass at 4.5 miles, just west of Republic Peak, and connects with the Cache Creek Trail to the Lamar Valley in Yellowstone Park. This hike follows the first portion of the trail through the creek valley to the headwall at the north face of Republic Peak. There are scenic vistas of the surrounding peaks and a beautiful display of wildflowers.

Driving directions: From downtown Cooke City, turn south off Highway 212 onto Republic Road to a road split. Take the right fork on the unpaved road past some homes. Curve left up the narrow mountain road, and drive 1.3 miles to the signed Republic Creek Trail on the right. The trailhead is just past some old cabins and remnants of the Irma Mine. Park in one of the small pullouts.

Hiking directions: Head south on the signed footpath, crossing a small feeder stream of Republic Creek. At a quarter mile, the trail levels out and leads through the dense forest with a lush understory of grasses and flowers. Cross a rocky streambed, and emerge in an expansive meadow dotted with trees and teeming with flowers. Continue south up the alpine valley between mountain peaks. At 1.5 miles the trail reaches Republic Meadow, the turn-around point for a 3-mile, round-trip hike.

To continue hiking, skirt the west edge of the meadow,

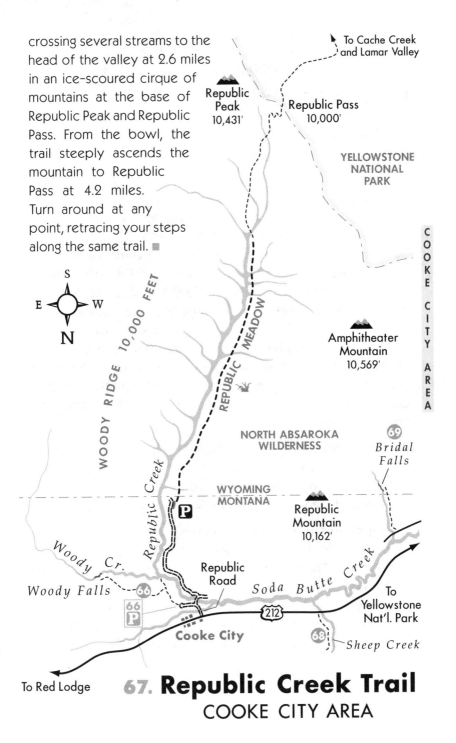

crossing several streams to the head of the valley at 2.6 miles in an ice-scoured cirque of mountains at the base of Republic Peak and Republic Pass. From the bowl, the trail steeply ascends the mountain to Republic Pass at 4.2 miles. Turn around at any point, retracing your steps along the same trail. ▦

To Cache Creek and Lamar Valley

Republic Peak
10,431'

Republic Pass
10,000'

YELLOWSTONE NATIONAL PARK

C O O K E   C I T Y   A R E A

S
E — W
N

WOODY RIDGE 10,000 FEET

REPUBLIC MEADOW

Amphitheater Mountain
10,569'

NORTH ABSAROKA WILDERNESS

69
Bridal Falls

WYOMING
MONTANA

Republic Mountain
10,162'

Republic Creek

Woody Cr.

Woody Falls

Republic Road

Soda Butte Creek

66

66
P

To Yellowstone Nat'l. Park

212

68
Sheep Creek

Cooke City

To Red Lodge

67. Republic Creek Trail
COOKE CITY AREA

68. Sheep Creek Falls
COOKE CITY AREA

Hiking distance: 0.6 miles round trip
Hiking time: .5 hours
Elevation gain: 200 feet
Maps: U.S.G.S. Cooke City
Rocky Mountain Surveys: Cooke City

Summary of hike: Sheep Creek forms on the east slope of Mineral Mountain just outside Yellowstone National Park. The creek tumbles 2.5 miles south, where it feeds Soda Butte Creek between Cooke City and Silver Gate. An unmaintained path leads to Sheep Creek Falls, a magnificent, full-bodied waterfall on the creek. The towering 10,000-foot peaks of Miller Mountain, Sunset Peak, and Mineral Mountain surround the drainage. Although it is only 0.3 miles to the thunderous cataract, it is not an easy hike. It is a scramble up the canyon, climbing over downfall timber. There is not a defined trail; rather, the hike just follows the watercourse of Sheep Creek. The route climbs through the burn area from the 1988 Yellowstone fires, now thick with regrowth.

Driving directions: The trailhead is located on Highway 212: 1.1 miles west of Cooke City and 1.6 miles east of Silver Gate. The parking pullout is located on the south side of the highway and the west side of the Sheep Creek bridge.

Hiking directions: From the parking pullout, cross to the north side of Highway 212. Walk upstream along the east side of Sheep Creek. The trail fades in and out. Scramble upstream, using Sheep Creek as your guide. After climbing over and around down trees for a quarter mile, the canyon curves to the right. From this spot, the magnificence of Sheep Creek Falls is directly in view. Return by heading back downstream to the highway. ■

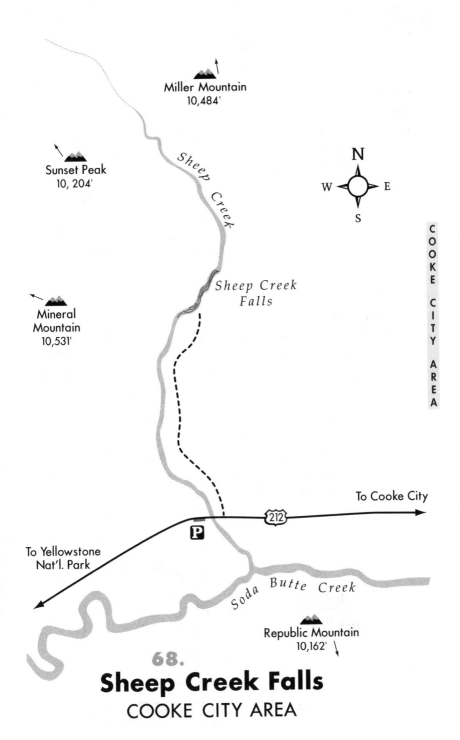

Miller Mountain
10,484'

Sunset Peak
10, 204'

Sheep Creek

Sheep Creek Falls

Mineral
Mountain
10,531'

N
W   E
S

C O O K E   C I T Y   A R E A

To Cooke City

212

P

To Yellowstone
Nat'l. Park

Soda Butte Creek

Republic Mountain
10,162'

68.

Sheep Creek Falls
COOKE CITY AREA

69. Bridal Falls
COOKE CITY AREA

Hiking distance: 0.6 miles round trip
Hiking time: 15 minutes
Elevation gain: 50 feet
Maps: U.S.G.S. Cooke City
         Rocky Mountain Surveys: Cooke City

Summary of hike: Bridal Falls (unofficially named) drops out of steep granite cliffs to a ledge. From the ledge, the water shoots out horizontally, dropping more than forty additional feet into a misty pool. Ferns and moss grow along these sheer rock walls. The trail is a short and easy path that parallels Wyoming Creek through the forest.

Driving directions: From downtown Silver Gate, turn south from Highway 212 onto Monument Avenue. Drive 0.2 miles to the end of the road. Turn left on Bannock and continue 0.8 miles to the Wyoming Creek bridge (the only bridge along the road). Park off road before crossing the bridge.

Hiking directions: From the road, walk upstream along the west side of Wyoming Creek. The path leads south for 0.3 miles to the base of the falls and pool. The mountain on the left (east) of the falls is Republic Mountain. To the right (west) is Wall Rock. Return along the same trail. ▦

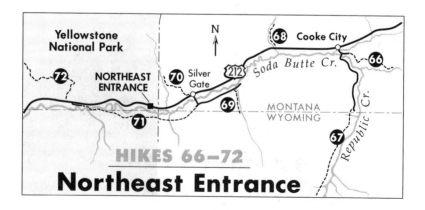

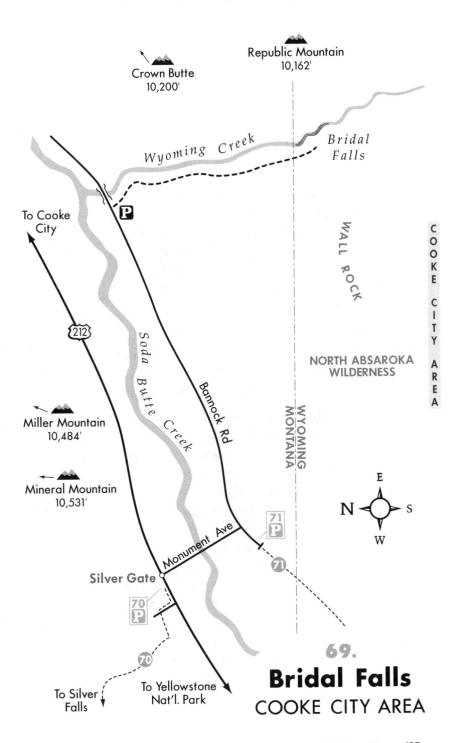

Crown Butte
10,200'

Republic Mountain
10,162'

Wyoming Creek

Bridal Falls

To Cooke
City

P

WALL ROCK

COOKE CITY AREA

212

Soda Butte Creek

Bannock Rd

NORTH ABSAROKA
WILDERNESS

WYOMING
MONTANA

Miller Mountain
10,484'

Mineral Mountain
10,531'

E

N ✦ S

W

71
P

Monument Ave

71

Silver Gate

70
P

70

69.
Bridal Falls
COOKE CITY AREA

To Silver
Falls

To Yellowstone
Nat'l. Park

70. Silver Falls
COOKE CITY AREA

Hiking distance: 2 miles round trip
Hiking time: 1 hour
Elevation gain: 350 feet
Maps: U.S.G.S. Cooke City and Cutoff Mountain
Trails Illustrated: Tower/Canyon

Summary of hike: Silver Creek, a feeder stream of Soda Butte Creek, tumbles out of Mineral Mountain and Meridian Peak at the Yellowstone National Park boundary. Silver Falls is a long and narrow waterfall that drops more than 100 feet over a limestone cliff. The hike to the falls is along the eastern border of Yellowstone National Park, beginning from the town of Silver Gate. The last section of the trail climbs over rocks along Silver Creek to the base of this beautiful falls.

Driving directions: Park at the far west end of Silver Gate on Highway 212. From the northeast entrance station of Yellowstone National Park, the trailhead is one mile east on Highway 212.

Hiking directions: Walk 0.1 mile west on Highway 212 towards Yellowstone National Park. Take the unpaved road on the right 30 yards uphill to the powerlines and private road sign. Take the trail on the left, following the powerpoles 20 yards to the trail arrow sign on the right. Bear right on the footpath through the dense forest to an unsigned three-way trail split. Take the middle fork, straight ahead, to an old grass-covered road and another trail arrow. Bear left on the road. A short distance ahead, the road curves right to another road at a T-junction. Follow the arrow sign to the left through the burn area, reaching the east bank of Silver Creek. Take the creekside trail upstream above the drainage. As you near the head of the canyon, the trail becomes rocky. Descend into the canyon to the trail's end at the base of Silver Falls. Return along the same path. ■

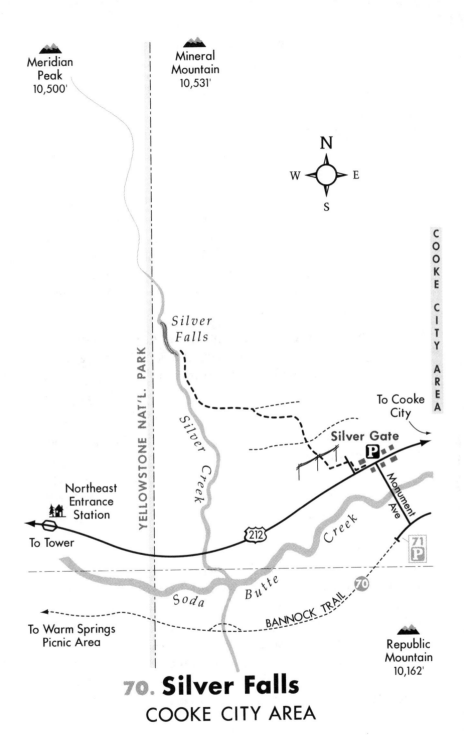

70. Silver Falls
COOKE CITY AREA

71. Bannock Trail
COOKE CITY AREA

Hiking distance: 4.8 miles round trip
Hiking time: 2.5 hours
Elevation gain: 130 feet
Maps: U.S.G.S. Cooke City and Cutoff Mountain
Trails Illustrated: Tower/Canyon

Summary of hike: The Bannock Trail is a short section of the Bannock Indian route once used to reach bison hunting grounds in Lamar Valley. The trail begins at Silver Gate in the North Absaroka Wilderness. The near-level terrain parallels Soda Butte Creek, a major tributary of the Lamar River, into Yellowstone National Park. The trail crosses several streams through open meadows and forest groves.

Driving directions: From downtown Silver Gate, turn south from Highway 212 onto Monument Avenue. Drive 0.2 miles, crossing over Soda Butte Creek, to the end of the road. Turn right on Bannock and continue 0.1 mile to the end of the road at the signed trailhead. Park in pullouts alongside the road.

Hiking directions: Head west past the trailhead sign along the base of Amphitheater Mountain. The trail skirts the south edge of the meadow under the shadow of Abiathar Peak and Barronette Peak. Past the meadow, meander through a lush lodgepole forest. Ford a wide tributary stream of Soda Butte Creek and continue west. (Downfall logs can be used to cross the stream 20 yards downstream.) Across the canyon are the bald peaks of Miller Mountain and Meridian Peak. At one mile a sign along the trail marks the boundary between the Shoshone National Forest and Yellowstone National Park. Weave through the quiet forest, reaching the banks of Soda Butte Creek at two miles. Follow the creekside ledge downstream to a clearing by a feeder stream. Across Soda Butte Creek is the Warm Creek picnic area. To access the picnic area, you must wade across the creek. To return, take the same trail back. ■

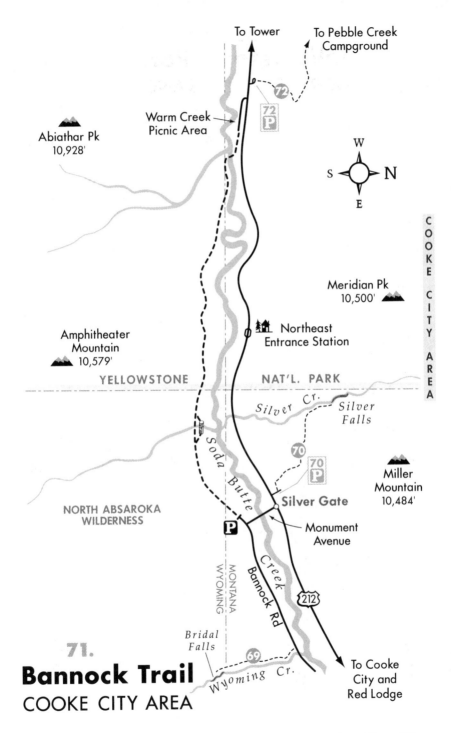

To Tower

To Pebble Creek Campground

Warm Creek Picnic Area

72

72 P

Abiathar Pk
10,928'

W

S ✦ N

E

COOKE CITY AREA

Meridian Pk
10,500'

Northeast
Entrance Station

Amphitheater
Mountain
10,579'

YELLOWSTONE   NAT'L. PARK

Silver Cr.

Silver
Falls

70

70 P

Miller
Mountain
10,484'

Soda Butte

NORTH ABSAROKA
WILDERNESS

Silver Gate

Monument
Avenue

P

MONTANA
WYOMING

Creek

Bannock Rd

212

71.
Bannock Trail
COOKE CITY AREA

Bridal
Falls

69

Wyoming Cr.

To Cooke
City and
Red Lodge

Yellowstone Park
NORTHEAST ENTRANCE

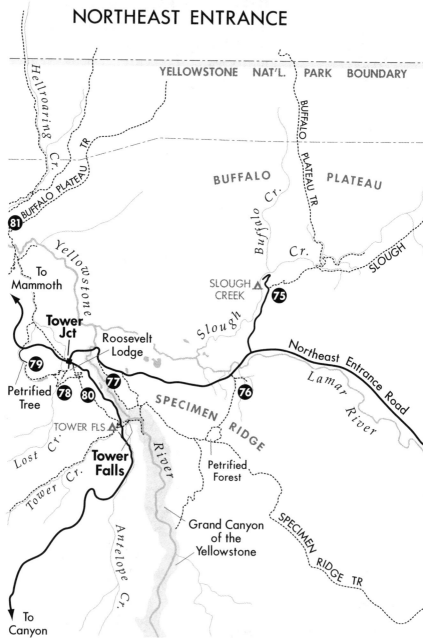

YELLOWSTONE   NAT'L.   PARK   BOUNDARY

BUFFALO

BUFFALO PLATEAU TR

PLATEAU

Buffalo Cr.

Cr.

SLOUGH

Hellroaring Cr.

BUFFALO PLATEAU TR

81

Yellowstone

To
Mammoth

SLOUGH
CREEK

75

Slough

**Tower
Jct**

Roosevelt
Lodge

Slough

Northeast Entrance Road

79

78 **80**

77

Petrified
Tree

SPECIMEN

76

Lamar River

TOWER FLS

RIDGE

Lost Cr.

River

Petrified
Forest

**Tower
Falls**

Tower Cr.

Grand Canyon
of the
Yellowstone

SPECIMEN

Antelope Cr.

RIDGE TR

To
Canyon

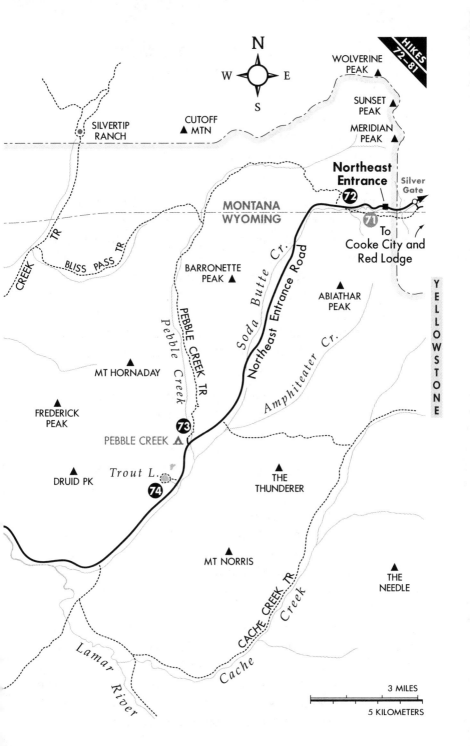

N
W E
S

WOLVERINE PEAK ▲

SUNSET PEAK ▲

MERIDIAN PEAK ▲

SILVERTIP RANCH

CUTOFF ▲ MTN

Northeast Entrance
72

Silver Gate

71

To Cooke City and Red Lodge

MONTANA
WYOMING

BLISS PASS TR.

CREEK TR.

BARRONETTE PEAK ▲

ABIATHAR PEAK ▲

Soda Butte Cr.

Northeast Entrance Road

Amphiteater Cr.

PEBBLE CREEK TR.

Pebble Creek

MT HORNADAY ▲

FREDERICK PEAK ▲

73

PEBBLE CREEK ▲

DRUID PK ▲

Trout L.

74

THE THUNDERER ▲

MT NORRIS ▲

THE NEEDLE ▲

CACHE CREEK TR.

Cache Creek

Lamar River

3 MILES

5 KILOMETERS

Y E L L O W S T O N E

72. Pebble Creek Trail from Warm Creek
N.E. YELLOWSTONE PARK

Hiking distance: 7 miles round trip (or 12-mile shuttle)
Hiking time: 4 hours
Elevation gain: 800 feet
Maps: U.S.G.S. Cutoff Mountain
Trails Illustrated: Tower/Canyon

Summary of hike: The Pebble Creek Trail is a 12-mile trail with trailheads at Warm Creek and the Pebble Creek Campground (Hike 73). This hike begins at the Warm Creek trailhead and climbs to the Upper Meadows in a glacial valley at the north end of Barronette Peak. From the wildflower-covered meadow are panoramic views of the Absaroka Range and many of its peaks. The trail parallels Pebble Creek through the scenic valley for miles before reentering the forest. This trail may be combined with Hike 73 for a 12-mile shuttle hike. (Reference the map on page 197.)

Driving directions: From the northeast entrance to Yellowstone National Park, drive 1.2 miles west to the signed Warm Creek Trailhead turnoff. Turn right (north) and drive 0.1 mile to the parking area at the end of the road.

From Pebble Creek Campground, drive 8 miles on the Northeast Entrance Road to the signed turnoff on the left (north).

Hiking directions: Follow the signed trail north, heading steadily uphill through the lush spruce and fir forest. At 0.4 miles, the trail bears left (west) on a more gradual slope. Continue climbing up the mountain. Near the top, emerge from the forest. Cross a talus slope with views of the Soda Butte Creek valley and the surrounding glacial peaks. Reenter the forest for the final ascent to the 8,200-foot saddle, the high point of the hike at 1.5 miles. Gradually descend 200 feet to the high mountain meadow and Pebble Creek. Carefully ford the creek and head downstream through the expansive meadow dotted with spruce and fir trees. The trail continues 1.8 miles west through the Upper Meadows past numerous trickling streams and vistas of the surrounding peaks. At 3.5 miles, the trail reaches a second creek crossing near the west end of the meadow. This is the turn-around spot.

To hike farther, the trail stays level for several miles before descending 1,000 feet to the Pebble Creek Campground, 8.5 miles ahead (Hike 73). ▦

To
Pebble Creek
Campground
(Hike 73)

Barronette
Peak
10,442'

MONTANA
WYOMING

YELLOWSTONE
NATIONAL PARK

Pebble Creek

Upper

Meadows

W

S ✦ N

E

Y
E
L
L
O
W
S
T
O
N
E

See
entire trail on
Hike 73

8,200'
saddle

To
Tower

NE Entrance Rd (212)

Soda Butte Creek

Abiathar
Peak
10,928'

P

Warm Springs
Picnic Area
(Hike 71)

To
Cooke City

72.
Pebble Creek Trail
from Warm Creek
N.E. YELLOWSTONE

73. Pebble Creek Trail
from PEBBLE CREEK CAMPGROUND
N.E. YELLOWSTONE PARK

Hiking distance: 5 miles round trip (or 12-mile shuttle)
Hiking time: 3 hours
Elevation gain: 1,200 feet
Maps: U.S.G.S. Abiathar Peak
Trails Illustrated: Tower/Canyon

Summary of hike: The Pebble Creek Trail is a 12-mile trail with trailheads at the Pebble Creek Campground and the Warm Creek picnic area (Hike 72). This hike begins at the Pebble Creek Campground. The forested trail, interspersed with small meadows, steadily climbs between 10,000-foot mountain peaks. This trail may be combined with Hike 72 for a 12-mile shuttle hike. For the one-way hike, it is recommended to begin from the Warm Creek Trailhead (Hike 72) for less elevation gain.

Driving directions: From the northeast entrance to Yellowstone National Park, drive 9.2 miles southwest to the signed Pebble Creek Campground turnoff. Turn right (north) and park in the day-use parking spaces 0.2 miles ahead on the left.

From Tower Junction, drive 19 miles on the Northeast Entrance Road towards Cooke City to the turnoff on the left (north).

Hiking directions: Walk towards Pebble Creek, crossing the wooden footbridge over the creek next to campsite 32 and the restrooms. Head through the small meadow and ascend the hillside. The Pebble Creek Trail from the Northeast Entrance Road merges with the campground trail on a knoll at 0.2 miles. Bear left and climb another short hill to a view of Barronette Peak's southern flank. Cross the level area to the base of the mountain. Begin the ascent up the steep canyon, staying above the creek to the east. Switchbacks lead to a small meadow at one mile, where there are great views of The Thunderer to the southeast. This is a good turn-around spot for a short hike.

To hike farther, continue through the lodgepole pine, spruce, and Douglas fir forest, crossing several tributary streams to the first crossing of Pebble Creek at 3.5 miles. Elevation gain continues gradually but steadily until reaching the Upper Meadows (Hike 72) and the Warm Creek trailhead, 8.5 miles from the first Pebble Creek crossing. ■

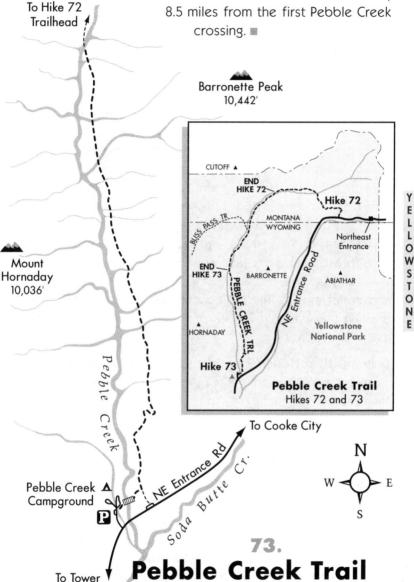

To Hike 72 Trailhead

Barronette Peak 10,442'

Mount Hornaday 10,036'

Pebble Creek

Pebble Creek Campground

NE Entrance Rd

To Cooke City

Soda Butte Cr.

To Tower

CUTOFF

END HIKE 72

Hike 72

BLISS PASS TR.

MONTANA
WYOMING

Northeast Entrance

END HIKE 73

BARRONETTE

ABIATHAR

PEBBLE CREEK TRL.

NE Entrance Road

HORNADAY

Yellowstone National Park

Hike 73

Pebble Creek Trail
Hikes 72 and 73

YELLOWSTONE

N
W · E
S

73.
Pebble Creek Trail
from Pebble Creek Cmpgrnd.
N.E. YELLOWSTONE

74. Trout Lake

N.E. YELLOWSTONE PARK

Hiking distance: 2.2 miles round trip
Hiking time: 1 hour
Elevation gain: 200 feet
Maps: U.S.G.S. Abiathar Peak and Mount Hornaday
Trails Illustrated: Tower/Canyon

Summary of hike: Trout Lake is a 12-acre backcountry lake fed by a stream formed on the steep mountains to its north and west. It is known for its excellent trout fishing. The round lake sits in a depression on a high bench above Soda Butte Creek Canyon along the base of Mount Hornaday and Druid Peak. The scenic tarn is surrounded by rolling meadows, evergreen forests, and a sheer rock mountain wall to the north. The short trail zigzags up to a small ridge in a Douglas fir and lodgepole pine forest, where the first views of Trout Lake emerge. From the crest, the trail drops into the scenic lake basin at the dam and outlet stream. The path circles the perimeter of the lake through the grassy, rolling terrain with views of mountains in every direction.

Driving directions: From the northeast entrance to Yellowstone National Park, drive 10.4 miles southwest to the unmarked trailhead pullout on the right (northwest). The pullout is 1.2 miles southwest of the Pebble Creek Campground.

From Tower Junction, drive 17.6 miles northeast towards Cooke City to the pullout on the left (northwest).

Hiking directions: From the parking pullout, hike west past the trail sign towards the Engelmann spruce and Douglas fir forest. Begin ascending the hillside to the forested ridge. Along the way, the cascading outlet stream of Trout Lake tumbles down the drainage to the left of the trail. At 0.6 miles, the trail reaches the southeast corner of Trout Lake at the outlet. Cross the log bridge over the creek. Once across, the trail follows the forested shoreline. A short distance ahead, the trail leaves the forest and emerges into open, rolling meadows with a wide variety of wildflowers. Continue along the shoreline, crossing a small bridge over the lake's inlet stream. Circle the perimeter of the lake back to the junction by the outlet stream, completing the loop. ■

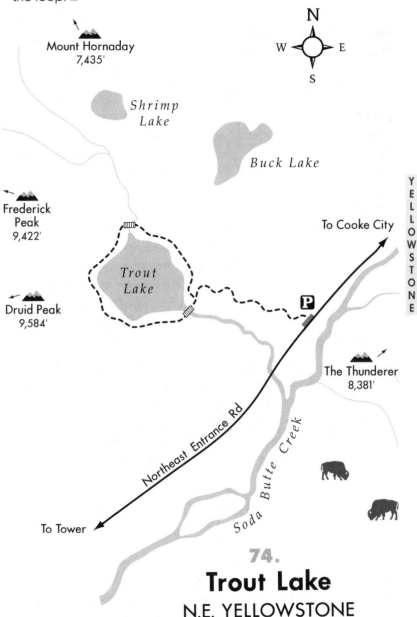

Mount Hornaday
7,435'

N

W — E

S

Shrimp
Lake

Buck Lake

Frederick
Peak
9,422'

To Cooke City

YELLOWSTONE

Trout
Lake

Druid Peak
9,584'

P

The Thunderer
8,381'

Northeast Entrance Rd

Soda Butte Creek

To Tower

74.

Trout Lake
N.E. YELLOWSTONE

75. Slough Creek
N.E. YELLOWSTONE PARK

Hiking distance: 2 miles round trip (to trail junction)
Hiking time: 1 hour
Elevation gain: 400 feet
Maps: U.S.G.S. Lamar Canyon
Beartooth Publishing: Absaroka Beartooth Wilderness
Trails Illustrated: Tower/Canyon

Summary of hike: Slough Creek is a slow-rolling, meandering creek in a gorgeous glacial valley. The creek is a popular fishing destination, well known for its cutthroat trout. The hike begins near the secluded Slough Creek Campground at the mouth of the canyon and follows a historic wagon road through open fir and aspen forests. (The road is still used by horse-drawn wagons for access to the Silver Tip Ranch, located just outside the park.) The trail emerges in the broad open valley at an ox-bow bend in Slough Creek. Beyond the crescent-shaped bend, the creek snakes through scenic, wildflower-laden meadows surrounded by mountains and imposing walls of granite rock. Straight north, and over several layers of mountains, is the main Boulder River Valley (Hike 91).

Driving directions: From the northeast entrance to Yellowstone Park, drive 22.2 miles southwest to the signed Slough Creek Campground turnoff on the right (north). Turn right and go 1.8 miles to the posted trailhead parking area on the right.
From Tower Junction, drive 5.8 miles on the Northeast Entrance Road towards Cooke City to the signed turnoff on the left (north).

Hiking directions: Head east on the old wagon road past the trailhead sign. Wind up the open forest past large glacial boulders, reaching a small saddle covered with flowers at a half mile. Curve right, looping around the large rock formation as the trail levels out. Begin the gradual descent through the forest, and emerge in the gorgeous meadow at the banks of Slough Creek, backed by a large granite wall. A short distance ahead is a signed junction with the Buffalo Plateau Trail on the left. This is the turn-around spot for a 2-mile round-trip hike.

To hike farther, the Buffalo Plateau Trail crosses the creek and meadow, climbing north up to Buffalo Plateau. The Slough Creek Trail continues east up the valley, crossing a ridge to the second meadow. An enjoyable third option is to follow the angler trails through the meadow along the banks of the tranquil, meandering creek. The area is so beautiful and vast, any route will be memorable. ▪

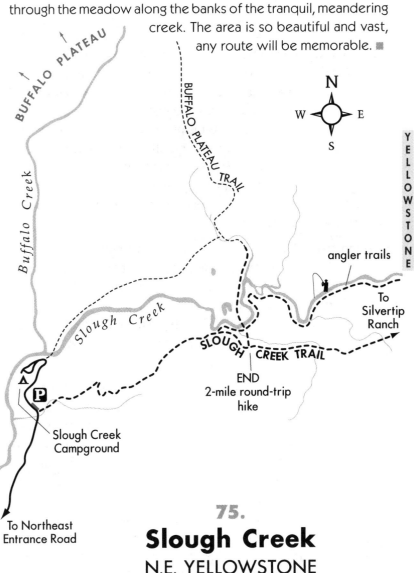

75.
Slough Creek
N.E. YELLOWSTONE

76. Petrified Forest
N.E. YELLOWSTONE PARK

Hiking distance: 3.5 miles round trip
Hiking time: 2 hours
Elevation gain: 1,600 feet
Maps: U.S.G.S. Lamar Canyon
      Trails Illustrated: Tower/Canyon

Summary of hike: The Petrified Forest on Specimen Ridge extends over 40 square miles and contains one of the most extensive petrified forests in the world. Lava flows engulfed and entombed the deciduous forest 50 million years ago, preserving the still-standing ancient remains. Among the specimens are redwoods, sycamores, oaks, and maples. This hike is the shortest route to the Petrified Forest and is brutally steep. The trail climbs nearly straight up the ridge with little finesse. The impressive fossilized forest and panoramic vistas are worth every step of the steep ascent.

Driving directions: From the northeast entrance to Yellowstone National Park, drive 23 miles southwest to the signed trailhead turnout on the left (south). It is located 0.8 miles past the Slough Creek Campground turnoff.

From Tower Junction, drive 5 miles on the Northeast Entrance Road towards Cooke City to the signed turnoff on the right (south).

Hiking directions: Follow the faint old road south for a hundred yards, then bear right on the distinct footpath. Cross the flat grass and sage meadow to the base of the mountain. Begin the ascent up the mountain, reaching a Douglas fir grove at one mile. Follow the ridge, curving to the right around the north flank of the mountain. Pass a larger stand of Douglas fir and continue steeply uphill, reaching a trail split near the top.

Begin the loop to the right, following the north side of the ridge. Just after emerging from the forest is a petrified tree stump on the right side of the trail. Another stump is embedded in the path. Traverse the narrow, cliff-hugging path past numerous massive stumps to a sloping meadow. Curve left, making the final ascent up the grassy hillside to the ridge and the Specimen Ridge Trail. Bear left and follow the ridge to the knoll. Mount Washburn rises in the south, and the Lamar Valley lies to the north. Side paths lead to the numerous petrified stumps. Leave the knoll and descend on the rocky path past many more fossilized trees, completing the loop at the treeline. Take the right fork and retrace your route back to the trailhead. ◾

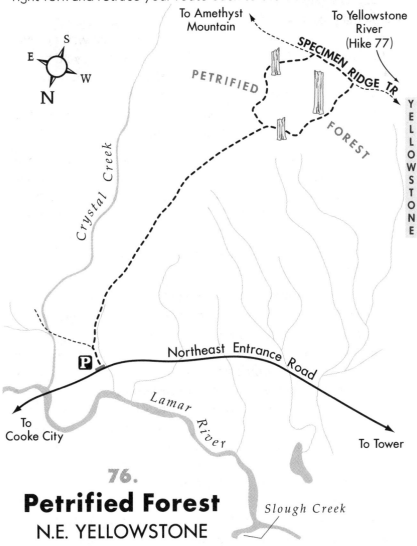

76.

Petrified Forest
N.E. YELLOWSTONE

77. Yellowstone River Picnic Area Trail
N.E. YELLOWSTONE PARK

Hiking distance: 4 miles round trip or 3.7 mile loop
Hiking time: 2 hours
Elevation gain: 300 feet
Maps: U.S.G.S. Tower Junction
Trails Illustrated: Tower/Canyon

Summary of hike: This easy hike parallels the northern end of the Grand Canyon of the Yellowstone and the Yellowstone River along the edge of the canyon rim. From 700 feet above the river, the hike offers continuous views of vertical basalt columns and eroded rock formations, including The Narrows (the narrowest section of the 23-mile-long canyon), Bumpus Butte, The Needle, Overhanging Cliff, Devil's Den, and the towers at Tower Falls.

Driving directions: From the northeast entrance to Yellowstone National Park, drive 26.8 miles southwest to the signed Yellowstone River Picnic Area on the left (southwest). It is located just before crossing the bridge over the Yellowstone River.

From Tower Junction, drive 1.2 miles on the Northeast Entrance Road towards Cooke City to the signed turnoff on the right (southwest).

Hiking directions: The signed trail begins on the east side of the picnic area. Head south, gaining 200 feet up the grassy hillside to the ridge. From the ridge are views across the canyon and down to the Yellowstone River. From here, the trail levels out and continues southeast along the ridge. At 1.5 miles, the canyon and trail curve left. The trail crosses the plateau and connects with the Specimen Ridge Trail (which heads east across the ridge) and the Bannock Indian Trail (which drops south into the canyon and down to the river). This junction is the turn-around point. Return to the trailhead along the same route for the views in reverse, or make a loop on the Specimen Ridge Trail.

For the 3.7-mile loop hike, at the junction with the Specimen Ridge Trail, take the downhill route to the north. Wind through aspen and Douglas fir groves and grassland meadows to the

Northeast Entrance Road at just over one mile. Follow the road to the left for 0.7 miles, returning to the trailhead.

From the Specimen Ridge Trail junction, it is 2 miles east across the ridge to the Petrified Forest (Hike 76). ▪

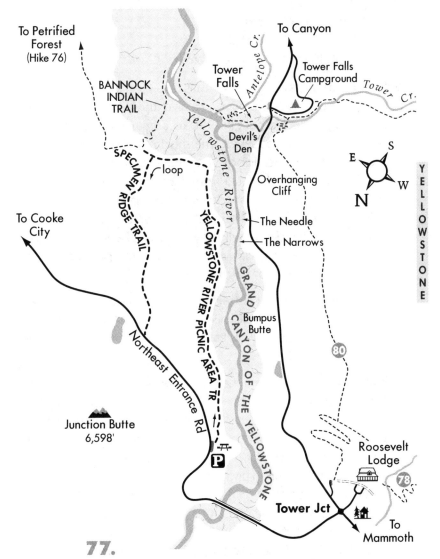

77.
Yellowstone River Picnic Area
N.E. YELLOWSTONE

78. Lost Creek Falls and Lost Lake
N.E. YELLOWSTONE PARK

Hiking distance: 4 miles round trip
Hiking time: 2 hours
Elevation gain: 450 feet
Maps: U.S.G.S. Tower Junction
Trails Illustrated: Tower/Canyon

Summary of hike: Lost Creek Falls is a 40-foot waterfall in a steep, dark-walled box canyon behind the historic Roosevelt Lodge, a log structure built in 1920 to commemorate a visit by President Theodore Roosevelt. The short path leads up the canyon through subalpine fir between moss-covered walls to the base of the falls. Another trail from the lodge leads to the brink of Lost Creek Falls and an overlook at the top of the falls.

This route also connects to Lost Lake, which sits in a beautiful grassy draw filled with wildflowers. The lake is bordered on both ends by forested hills. From Lost Lake, the path continues to the ancient remains of Petrified Tree (Hike 79).

Driving directions: The trailhead is at Roosevelt Lodge at Tower Junction, located 28 miles from the northeast entrance to Yellowstone National Park. Park on the west side of the parking lot near the lodge.

Hiking directions: From the parking area, walk to the back of Roosevelt Lodge. The trailhead is easily found directly behind the lodge. There are two trails. To begin, take the left trail 0.2 miles to a magnificent view of Lost Creek Falls from its base. This short trail is surrounded by steep canyon cliffs.

Return to the trailhead and take the other fork towards Lost Lake, which immediately crosses a footbridge over Lost Creek. Continue up switchbacks through a dense Douglas fir forest to the top of the hill at 0.6 miles and a trail junction. The right trail goes to Lost Lake. First, take the left fork 0.6 miles to an overlook of Lost Creek Falls. From here, the trail continues to Tower Falls, Hike 80.

Return 0.6 miles back to the Lost Lake trail junction. Take the west fork 0.2 miles to Lost Lake. The trail follows the north shore of the lake and continues a half mile to Petrified Tree (Hike 79). After exploring the lake, take the same trail back to Roosevelt Lodge. ▪

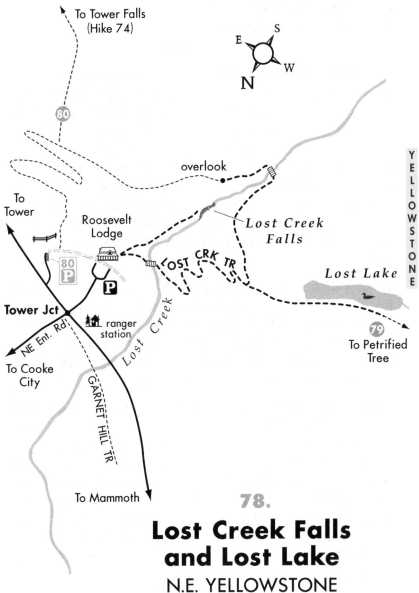

78.

Lost Creek Falls
and Lost Lake
N.E. YELLOWSTONE

79. Lost Lake from Petrified Tree
N.E. YELLOWSTONE PARK

Hiking distance: 1 mile round trip
Hiking time: 40 minutes
Elevation gain: Level
Maps: U.S.G.S. Tower Junction
Trails Illustrated: Tower/Canyon

Summary of hike: Lost Lake is a six-acre mountain lake that sits in a long, tree-lined valley surrounded by steep, forested hillsides. Yellow pond lilies line the shores of the shallow, pastoral lake. This hike begins from Petrified Tree, an old redwood tree buried and entombed in ash and mud from volcanic eruptions 50 million years ago. The trail from Petrified Tree to Lost Lake follows the grassy meadows through a narrow, open valley filled with wildflowers to the head of the lake. The path continues along the north side of the lake to Roosevelt Lodge, Hike 78. (For more petrified trees, see Hike 76—the Petrified Forest.)

Driving directions: From Tower Junction (located 28 miles from the northeast entrance to Yellowstone National Park) turn right (west). Drive 1.4 miles northwest towards Mammoth to the signed Petrified Tree turnoff on the left (south). Turn left and continue 0.5 miles on the paved road to the signed trailhead and parking area at the end of the road.

Hiking directions: Take the short walk up the ramp to view the fenced, 50-million-year-old petrified redwood tree. Return to the parking lot and pick up the signed trail at the end of the lot across the road. Head south into the meadow. Curve around the forested hill in the lush draw, thick with grasses and flowers. As the ravine narrows, the path follows the banks of a trickling stream. Soon the canyon opens up to a wide meadow and curves east, contouring around the hillside on the left. The trail reaches the west end of Lost Lake at a half mile. Follow the north shore of the lily pad-rimmed lake.

To hike farther, the trail continues to Lost Creek Falls and Roosevelt Lodge (Hike 78). It also connects with the trail to Tower Falls (Hike 80). ■

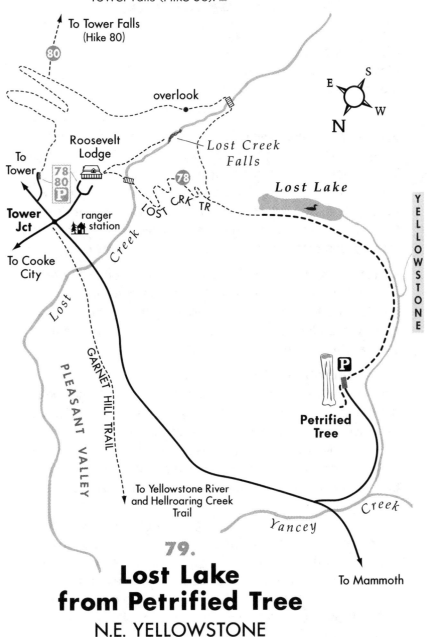

79.
Lost Lake
from Petrified Tree
N.E. YELLOWSTONE

80. Roosevelt Lodge to Tower Falls Campground
N.E. YELLOWSTONE PARK

Hiking distance: 5 miles round trip
Hiking time: 2.5 hours
Elevation gain: 400 feet
Maps: U.S.G.S. Tower Junction
Trails Illustrated: Tower/Canyon

Summary of hike: This hike begins near the historic Roosevelt Lodge, a beautiful log structure built in 1920. The trail crosses large meadows and open forests to the Tower Falls Campground across from Tower Falls. The connector trail parallels the Tower-Canyon Road, but the route is up and over a ridge, isolated in the remote backcountry. The well-defined trail is not heavily traveled and offers expansive views of the surrounding terrain.

Driving directions: From Tower Junction (located 28 miles from the northeast entrance to Yellowstone National Park) turn left (east). Drive 0.2 miles east towards Tower Falls to the Roosevelt Lodge horse stables on the right (south). Turn right and park in the parking area.

Hiking directions: Facing the stable information building, walk around the right side of the building. Follow the road to the forested hillside. Curve left along the base of the hill around the back side of the cabins and stables. The pack trail climbs the hill. Long, sweeping switchbacks lead up to the ridge and a signed junction at 0.6 miles. The right fork crosses Lost Creek back to Roosevelt Lodge (Hike 78) or continues to Lost Lake and Petrified Tree (Hike 79).

Take the left fork across the sage-covered meadow. Traverse the southern flank of the forested draw to a ridge at an aspen grove. Wind through open forests and cross the rolling, flowering meadows dotted with trees. The views extend from The Narrows of the Yellowstone River and across the Lamar Valley to The Thunderer. At 2.5 miles, short, steep switchbacks quickly descend the hillside to Tower Creek. Cross the wooden bridge over the creek to a junction. The left fork leads to the Hamilton Store and Tower Falls. The right fork leads 0.2 miles to a signed junction with the Tower Creek Trail (on the right) and the Tower Falls Campground (on the left).

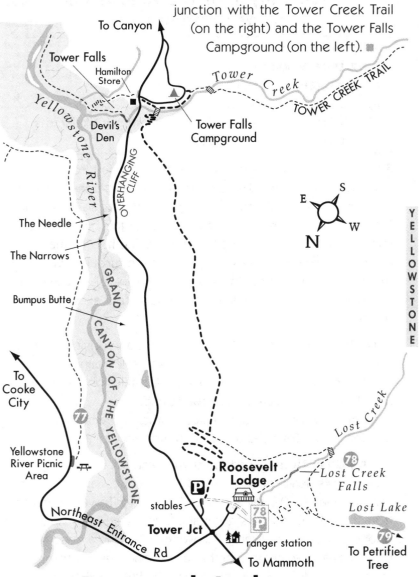

80. Roosevelt Lodge to Tower Falls Campground
N.E. YELLOWSTONE

81. Hellroaring Creek and Black Canyon of the Yellowstone

N.E. YELLOWSTONE PARK

Hiking distance: 4 miles round trip
Hiking time: 2 hours
Elevation gain: 700 feet
Maps: U.S.G.S. Tower Junction
  Beartooth Publishing: Absaroka Beartooth Wilderness
  Trails Illustrated Tower/Canyon

Summary of hike: Hellroaring Creek is a wide rocky creek that flows from the Absaroka-Beartooth Wilderness into the Yellowstone River. At the creek, pyramid-shaped Hellroaring Mountain lies to the north, the park's largest granite mountain, and Buffalo Plateau lies to the east. The hike to the creek crosses a suspension bridge high above the turbulent water of the Yellowstone River in the steep and narrow Black Canyon of the Yellowstone. Hellroaring Creek also offers excellent trout fishing.

Driving directions: From Tower Junction, drive 3.7 miles northwest towards Mammoth to the signed Hellroaring trailhead turnoff and turn right (north). Continue 0.2 miles on the unpaved road to the parking area at the road's end.

From Mammoth, drive 14.5 miles southeast towards Tower to the Hellroaring Trailhead turnoff and turn left (north).

Hiking directions: Head northeast across the rolling hills. Switchbacks lead down towards the Black Canyon of the Yellowstone. At 0.8 miles, a trail leading to Tower intersects from the right. Continue straight ahead to the sturdy suspension bridge crossing the surging Yellowstone River in a deep gorge. Cross the narrow bridge over the canyon, and head north through the forested draw to a junction with the Buffalo Plateau Trail at 1.5 miles. Continue north across the open sagebrush hills, reaching a pond and a trail split at two miles. The left fork follows the edge of the pond to tree-lined Hellroaring Creek. Across the creek, the Yellowstone River Trail parallels the north side of the river 16 miles to Gardiner. The right fork heads upstream to a patrol cabin at just under a mile and a stock bridge shortly after. Return by retracing your route. ■

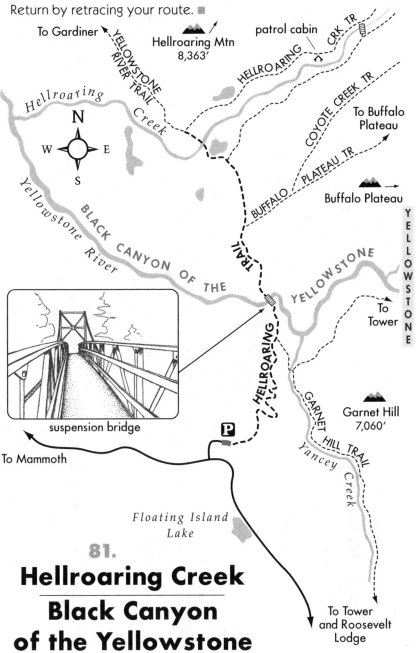

To Gardiner

YELLOWSTONE RIVER TRAIL

Hellroaring Mtn
8,363'

patrol cabin

HELLROARING CRK TR

COYOTE CREEK TR

To Buffalo Plateau

Hellroaring Creek

N
W E
S

BUFFALO PLATEAU TR

Buffalo Plateau

Yellowstone River

BLACK CANYON OF THE

TRAIL

YELLOWSTONE

YELLOWSTONE

To Tower

HELLROARING

GARNET HILL TRAIL

Garnet Hill
7,060'

suspension bridge

To Mammoth

P

Yancey Creek

Floating Island Lake

81.
Hellroaring Creek
Black Canyon of the Yellowstone

To Tower and Roosevelt Lodge

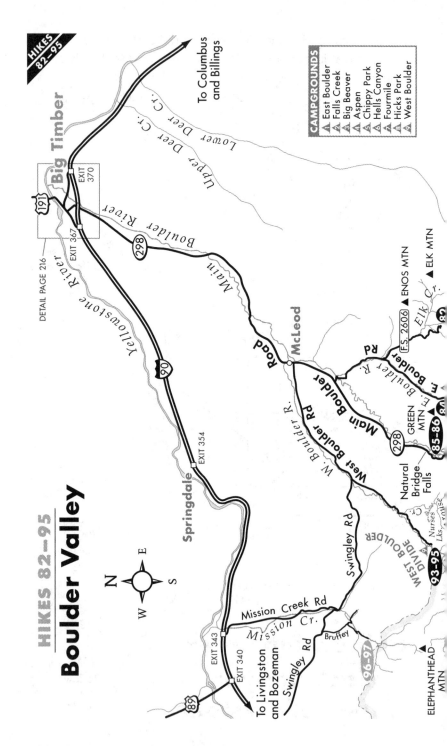

Boulder Valley

To Columbus
and Billings

Big Timber

Lower Deer Cr.

Upper Deer Cr.

EXIT
370

191

298

Main *Boulder River*

DETAIL PAGE 216

EXIT 367

Yellowstone River

90

EXIT 354

Springdale

N
E
S
W

Road

W. Boulder R.

McLeod

Main Boulder

West Boulder Rd

E. Boulder R.

Rd

F.S. 2606 ▲ ENOS MTN

Elk Cr.

▲ ELK MTN

GREEN
MTN ▲

298

85-86

E. Boulder

Natural
Bridge
Falls

W. Boulder Cr.

Nurses Lks.

Rouse

WEST BOULDER

DIVIDE

93-95

Swingley Rd

EXIT 343

Mission Creek Rd

Mission Cr.

Bruffey

96-97

Swingley Rd

EXIT 340

To Livingston
and Bozeman

89

ELEPHANTHEAD
MTN ▲

CAMPGROUNDS

△ East Boulder
△ Falls Creek
△ Big Beaver
△ Aspen
△ Chippy Park
△ Hells Canyon
△ Fourmile
△ Hicks Park
△ West Boulder

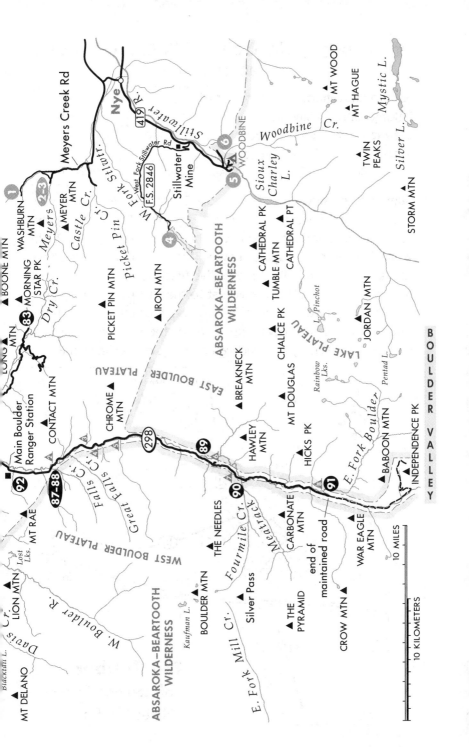

82. Lodgepole Trail to Elk Creek Divide
EAST BOULDER VALLEY

Hiking distance: 8 miles round trip
Hiking time: 4.5 hours
Elevation gain: 1,000 feet
Maps: U.S.G.S. Enos Mountain
        Beartooth Publishing: Absaroka Beartooth Wilderness

Summary of hike: The Lodgepole Trail is located in the East Boulder River drainage at the end of Elk Creek Road. The lightly-used, ten-mile-long trail connects the East Boulder to the northwest Stillwater drainage at Lower Deer Creek and Lodgepole Creek (Hike 1). This hike follows the first four miles of the trail through the Custer National Forest to the Elk Creek Divide, lying between the two drainages. The west end of the trail traverses through alpine meadows with vistas of the surrounding mountains. After reaching the headwater springs of Elk Creek, the trail

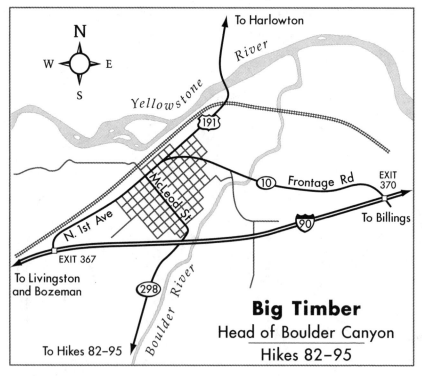

climbs steeply up to the 7,400-foot saddle at Elk Creek Divide, where there are far-reaching vistas that span across the Boulder drainage and the Stillwater drainage.

Driving directions: From I-90, there are two exits into the town of Big Timber—Exit 367 and Exit 370. (See map on page 216.) From Exit 367, drive one mile to McLeod Street (Highway 298). From Exit 370, drive 2.4 miles to McLeod Street (Highway 298). Turn south on McLeod Street, passing through downtown and over I-90.

Continuing south on Highway 298, drive 19.2 miles south into the Boulder River Valley to East Boulder Road on the left. The turnoff is 3.1 miles past the town of McLeod. Turn left and drive 3.4 miles to a road fork with Forest Service Road 2606, signed for Elk Creek. The East Boulder Road continues to the right. Stay to the left on F.S. Road 2606, and continue 4.5 miles uphill to the trailhead at the end of the road. The trailhead is on the left, where the road fades into a grassy meadow.

Hiking directions: Pass the trailhead sign and enter the shade of a lodgepole pine forest. Traverse the hillside, heading east on an easy uphill grade. Pass through a trail gate, and drop down to West Sheep Creek, a tributary of Elk Creek. Cross the creek and stroll through the pastoral forest to flower-filled meadows rimmed with aspen groves and vistas of Long Mountain and Boone Mountain. Climb to a minor ridge overlooking Skookum Joe Canyon and a view of Elk Mountain. Gently descend into the canyon to cascading East Sheep Creek at two miles. Rock-hop over the creek, and pass through another trail gate. Head up the slope through meadows dotted with pines and aspens. Pass a spring on the left with a horse trough. Climb to the top of a rise with 360-degree vistas. Begin the final and steep ascent to the Elk Creek Divide in a 7,400-foot saddle on Elk Mountain. The trail fades away by a junction with a sign posted on a pine tree. This is the turn-around point.

The Boone Peak Trail veers downhill to the left and leads to the Middle Fork and the West Fork of Upper Deer Creek. Curving to the right, the Lodgepole Trail continues to Lower Deer Creek and into the Stillwater drainage (Hike 1). The Lodgepole Trail also connects with another segment of the Boone Peak Trail, which heads south across the ridge of Elk Mountain. ■

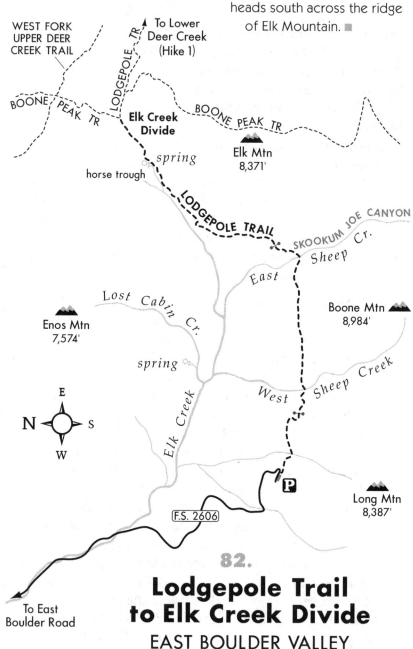

WEST FORK
UPPER DEER
CREEK TRAIL

LODGEPOLE TR

To Lower
Deer Creek
(Hike 1)

BOONE PEAK TR

Elk Creek
Divide

BOONE PEAK TR

Elk Mtn
8,371'

spring

horse trough

LODGEPOLE TRAIL

SKOOKUM JOE CANYON

Sheep Cr.

East

Lost Cabin Cr.

Boone Mtn
8,984'

Enos Mtn
7,574'

spring

Elk Creek

West Sheep Creek

N E S W

P

Long Mtn
8,387'

F.S. 2606

To East
Boulder Road

82.

Lodgepole Trail
to Elk Creek Divide
EAST BOULDER VALLEY

83. Dry Fork Trail to
Moccasin Lake and Meyers Creek Pass
EAST BOULDER VALLEY

Hiking distance: 9 miles round trip
Hiking time: 5 hours
Elevation gain: 1,700 feet
Maps: U.S.G.S. Enos Mountain and Picket Pin Mountain
Beartooth Publishing: Absaroka Beartooth Wilderness

Summary of hike: This trail in the East Boulder drainage parallels Dry Fork Creek, a perennial tributary of the East Boulder River. The Dry Fork Trail begins at the end of East Boulder Road and gains substantial elevation up to Meyers Creek Pass between the East Boulder and northwest Stillwater drainages. The pass lies on an 8,111-foot saddle on the boundary of the Gallatin and Custer national forests, where panoramic vistas span across the remote backcountry. En route, the path leads through a scenic valley, meadows, and forests to Moccasin Lake, a beautiful oblong lake in a natural depression. The tarn is surrounded by meadows and backed by forested mountains. Past Meyers Creek Pass, the trail continues down into the Meyers Creek drainage (Hike 3).

Driving directions: From I-90, there are two exits into the town of Big Timber—Exit 367 and Exit 370. (See map on page 216.) From Exit 367, drive one mile to McLeod Street (Highway 298). From Exit 370, drive 2.4 miles to McLeod Street (Highway 298). Turn south on McLeod Street, passing through downtown and over I-90.

Continuing south on Highway 298, drive 19.2 miles south into the Boulder River Valley to East Boulder Road on the left. The turnoff is 3.1 miles past the town of McLeod. Turn left and drive 3.4 miles to a signed road fork with Forest Service Road 2606. Turn right, staying on the East Boulder Road, and continue 8.1 miles uphill to Forest Service Road 6645 on the left (signed as Dry Fork Road). The turnoff is at the end of the public road and a half mile past the Lewis Gulch turnoff. Turn left on F.S. Road 6645, and drive 1.2 miles to a pullout on the left, just after crossing a cattle guard.

F.S. Road 6645 continues for two miles, but there are a few rocky, rough spots, and this scenic area is best seen on foot.

Hiking directions: Walk past the forest service gate, and cross a tributary of the East Boulder River. Wind through the forest on Forest Service Road 6645, a rough, narrow dirt road. Drop into an expansive meadow with a view of Boone Mountain and Morning Star Peak. Head through the meadow and cross a cattle guard. Veer left, meandering through aspen groves on the level road. Parallel Dry Fork Creek in the scenic, open valley surrounded by the forested mountains. Follow the two-track road and enter the forest, gently gaining elevation. Cross another cattle guard to the end of Forest Service Road 6645 at 2.4 miles. Less than 0.1 mile ahead is a junction with the Placer Basin Trail on the right, which follows Blacktail Creek and leads to Placer Basin 7 miles ahead.

Stay on the Dry Fork Trail straight ahead through a mix of meadows and forest. The two-track road narrows to a footpath and climbs the south canyon slope through lodgepole pines. Walk through a flower-filled meadow and ascend the forested slope. Follow a long, narrow meadow downhill to Moccasin Lake on the right at 3.7 miles. This is a good destination and turn-around spot.

To reach Meyers Creek Pass, continue southeast past the lake, climbing 0.8 miles and gaining 600 feet to the pass. The 8,111-foot wide, grassy saddle is marked with a cairn. From the summit are 360-degree panoramas of Moccasin Lake, the Dry Fork Creek drainage, the East Boulder River Valley, Morning Star Peak, Boone Mountain, Long Mountain, Meyer Mountain, and Washburn Mountain.

To extend the hike, the Meyers Creek Trail (Hike 3) descends through the Custer National Forest, following the south fork and main fork of Meyers Creek. ∎

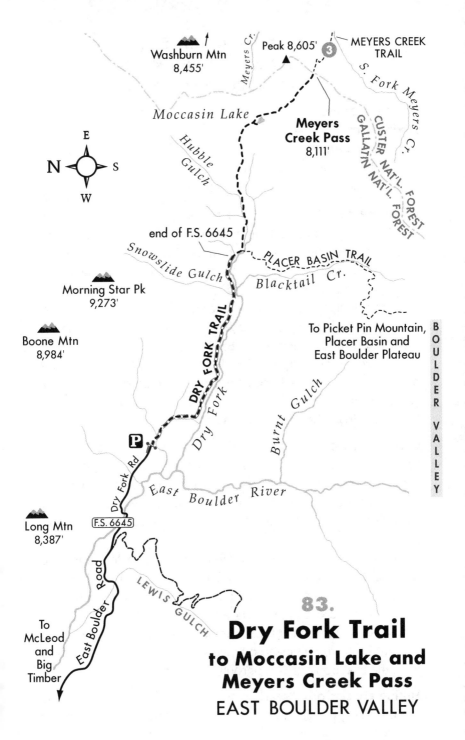

Washburn Mtn
8,455'

Meyers Cr.

Peak 8,605'

MEYERS CREEK
TRAIL

3

S. Fork Meyers Cr.

Moccasin Lake

**Meyers
Creek Pass**
8,111'

CUSTER NAT'L. FOREST

GALLATIN NAT'L. FOREST

Hubble Gulch

E
N ☼ S
W

end of F.S. 6645

Snowslide Gulch

PLACER BASIN TRAIL

Blacktail Cr.

Morning Star Pk
9,273'

To Picket Pin Mountain,
Placer Basin and
East Boulder Plateau

B
O
U
L
D
E
R

V
A
L
L
E
Y

Boone Mtn
8,984'

DRY FORK TRAIL

Dry Fork

Burnt Gulch

P

Dry Fork Rd

East Boulder River

Long Mtn
8,387'

F.S. 6645

East Boulder Road

LEWIS GULCH

To
McLeod
and
Big
Timber

83.

Dry Fork Trail
to Moccasin Lake and
Meyers Creek Pass
EAST BOULDER VALLEY

84. Green Mountain Trail from East Fork Boulder River

EAST BOULDER VALLEY

Hiking distance: 5 miles round trip
Hiking time: 3 hours
Elevation gain: 1,100 feet
Maps: U.S.G.S. McLeod Basin
        Beartooth Publishing: Absaroka Beartooth Wilderness

Summary of hike: Green Mountain is a 7,300-foot mountain at the mouth of the Main Boulder Valley. The low mountain separates the Main Boulder Valley from the East Boulder Valley. The Green Mountain Trail, constructed by the Montana Conservation Corps, connects the two drainages. The six-mile-long trail passes through grasslands and heavily timbered forest, including limber pine, lodgepole pine, and Douglas fir. The Main Boulder trailhead is by Natural Bridge Falls (Hikes 85 and 86). This hike begins in the East Boulder Valley by the East Boulder Campground. The hike heads west along the base of Green Mountain and climbs to a grassy 6,580-foot saddle between Green Mountain and Tepee Mountain. From the grassy plateau are views into both valleys.

Driving directions: From I-90, there are two exits into the town of Big Timber—Exit 367 and Exit 370. (See map on page 216.) From Exit 367, drive one mile to McLeod Street (Highway 298). From Exit 370, drive 2.4 miles to McLeod Street (Highway 298). Turn south on McLeod Street, passing through downtown and over I-90.

Continuing south on Highway 298, drive 19.2 miles south into the Boulder River Valley to East Boulder Road on the left. The turnoff is 3.1 miles past the town of McLeod. Turn left and drive 3.4 miles to a signed road fork with Forest Service Road 2606. Turn right, staying on the East Boulder Road, and continue 4.3 miles uphill to the trailhead on the right. Park off the road across from the East Boulder Campground entrance.

Hiking directions: Head up the hillside, traversing the slope while walking parallel to the road. Veer right, continuing up the hill through a meadow with scattered pines. Switchback to the left, weaving gently through the forest. Skirt the southern base of Green Mountain above stream-fed Fuller Gulch as southern and eastern views open up of Contact Mountain, Tepee Mountain, and Long Mountain. Descend a short distance into Fuller Gulch, then curve right and continue the ascent, skirting the north edge of a large meadow surrounded by aspen groves. The views include Boone Mountain, Morning Star Peak, and Picket Pin Mountain. Walk through another meadow with a spring and horse trough. Ascend the grassy slope to the 6,580-foot plateau on a saddle between Green Mountain and Tepee Mountain. Cross the exposed saddle and pass through a fenceline. Continue across the level, tree-rimmed plateau to a trail sign at 2 miles. This is our turn-around spot. After savoring the vistas across the Main Boulder drainage, including Mount Rae, Baker Mountain, and the West Boulder Plateau, return by retracing your route.

To extend the hike, the trail heads downhill 3.5 miles to Natural Bridge Falls (Hike 85). ▪

85. Green Mountain Trail from the Main Fork Boulder River
MAIN BOULDER VALLEY

Hiking distance: 7 miles round trip
Hiking time: 4 hours
Elevation gain: 1,500 feet
Maps: U.S.G.S. McLeod Basin
      Beartooth Publishing: Absaroka Beartooth Wilderness

Summary of hike: Green Mountain is a 7,300-foot mountain at the mouth of the Main Boulder Valley. The low mountain separates the Main Boulder Valley from the East Boulder Valley. The Green Mountain Trail, constructed by the Montana Conservation Corps, connects the two drainages. The six-mile trail climbs through a transition area from native grasslands and wildflowers to heavily timbered forest. The views span across the whole Boulder Valley. The East Boulder trailhead—Hike 84—is located at the

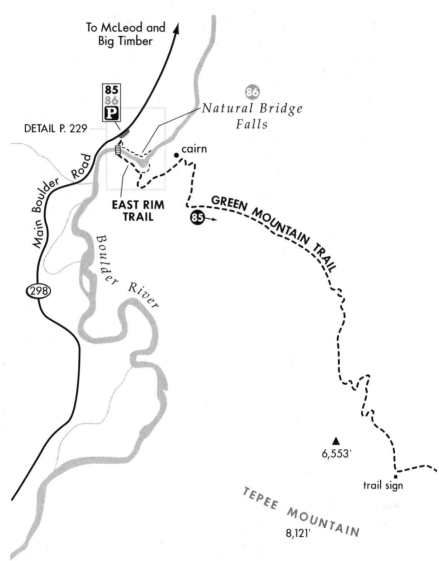

To McLeod and
Big Timber

85
86
P

DETAIL P. 229

*Natural Bridge
Falls*

86

cairn

Main Boulder Road

Boulder River

**EAST RIM
TRAIL**

85

GREEN MOUNTAIN TRAIL

298

▲
6,553'

trail sign

TEPEE MOUNTAIN
8,121'

Green Mountain Trail

HIKE 84
East Fork Boulder River Trailhead

HIKE 85
Main Fork Boulder River Trailhead

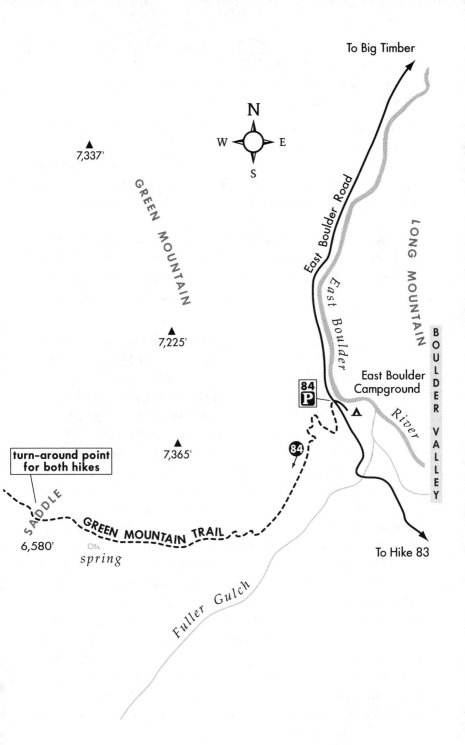

To Big Timber

N
W   E
S

7,337'

GREEN MOUNTAIN

East Boulder Road

East Boulder

LONG MOUNTAIN

7,225'

84
P

East Boulder
Campground

River

B
O
U
L
D
E
R
V
A
L
L
E
Y

84

7,365'

turn-around point
for both hikes

SADDLE

6,580'

spring

GREEN MOUNTAIN TRAIL

To Hike 83

Fuller Gulch

East Boulder Campground. This hike begins in the Main Boulder Valley by Natural Bridge State Monument. The trail leads to a grassy plateau on a saddle that straddles the East Boulder and Main Boulder Valleys, with views into both river-fed corridors.

Driving directions: From I-90, there are two exits into the town of Big Timber—Exit 367 and Exit 370. (See map on page 216.) From Exit 367, drive one mile to McLeod Street (Highway 298). From Exit 370, drive 2.4 miles to McLeod Street (Highway 298). Turn south on McLeod Street, passing through downtown and over I-90.

Continuing south on Highway 298, drive 26 miles south into the Boulder River Valley to the signed turnoff on the left for Natural Bridge Falls. The turnoff is 10 miles past the town of McLeod. (Highway 298 is also called the Main Boulder Road.) Turn left and park in the lot.

Hiking directions: Walk to the trailhead map and a paved trail split. To the left is the Natural Bridge Trail—see Hike 86 map for detailed trails. Take the right fork on the East Rim Trail. Follow the paved, rock-lined path. Cross the bridge over the Boulder River, overlooking the limestone rock gorge and raging whitewater. Continue following the gravel path, passing overlooks of the majestic gorge and churning river. Descend to a signed junction with the Green Mountain Trail at a quarter mile. The left fork stays on the East Rim Trail and another overlook.

Veer to the right and head up the hillside, overlooking the chasm and the Natural Bridge trail system. Traverse the hill to a cairn atop a ridge with an expansive 360-degree vista that includes Mount Rae and Baker Mountain. Curve right and zig-zag down 5 switchbacks to the bottom of a gulch. Head up the opposite wall to a vast meadow stretching along the western base of Green Mountain. Cross the open grassland, marked with cairns, between Green Mountain and Tepee Mountain. Gradually but steadily gain elevation and enter a grove of pines. Climb 6 more switchbacks into a lodgepole pine forest, and weave uphill to a plateau with a tree-rimmed meadow. Walk through the meadow to a trail sign at 3 miles. Continue uphill to the open, grassy summit on a 6,580-foot saddle between Green Mountain and Tepee Mountain. The views drop into the East Boulder River Valley and span across to Long Mountain, Boone Mountain, Morning Star Peak, and Picket Pin Mountain. Pass through a fence-line, and cross the open saddle to the east edge of the summit at 3.5 miles. This is our turn-around spot.

To extend the hike, the trail continues 2 miles downhill into the East Boulder Valley to the trailhead by the East Boulder Campground (Hike 84). ▪

86. Natural Bridge Falls
NATURAL BRIDGE STATE MONUMENT
MAIN BOULDER VALLEY

Hiking distance: 1 mile round trip
Hiking time: 45 minutes
Elevation gain: 100 feet
Maps: U.S.G.S. McLeod Basin
　　　　Beartooth Publishing: Absaroka Beartooth Wilderness

B
O
U
L
D
E
R

V
A
L
L
E
Y

Summary of hike: Natural Bridge State Monument is located in the Main Boulder River Valley 25 miles south of the town of Big Timber. The area is named for a limestone arch that once spanned the Boulder River. The 25-foot natural arch collapsed in July 1988. Natural Bridge Falls, a 105-foot cataract on the river, surges through the Madison limestone chasm. The waterfall changes throughout the seasons. In the early spring, the surging cataract drops more than 100 feet over the limestone precipice in the river-carved gorge. In late spring, two smaller waterfalls are visible under the main falls. During the summer, the water disappears into a riverbed hole and tumbles out of the lower caverns at the base of the waterfall, revealing the bedrock.

The Natural Bridge Trail is a paved and handicapped acces-sible path that follows the Boulder River along ledges and steep cliffs. The popular trail contains several scenic overlooks with interpretive panels. The observation stations explain the geo-logical events that shaped the topography. Fossilized sea shells dating back millions of years can be seen in the sedimentary rocks. The East Rim Trail, on the opposite side of the gorge, is a natural path that leads to an impressive viewing spot of the river canyon, falls, and pool.

Driving directions: From I-90, there are two exits into the town of Big Timber—Exit 367 and Exit 370. (See map on page 216.) From Exit 367, drive one mile to McLeod Street (Highway 298). From Exit 370, drive 2.4 miles to McLeod Street (Highway 298). Turn south on McLeod Street, passing through downtown and over I-90.

Continuing south on Highway 298, drive 26 miles south into the Boulder River Valley to the signed turnoff on the left for Natural Bridge Falls. The turnoff is 10 miles past the town of McLeod. (Highway 298 is also called the Main Boulder Road.) Turn left and park in the lot.

Hiking directions: Walk to the trailhead map and a paved trail split. The East Rim Trail bears right. Begin to the left on the Natural Bridge Trail to an overlook of the Boulder River and the rocky limestone gorge. Continue 25 yards to a Y-fork. Begin a short loop on the right fork and descend steps to five more lookout points with interpretive panels and differing views of the magnificent, 100-foot deep chasm. The paved path ends at the sixth overlook. Bear left on the unpaved upper trail to complete the loop.

Return to the trailhead junction, and take the signed East Rim Trail. Follow the paved, rock-lined path. Cross the bridge over the Boulder River, overlooking the sedimentary rock gorge and turbulent whitewater. Continue following the gravel path to another overlook of the gorge, where a dirt footpath descends to the base of the canyon. The main trail continues up the hill to another overlook down the canyon. Descend to a signed junction with the Green Mountain Trail (Hike 85). Walk straight ahead, staying on the East Rim Trail, and make a U-bend. Descend along the canyon's east precipice, with spectacular views of the unusual geologic formations, powerful waterfall, and pool. The designated trail soon ends. Side paths continue along the rim and down into the canyon. ▪

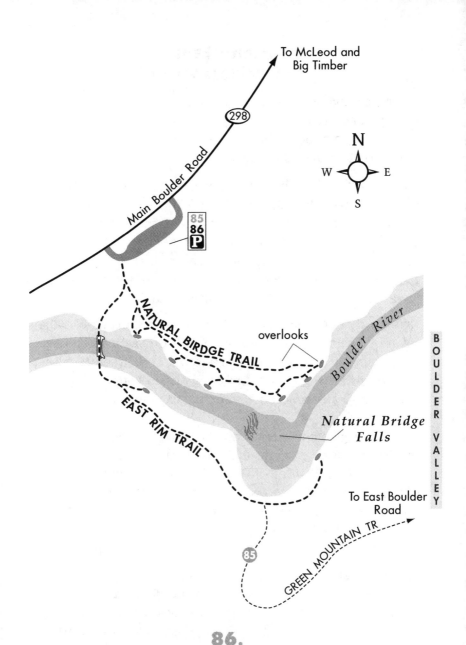

To McLeod and
Big Timber

298

Main Boulder Road

N
W · E
S

85
86
P

NATURAL BIRDGE TRAIL

overlooks

Boulder River

EAST RIM TRAIL

B
O
U
L
D
E
R

V
A
L
L
E
Y

*Natural Bridge
Falls*

To East Boulder
Road

85

GREEN MOUNTAIN TR

86.
Natural Bridge Falls
NATURAL BRIDGE STATE MONUMENT
MAIN BOULDER VALLEY

87. Trinity Falls
MAIN BOULDER VALLEY

Hiking distance: 2.5 miles round trip
Hiking time: 1.5 hours
Elevation gain: 500 feet
Maps: U.S.G.S. Chrome Mountain

Summary of hike: This short, relatively easy trail to Trinity Falls is a hidden gem. The falls is a majestic 70-foot cataract on Great Falls Creek, a quarter mile from the creek's confluence with the Boulder River. The four-tier falls, unofficially named by one of the local church camps, sits in a box canyon by an old mine cave. The trail begins on the Great Falls Creek Trail and also includes a lower 30-foot waterfall by an old miner's cabin.

Driving directions: From I-90, there are two exits into the town of Big Timber—Exit 367 and Exit 370. (See map on page 216.) From Exit 367, drive one mile to McLeod Street (Highway 298). From Exit 370, drive 2.4 miles to McLeod Street (Highway 298). Turn south on McLeod Street, passing through downtown and over I-90.

Continuing south on Highway 298, drive 31 miles south into the Boulder River Valley to the signed trailhead turnoff on the right. (The first 26 miles of Highway 298 are paved.) The turn-off is 15 miles past the town of McLeod and 2.6 miles past the signed Main Boulder Ranger Station. Turn right and drive 0.1 mile up the hill to the trailhead at the end of the road. (Highway 298 is also called the Main Boulder Road.)

Hiking directions: Head south past the trailhead sign and enter the pine forest. Follow the Boulder River upstream to a Y-fork. The left trail fork follows the course of the river. Curve right, staying on the Great Falls Creek Trail. Walk 40 yards to another signed junction. The right fork, straight ahead, leads less than a quarter mile to an old mine. Bear left. The Great Falls Creek Trail, a footpath, immediately veers right and climbs the hillside (Hike 88). The route to Trinity Falls stays on the wide path straight ahead, continuing south and rejoining the river route.

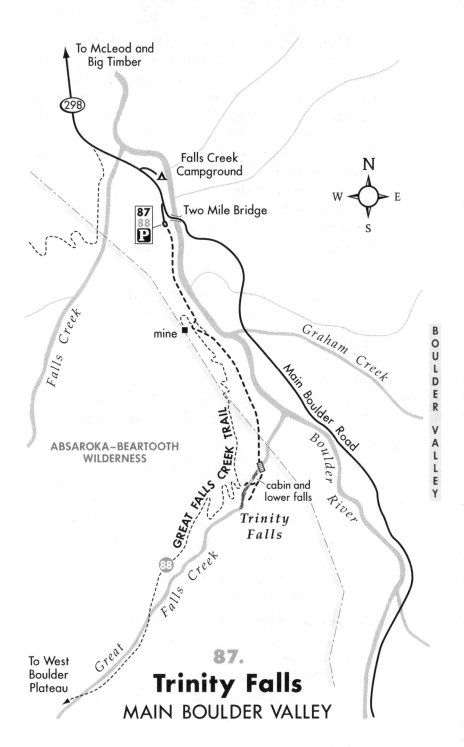

To McLeod and
Big Timber

298

Falls Creek
Campground

Two Mile Bridge

87
88
P

N
W · E
S

mine

Falls Creek

Graham Creek

BOULDER VALLEY

Main Boulder Road

GREAT FALLS CREEK TRAIL

ABSAROKA–BEARTOOTH
WILDERNESS

Boulder River

cabin and
lower falls

*Trinity
Falls*

88

Falls Creek

To West
Boulder
Plateau

Great

87.
Trinity Falls
MAIN BOULDER VALLEY

Head up the hill, pass through a flat meadow, and traverse the hillside. Stay within view of the Boulder River to the Trinity Falls sign at 0.8 miles. Go to the right and ascend the hill to Great Falls Creek. Cautiously cross downfall logs over the rocky, cascading creek. Continue up the southeast side of the tumbling whitewater to the lower falls in a rocky gorge by an old log cabin once inhabited by a miner. Pass the 30-foot lower falls and the old miner's cabin. Cross the creek again on another log to a mine cave in a box canyon and 70-foot Trinity Falls. After enjoying the area, return by retracing your steps.

To extend the hike, return to the junction with the Great Falls Creek Trail and continue with Hike 88 on the upper trail. ▪

88. Great Falls Creek Trail
MAIN BOULDER VALLEY

Hiking distance: 4.8 miles round trip
Hiking time: 3 hours
Elevation gain: 1,400 feet
Maps: U.S.G.S. Chrome Mountain and West Boulder Plateau
　　　　Beartooth Publishing: Absaroka Beartooth Wilderness

Summary of hike: The Great Falls Creek Trail climbs 4,250 feet over 8 miles to Upper Great Falls Creek Lake, the creek's headwaters just above the timberline. The lake is a mile shy of the pass atop the West Boulder Plateau. This hike, within the Absaroka-Beartooth Wilderness, follows the first 2.4 miles of the trail, zigzagging 1,400 feet up the north canyon wall. The forested trail overlooks the turbulent cascades of Great Falls Creek. For extended hiking, the trail continues over the plateau and descends into the West Boulder drainage along Falls Creek.

Driving directions: From I-90, there are two exits into the town of Big Timber—Exit 367 and Exit 370. (See map on page 216.) From Exit 367, drive one mile to McLeod Street (Highway 298). From Exit 370, drive 2.4 miles to McLeod Street (Highway 298). Turn south on McLeod Street, passing through downtown and over I-90.

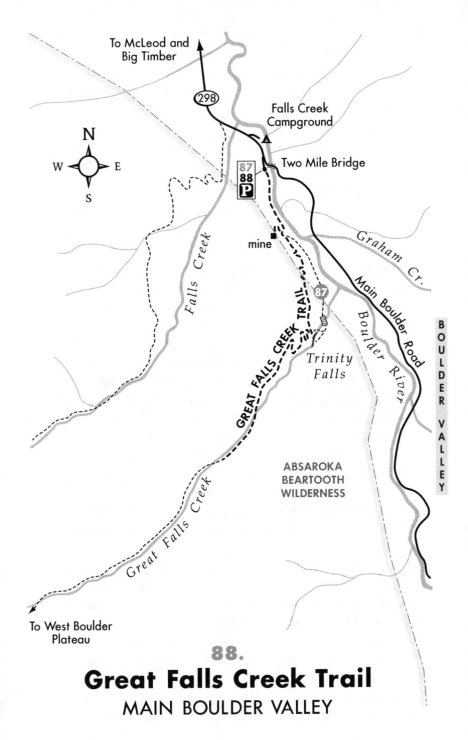

To McLeod and
Big Timber

298

Falls Creek
Campground

Two Mile Bridge

87
88
P

mine

Graham Cr.

N
W E
S

Falls Creek

GREAT FALLS CREEK TRAIL

87

Trinity
Falls

Main Boulder Road

Boulder River

BOULDER VALLEY

Great Falls Creek

ABSAROKA
BEARTOOTH
WILDERNESS

To West Boulder
Plateau

88.
Great Falls Creek Trail
MAIN BOULDER VALLEY

Continuing south on Highway 298, drive 31 miles south into the Boulder River Valley to the signed trailhead turnoff on the right. (The first 26 miles of Highway 298 are paved.) The turnoff is 15 miles past the town of McLeod and 2.6 miles past the signed Main Boulder Ranger Station, just below Two-Mile Bridge on the west side of the road. Turn right and drive 0.1 mile up the hill to the trailhead at the end of the road. (Highway 298 is also called the Main Boulder Road.)

Hiking directions: Head south past the trailhead sign and enter the pine forest. Follow the Boulder River upstream to a Y-fork. The left trail fork follows the course of the river. Curve right, staying on the Great Falls Creek Trail. Walk 40 yards to another signed junction. The right fork, straight ahead, leads less than a quarter mile to an old mine. Bear left to an immediate fork. The lower trail, straight ahead, leads to Trinity Falls (Hike 87).

For this hike, veer right on the Great Falls Creek Trail (a footpath) and climb the hillside. Traverse the mountain slope, climbing south, and zigzag up four switchbacks. Enter the Absaroka-Beartooth Wilderness at just under one mile. The grade of the trail eases up and leaves the sounds of the Boulder River to the quiet of the forest. Begin climbing again to the northern slope above thunderous Great Falls Creek and Trinity Falls. A very unstable and steep path descends to the falls. If you choose to take this precarious path, use extreme caution. (Hike 87 is the best way to see the falls.)

The Great Falls Creek Trail cuts to the right and weaves back and forth on five more switchbacks. Follow the north wall of the canyon high above the tumbling whitewater. The continuous cascades and waterfalls are intermittently viewed through the trees. Drop down to the creek by a beautiful cascade at 2.4 miles. The trail continues across the creek. If you choose to continue, use caution crossing Great Falls Creek on the old downfall logs. The path parallels the creek upstream through the forest for a half mile to another creek crossing. Choose your own turnaround spot.

To extend the hike, the trail continues up the canyon along Great Falls Creek to the West Boulder Plateau at 9 miles. ▪

89. Placer Basin Trail
MAIN BOULDER VALLEY

Hiking distance: 4 miles round trip
Hiking time: 2 hours
Elevation gain: 1,000 feet
Maps: U.S.G.S. Chrome Mountain and Mount Douglas
       Beartooth Publishing: Absaroka Beartooth Wilderness

Summary of hike: The Placer Basin Trail climbs 6 miles up the east side of the main Boulder drainage to the 9,400-foot East Boulder Plateau. This hike includes the first two miles of the trail along Hawley Creek. The trail enters the Absaroka-Beartooth Wilderness and climbs a thousand feet to a high alpine saddle with dramatic vistas of the surrounding mountains. Near the trailhead, by Camp Mimanagish, the trail crosses a footbridge over the tumbling Boulder River. For extended hiking, the trail continues up a steep incline to Breakneck Plateau at the south end of East Boulder Plateau.

Driving directions: From I-90, there are two exits into the town of Big Timber—Exit 367 and Exit 370. (See map on page 216.) From Exit 367, drive one mile to McLeod Street (Highway 298). From Exit 370, drive 2.4 miles to McLeod Street (Highway 298). Turn south on McLeod Street, passing through downtown and over I-90.

Continuing south on Highway 298, drive 40.3 miles south into the Boulder River Valley to the posted Placer Basin Trailhead on the right. (The first 26 miles of Highway 298 are paved.) The parking area is 24.2 miles past the town of McLeod and 1.2 miles past the posted Speculator Creek Trailhead. Turn right and park. (Highway 298 is also called the Main Boulder Road.)

Hiking directions: From the Placer Basin Trail sign, walk over the small rise to the Main Boulder Road. Cross the road and cross the bridge over the Boulder River. Enter the lodgepole pine forest and head south, parallel to the east side of the river. The cabins of Camp Mimanagish can be seen across the river. Climb up the hillside to views of the canyon, river and mountains,

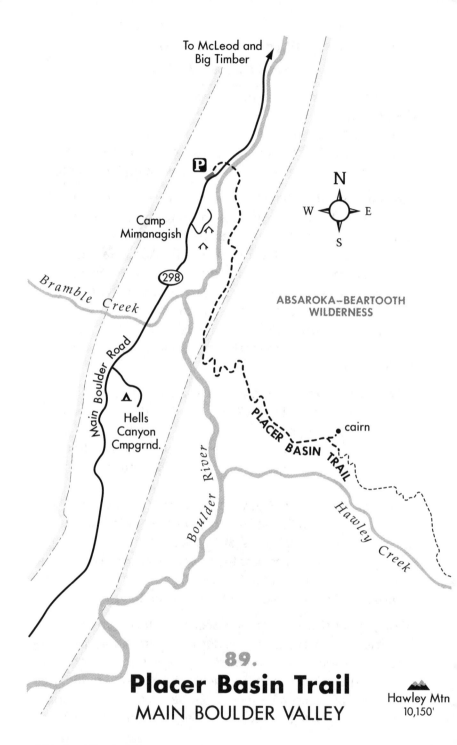

To McLeod and
Big Timber

P

N

W   E

S

Camp
Mimanagish

298

Bramble Creek

ABSAROKA–BEARTOOTH
WILDERNESS

Main Boulder Road

Hells
Canyon
Cmpgrnd.

Boulder River

PLACER BASIN TRAIL

• cairn

Hawley Creek

89.
Placer Basin Trail
MAIN BOULDER VALLEY

Hawley Mtn
10,150'

including Carbonate Mountain and The Needles. Walk through a garden of mossy granite boulders, and enter the Absaroka-Beartooth Wilderness at 0.8 miles. Skirt the base of a talus slope, and ascend the mountain with the aid of six switchbacks to a sloping meadow. Pass through the meadow and enjoy the wide vistas. Bend to the right, with a head-on view of rounded Hawley Mountain. Continue climbing to a vast meadow with east views of Breakneck Mountain, Snowy Peak, Mount Douglas, and the layers of mountains beyond the Boulder Valley. Weave through the meadow and reenter the forest to a saddle at the upper end of the meadow, where there is a junction with a cairn. For this hike, walk 30 yards straight ahead to a flat, scenic area, perfect for a lunch break or a rest.

To extend the hike, the Placer Basin Trail continues up the Hawley Creek drainage through a tree-rimmed grassland. The route steadily climbs 4 miles, parallel to Hawley Creek and the North Fork Hawley Creek, to the 9,400-foot alpine terrain of the East Boulder Plateau, just north of Breakneck Mountain. The trail travels across the plateau to Placer Basin and Picket Pin Mountain, connecting to the Dry Fork Trail (Hike 83). ▪

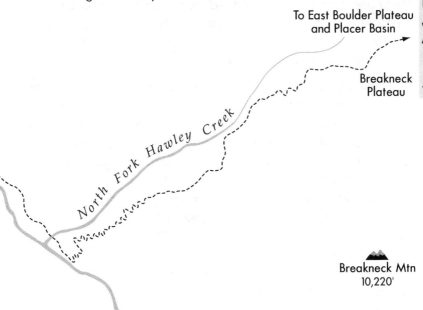

To East Boulder Plateau
and Placer Basin

Breakneck
Plateau

BOULDER VALLEY

North Fork Hawley Creek

Breakneck Mtn
10,220'

90. Fourmile Trail—Trail Creek—Meatrack Trail Loop
MAIN BOULDER VALLEY

Hiking distance: 9.3-mile loop
Hiking time: 5 hours
Elevation gain: 1,500 feet
Maps: U.S.G.S. Mount Douglas and The Needles
       Beartooth Publishing: Absaroka Beartooth Wilderness

Summary of hike: The headwaters of Fourmile Creek form on the upper eastern slope of The Pyramid, just below Silver Pass. Meatrack Creek begins from high alpine lakes on the southern slope of Boulder Mountain. The creeks are located deep within the Absaroka-Beartooth Wilderness.

Fourmile Trail and Meatrack Trail follow the stream-fed canyons up the west side of the main Boulder drainage. The trails lead to Silver Pass, a narrow ridge that straddles the spine of the Absaroka Range. This hike makes a 9-mile loop on the lower end of the trails via the forested 2.5-mile Trail Creek Trail. The connector trail crosses a saddle between the two canyons. The route overlooks the cascading whitewater of both creeks and visits Meatrack Meadows, an expansive meadow stretching across both sides of Meatrack Creek.

Driving directions: From I-90, there are two exits into the town of Big Timber—Exit 367 and Exit 370. (See map on page 216.) From Exit 367, drive one mile to McLeod Street (Highway 298). From Exit 370, drive 2.4 miles to McLeod Street (Highway 298). Turn south on McLeod Street, passing through downtown and over I-90.

Continuing south on Highway 298, drive 42.7 miles south into the Boulder River Valley to the signed trailhead parking area on the left. (The first 26 miles of Highway 298 are paved.) The turn-off is 26.7 miles past the town of McLeod and 4 miles past the well-signed Speculator Creek Trailhead. (Highway 298 is also called the Main Boulder Road.)

Hiking directions: Cross the road to the trailhead gate by the information kiosk. Walk past the forest service rental cabin on the left, and head up the Fourmile Trail through a lodgepole pine forest. Immediately enter the Absaroka-Beartooth Wilderness, and cross a bridge over a cascading stream. Steadily climb at a moderate grade to a signed junction at 0.8 miles. The loop can be hiked in either direction.

For this hike, bear left on the Meatrack Trail, hiking the loop clockwise. Descend to a bridge at the turbulent whitewater of Fourmile Creek. Cross the bridge and weave through the forest to Meatrack Creek. Head up the boulder-filled canyon, parallel to the north side of the tumbling creek. Cross a log bridge over a small stream and wetland. Stay close to the creek, and enter a meadow with a view of Carbonate Mountain to the south. At 4 miles, drop down into Meatrack Meadow to a posted junction. The Meatrack Trail continues to Silver Pass and also connects with Trail 24 to Bridge Creek.

Bear right on the Trail Creek Trail. Zigzag up the north canyon slope on a short but steep climb up to a forested 8,000-foot saddle. Cross the saddle and gradually descend into Fourmile Canyon, crossing three branches of the Trail Creek headwaters. Weave down the drainage to Fourmile Creek at 6 miles. Wade or rock-hop across the creek to a T-junction with the Fourmile Trail.

Go to the right and head down-canyon, crossing four consecutive tributary streams. Steadily descend, crossing a few more streams while meandering through meadows. At 8.2 miles, views open up across the Boulder Valley. Continue downhill, completing the loop at 8.5 miles. Return to the trailhead straight ahead. ▩

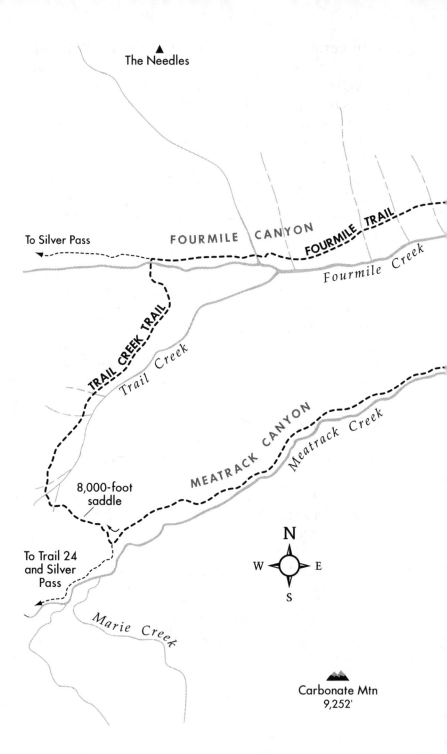

The Needles

To Silver Pass

FOURMILE CANYON

FOURMILE TRAIL

Fourmile Creek

TRAIL CREEK TRAIL

Trail Creek

MEATRACK CANYON

Meatrack Creek

8,000-foot
saddle

To Trail 24
and Silver
Pass

Marie Creek

N
W E
S

Carbonate Mtn
9,252'

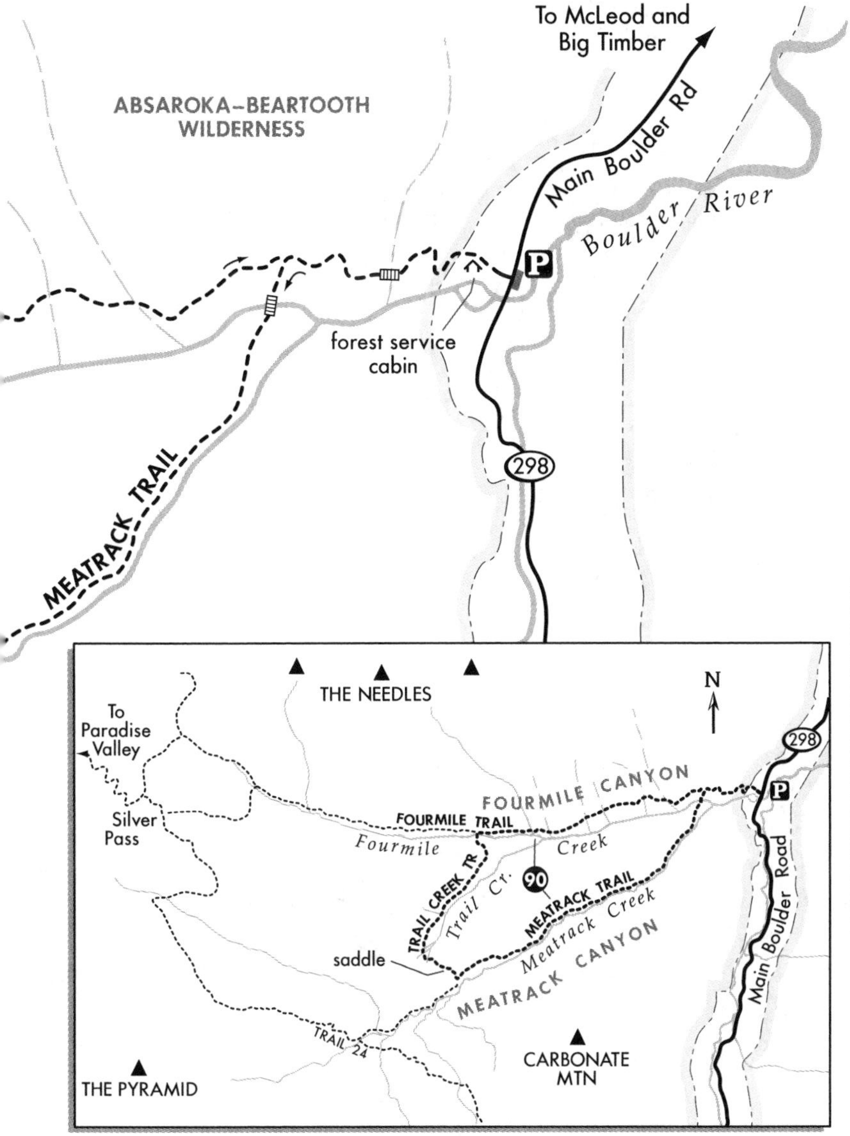

To McLeod and
Big Timber

Main Boulder Rd

Boulder River

P

forest service
cabin

298

MEATRACK TRAIL

BOULDER VALLEY

The Needles

To
Paradise
Valley

Silver
Pass

N

298

P

FOURMILE CANYON

FOURMILE TRAIL

Fourmile   Creek

TRAIL CREEK TR.

Trail Cr.

90

MEATRACK TRAIL

Meatrack Creek

MEATRACK CANYON

saddle

Main Boulder Road

TRAIL 24

CARBONATE
MTN

THE PYRAMID

90.
Fourmile Trail–Trail Creek–
Meatrack Trail Loop
MAIN BOULDER VALLEY

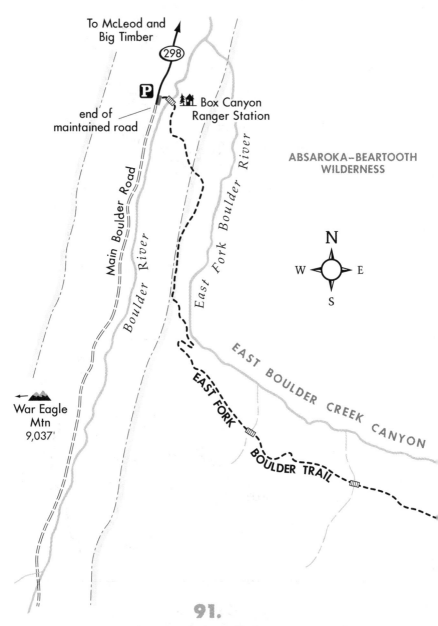

298

P

end of
maintained road

Box Canyon
Ranger Station

ABSAROKA–BEARTOOTH
WILDERNESS

Main Boulder Road

Boulder River

East Fork Boulder River

N

W — E

S

War Eagle
Mtn
9,037'

EAST BOULDER CREEK CANYON

EAST FORK

BOULDER TRAIL

91.

East Fork Boulder Trail
to East Fork Boulder River Bridge
MAIN BOULDER VALLEY

91. East Fork Boulder Trail
to East Fork Boulder River Bridge
MAIN BOULDER VALLEY

Hiking distance: 7.5 miles round trip
Hiking time: 3.5 hours
Elevation gain: 800 feet
Maps: U.S.G.S. Mount Douglas and Haystack Peak
Beartooth Publishing: Absaroka Beartooth Wilderness

Summary of hike: The East Fork Boulder Trail begins at the Box Canyon Trailhead at the end of the maintained Boulder Valley road. The trail, an old wagon road, parallels the East Fork Boulder River 9 miles to the Slough Creek Divide, eventually leading to the Slough Creek Campground in Yellowstone National Park (Hike 75). It is also a popular 12-mile route east to the Lake Plateau via the Rainbow Creek Trail. (Continuing east over the Lake Plateau leads into the Stillwater drainage.)

This hike enters the Absaroka–Beartooth Wilderness and gently climbs the first 3.5 miles of the trail through conifer forests and open meadows along the East Fork Boulder River. Baboon Mountain rises steeply to the south. The trail leads to a log bridge over the river and a swimming hole.

B
O
U
L
D
E
R

V
A
L
L
E
Y

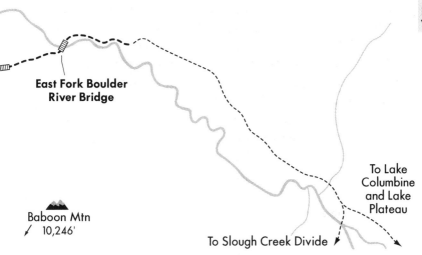

East Fork Boulder
River Bridge

Baboon Mtn
10,246'

To Slough Creek Divide

To Lake
Columbine
and Lake
Plateau

Driving directions: From I-90, there are two exits into the town of Big Timber—Exit 367 and Exit 370. (See map on page 216.) From Exit 367, drive one mile to McLeod Street (Highway 298). From Exit 370, drive 2.4 miles to McLeod Street (Highway 298). Turn south on McLeod Street, passing through downtown and over I-90.

Continuing south on Highway 298, drive 48.5 miles south into the Boulder River Valley to the Box Canyon Trailhead parking area at the end of the maintained road. (The first 26 miles of Highway 298 are paved.) The parking area is 32.4 miles past the town of McLeod and 2.1 miles past Hicks Park Campground. (Highway 298 is also called the Main Boulder Road.)

Hiking directions: Cross the bridge over the Boulder River, and pass the Box Canyon Ranger Station on the left. Weave through the mixed conifer forest on a gentle uphill grade. At 0.3 miles, enter the Absaroka-Beartooth Wilderness. Top a small rise and descend into East Boulder Creek Canyon. Gradually descend towards the river, walking parallel to the river. Climb up the hillside on two switchbacks, and stroll through the forest. Cross a rock and gravel bridge over a stream, and meander through the wooded area. Walk over a tributary on a log bridge to expansive vistas of the surrounding mountains, including Baboon Mountain and views down the canyon. Cross another log bridge in a small meadow, and continue to the East Fork Boulder River Bridge, a large log bridge. Beneath the bridge is a pool, popular with fishermen and water-loving dogs. Cross the bridge and follow the north edge of the tumbling river for a quarter mile. The river bends to the right, and the trail leaves the waterway, climbing through dense forest. This is a good turn-around spot.

To extend the hike, the trail connects with the Rainbow Creek Trail in 2.5 miles. The trail follows Rainbow Creek northeast to the Lake Plateau, 8 miles from the trailhead. En route, the trail connects with the Lake Columbine Trail, which heads south to Lake Columbine—8.5 miles from the trailhead—and on to the Slough Creek Divide at 9.5 miles. ■

92. Grouse Creek Trail from the Main Boulder (east trailhead)

BURRIS FLAT

MAIN BOULDER VALLEY

Hiking distance: 8 miles round trip
Hiking time: 4.5 hours
Elevation gain: 1,800 feet
Maps: U.S.G.S. McLeod Basin and Mount Rae
    Beartooth Publishing: Absaroka Beartooth Wilderness

Summary of hike: The east end of the Grouse Creek Trail begins from the historic Main Boulder Ranger Station in the Gallatin National Forest. The restored pine-log station, built in 1903, is among the oldest continually used forest service facilities in the nation. From the ranger station, this hike gains substantial elevation up the west flank of the main Boulder canyon, heading up to the scenic plateau between the main Boulder and West Boulder drainages. Near the top, the trail climbs over a saddle between Baker Mountain and Mount Rae to Burris Flat, where the open grasslands allow for expansive views. The path continues across the plateau to Nurses Lakes, a series of eleven shallow tarns, then descends into the West Boulder by the West Boulder Campground (Hike 93).

Driving directions: From I-90, there are two exits into the town of Big Timber—Exit 367 and Exit 370. (See map on page 216.) From Exit 367, drive one mile to McLeod Street (Highway 298). From Exit 370, drive 2.4 miles to McLeod Street (Highway 298). Turn south on McLeod Street, passing through downtown and over I-90.

Continuing south on Highway 298, drive 28.4 miles south into the Boulder River Valley to the historic Main Boulder Ranger Station on the right. (The first 26 miles of Highway 298 are paved.) The ranger station is 12.3 miles past the town of McLeod and 2.5 miles past the signed Natural Bridge turnoff. Turn right and drive 0.1 miles up the hill to the trailhead parking spaces. (Highway 298 is also called the Main Boulder Road.)

BOULDER VALLEY

Hiking directions: Walk past the trailhead sign and through the trail gate. Wind up the grassy, exposed slope with 360-degree vistas of the Boulder River Valley, Mount Rae, Baker Mountain, Teepee Mountain, Green Mountain, and Contact Mountain. Steadily climb while savoring the views. Enter an aspen grove, top a slope, and curve into a side canyon on the southern edge of Baker Mountain. Head through a pine forest and pass through another trail gate. Traverse the north-facing slope in the lush, shaded canyon. Cross a tributary of the Boulder River to an exposed east-facing slope with additional views of the Boulder Valley. Continue climbing to just under 7,000 feet, with new vistas across the West Boulder Valley at 3 miles. Descend the hill into Burris Flat, with a view of Mount Rae and the burn area from the 2006 Derby Fire. Pass through another gate to the floor of the grassland. Veer 50 yards to the right to a half-standing log cabin on the right. Bear left and stroll through the grasslands on the north side of Burris Flat. Cross over a stream to a signed junction at 4 miles. This is our turn-around spot.

To extend the hike, the Grouse Creek Trail continues 3 miles to the West Boulder Trailhead (Hike 93). From the turn-around point, bear right and walk 0.15 miles on the dirt road, leaving Burris Flat and overlooking Taylor Flat, to the signed Grouse Creek Trail on the left. Leave the road on the two-track trail, with a view of the first of the many Nurses Lakes on the right. Meander through the forest, passing a series of lakes, ponds, grassy wetlands, and a couple of cabins on the right (one with a grass-covered roof). Pass through a trail gate, re-entering the Gallatin National Forest. Stroll through aspen groves, open forest, and flower-filled meadows. A view into the West Boulder Valley includes Lion Mountain, Shell Mountain, Davis Creek Canyon, and the West Boulder Divide at 5.5 miles. From here, the trail descends 1.5 miles to the valley floor. Choose your own turn-around spot. ▪

93. Grouse Creek Trail
from the West Boulder (west trailhead)

NURSES LAKES and BURRIS FLAT

WEST BOULDER VALLEY

Hiking distance: 6 miles round trip
Hiking time: 3 hours
Elevation gain: 900 feet
Maps: U.S.G.S. Mount Rae
         Beartooth Publishing: Absaroka Beartooth Wilderness

Summary of hike: The Grouse Creek Trail is a 7-mile trail that connects the West Boulder River Valley to the main Boulder River Valley, leading over the plateau between the two drainages. Hike 92 begins from the main Boulder, while this hike begins from the West Boulder, the easier of the hikes up to the scenic plateau. The trail climbs up the east slope of the valley to Nurses Lakes, a series of 11 small (and fishless) lakes and ponds. After the grassy wetlands, the trail weaves past Taylor Flat and Burris Flat, crossing the 6,500-foot plateau before descending into the main Boulder Valley between Baker Mountain and Mount Rae.

Driving directions: From I-90, there are two exits into the town of Big Timber—Exit 367 and Exit 370. (See map on page 216.) From Exit 367, drive one mile to McLeod Street (Highway 298). From Exit 370, drive 2.4 miles to McLeod Street (Highway 298). Turn south on McLeod Street, passing through downtown and over I-90.

Continuing south on Highway 298, drive 16.7 miles south into the Boulder River Valley to the posted West Boulder Road on the right. The turnoff is located 0.6 miles past the town of McLeod. Turn right and continue 7.4 miles to a posted junction. Bear left, staying on West Boulder Road, and drive 6 miles to a Y-fork at the West Boulder Campground. Stay to the left and park 100 yards ahead in the large trailhead parking area.

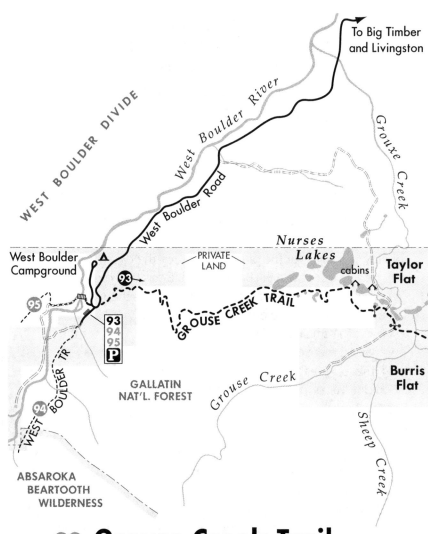

92. **Grouse Creek Trail from the Main Boulder**
MAIN BOULDER VALLEY

93. **Grouse Creek Trail from the West Boulder**
WEST BOULDER VALLEY

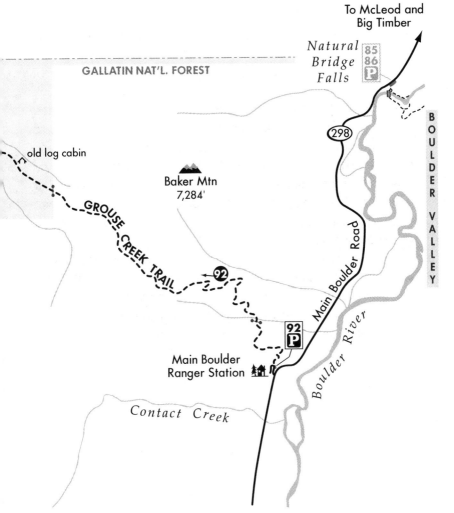

N

W   E

S

To McLeod and
Big Timber

Natural
Bridge
Falls

85
86
P

GALLATIN NAT'L. FOREST

old log cabin

298

GROUSE CREEK TRAIL

▲ Baker Mtn
7,284'

92

92
P

Main Boulder
Ranger Station

Main Boulder Road

Boulder River

B O U L D E R

V A L L E Y

Contact Creek

Hiking directions: Walk back down West Boulder Road to the Y-fork. Cross the cattle guard to the posted Grouse Creek Trail on the right. Bear right and head through the meadow to the hill. Curve left and climb the hill, weaving through the forest. At a quarter mile, enter the Gallatin National Forest. Continue up the east slope of the West Boulder Valley on an easy grade with the aid of four switchbacks. Pass through meadows and forest to the plateau, with views of Lion Mountain, Shell Mountain, Davis Creek Canyon, and the West Boulder Divide. At 1.4 miles, the trail levels out and strolls through aspen groves and flower-filled meadows. Gradually descend through the open forest, skirting the south side of the first of the Nurses Lakes at 1.8 miles. The shallow lake sits in a basin surrounded by a grassy rim. Continue past a series of lakes, ponds, grassy wetlands, and a couple of cabins on the left (one with a grass-covered roof). Pass through a trail gate, leaving the national forest and entering private land on a trail easement. Walk about 200 yards to a dirt road. Go to the right and follow the road, overlooking the expansive grassland of Taylor Flat on the left. Walk less than 0.2 miles on the road to a fence, a signed junction, and an overlook of Burris Flat, where the fire damage from the Derby Fire of 2006 can be seen. This is our turn-around spot. The trail continues 4 miles to the Main Boulder Ranger Station (Hike 92).

To extend the hike, bear left and walk along the north side of Burris Flat. Cross over a stream and curve right by a half-standing log cabin on the left. Climb the knoll to the trail sign by a gate. The trail climbs up and over the hill, dropping down into the Main Boulder drainage. Choose your own turn-around spot. ∎

94. West Boulder Trail to West Boulder Meadows
WEST BOULDER VALLEY

Hiking distance: 7 miles round trip
Hiking time: 3.5 hours
Elevation gain: 350 feet
Maps: U.S.G.S. Mount Rae
Beartooth Publishing: Absaroka Beartooth Wilderness

Summary of hike: The West Boulder River forms on the northeast slope of 11,212-foot Mount Cowen, the highest peak in the Absaroka Range, and the snowfields atop 10,620-foot Boulder Mountain. The West Boulder Trail, a portal into the Absaroka-Beartooth Wilderness, extends 16 miles up the glacially carved mountain valley, passing the river's headwaters and skirting the eastern base of Mount Cowen to Mill Creek Pass. This hike follows the first 3.5 miles of the trail to West Boulder Meadows. The vast mountain meadow sits at the eastern foot of 7,948-foot Lion Mountain. Rivulets of the river lace through the lush meadow grasses. The scenic trail follows the river at a gentle grade through meadows and intermittent forests of aspen and mixed pine. Throughout the hike are great views of the West Boulder River, the forested hillsides, and the surrounding snow-capped mountains.

Driving directions: From I-90, there are two exits into the town of Big Timber—Exit 367 and Exit 370. (See map on page 216.) From Exit 367, drive one mile to McLeod Street (Highway 298). From Exit 370, drive 2.4 miles to McLeod Street (Highway 298). Turn south on McLeod Street, passing through downtown and over I-90.

Continuing south on Highway 298, drive 16.7 miles south into the Boulder River Valley to the posted West Boulder Road on the right. The turnoff is located 0.6 miles past the town of McLeod.

Turn right and continue 7.4 miles to a posted junction. Bear left, staying on West Boulder Road, and drive 6 miles to a Y-fork at the West Boulder Campground. Stay to the left and park 100 yards ahead in the large trailhead parking area.

Hiking directions: From the far (south) end of the parking area, cross the cattle guard and walk 160 yards south on the dirt road. Leave the road and veer left on the signed West Boulder Trail. Climb the forested hillside, and pass a couple of small flower-covered meadows surrounded by mountains. Pass through a trail gate at 0.3 miles, and enter the Gallatin National Forest. Cross the hillside on the undulating path. Pass through the burn area from the Derby Fire of 2006. Enter the Absaroka-Beartooth Wilderness, and continue to the West Boulder River Bridge at one mile. Cross the wooden bridge over the river, and curve right a short distance downstream. Zigzag up three switchbacks and traverse the mountainside, passing a private entrance to the Burnt Leather Ranch. Head south high above the river, with a great vista up the West Boulder Canyon to Mount Cowen. At 1.8 miles, gradually descend to the north end of lush West Boulder Meadows. Side paths on the left lead down to the meandering river, and fishermen trails follow the river upstream. The West Boulder Trail follows the hillside between the grass-filled meadow and the steep east cliffs of Lion Mountain, pock-marked with caves. Stroll through the mountain meadow, dotted with boulders and a few skeleton trees from the fire. Drop down and cross a stream to a metal gate. Go through the gate, top a small rise, and descend to cascading Basin Creek. This is our turn-around spot.

To extend the hike, rock-hop over the creek and continue through the meadow. Parallel the west side of the river, reaching a junction with the Falls Creek Trail at 7.8 miles. Another 2.6 miles past Falls Creek is Beaver Meadows. ▪

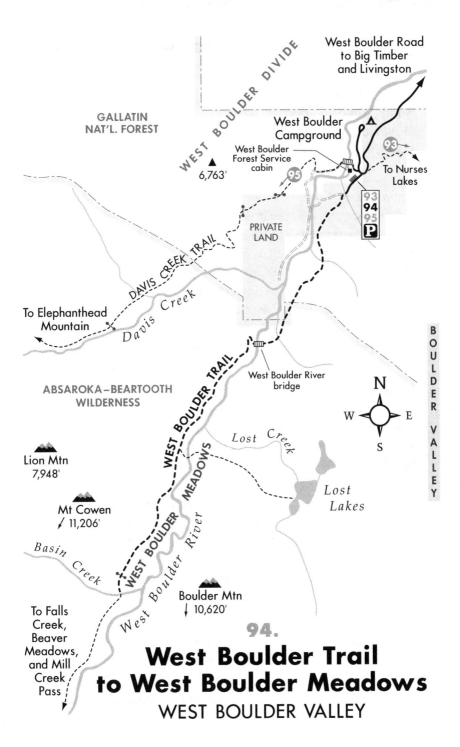

West Boulder Road
to Big Timber
and Livingston

GALLATIN
NAT'L. FOREST

WEST BOULDER DIVIDE

West Boulder
Campground

West Boulder
Forest Service
cabin

95

93

To Nurses
Lakes

▲ 6,763'

PRIVATE
LAND

93
94
95
P

DAVIS CREEK TRAIL

To Elephanthead
Mountain

Davis Creek

Davis Creek

WEST BOULDER TRAIL

West Boulder River
bridge

ABSAROKA–BEARTOOTH
WILDERNESS

Lost Creek

N
W E
S

B O U L D E R   V A L L E Y

Lion Mtn
7,948'

WEST BOULDER MEADOWS

Lost
Lakes

Mt Cowen
⤢ 11,206'

Basin Creek

WEST BOULDER TRAIL

West Boulder River

Boulder Mtn
⤢ 10,620'

To Falls
Creek,
Beaver
Meadows,
and Mill
Creek
Pass

94.

West Boulder Trail
to West Boulder Meadows
WEST BOULDER VALLEY

95. Davis Creek Trail to Blacktail Creek
WEST BOULDER VALLEY

Hiking distance: 10 miles round trip
Hiking time: 6 hours
Elevation gain: 1,000 feet
Maps: U.S.G.S. Mount Rae and Livingston Peak
         Beartooth Publishing: Absaroka Beartooth Wilderness

Summary of hike: The Davis Creek Trail heads west out of the West Boulder Valley towards Elephanthead Mountain and Mount Delano, connecting with trails to Paradise Valley, the next valley to the west. The trail begins from the West Boulder Campground, crosses Davis Creek on a footbridge, then parallels the west side of the wide creek below Shell Mountain and Lyon Mountain for 10 miles to the Deep Creek Divide. This hike follows the first five miles of the trail to Blacktail Creek at its confluence with Davis Creek. The remote path weaves through intermittent timber, open meadows, and a quarter mile of private ranch land.

Driving directions: From I-90, there are two exits into the town of Big Timber—Exit 367 and Exit 370. (See map on page 216.) From Exit 367, drive one mile to McLeod Street (Highway 298). From Exit 370, drive 2.4 miles to McLeod Street (Highway 298). Turn south on McLeod Street, passing through downtown and over I-90.

Continuing south on Highway 298, drive 16.7 miles south into the Boulder River Valley to the posted West Boulder Road on the right. The turnoff is located 0.6 miles past the town of McLeod. Turn right and continue 7.4 miles to a posted junction. Bear left, staying on West Boulder Road, and drive 6 miles to a Y-fork at the West Boulder Campground. Stay to the left and park 100 yards ahead in the large trailhead parking area.

Hiking directions: Walk 100 yards back to the campground road fork. Veer left 50 yards into the camp to another fork. Stay left and pass through the gate by the West Boulder forest service cabin. Curve right, passing the rental cabin to Davis

Creek. Cross the Davis Creek Bridge and bear left past the trail sign. Head west, traversing the grassy hillside above and parallel to the scenic creek. Bear right, leaving the old road, and head up the hill. About 50 yards ahead, make a horseshoe left bend and continue traversing the hill to what appears as the end of the trail by tall brush. Switchback to the right and follow the mountain slope above the Burnt Leather Ranch, with far-reaching vistas into the West Boulder Valley. Pass a trail gate and enter a quarter-mile easement through the ranch land. Pass through another gate, returning to the national forest.

Stroll through the forest at an easy grade, staying on the Davis Creek Trail past a couple of signed forks. Cross the gently rolling terrain, skirting the base of Shell Mountain, to Crystal Creek at 2 miles. Cross the small stream to an overlook of the tumbling waters of Davis Creek. Pass through another gate to the edge of Davis Creek. Follow the creek upstream a short distance, and enter a lodgepole pine forest. Meander through the dense forest for nearly a mile. Cross a small meadow, with a view of Shell Mountain to the northwest and Lyon Mountain across Davis Creek. Descend and rock hop over an unnamed stream, then drop into a large meadow under the shadow of Mount Delano. Reenter the forest to Canyon Creek at 4 miles. Cross the creek on rocks and continue one mile west to Blacktail Creek. This is our turn-around spot.

To extend the hike, cross the creek to a signed junction. The Davis Creek Trail continues to the left and heads southwest. The trail parallels Davis Creek for 3.7 miles to the 9,112-foot Deep Creek Divide, connecting with the South Fork Deep Creek Trail and Paradise Valley (Hike 101). The Blacktail Creek Trail bears right, leading 2.5 miles to Blacktail Lake and 2.8 miles to Elephanthead Mountain (Hike 96). ▓

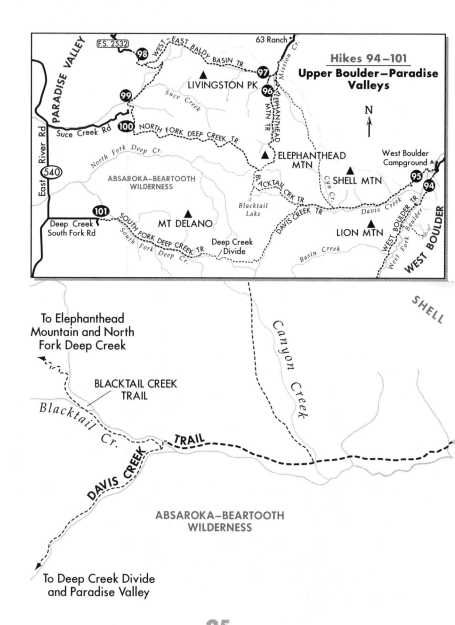

PARADISE VALLEY

F.S. 2532

98

WEST–EAST BALDY BASIN TR

63 Ranch

Mission Cr.

97

LIVINGSTON PK

96

Suce Creek

99

ELEPHANTHEAD MTN TR

N

Suce Creek Rd

100

NORTH FORK DEEP CREEK TR

East River Rd

540

North Fork Deep Cr.

ELEPHANTHEAD MTN

West Boulder Campground

ABSAROKA–BEARTOOTH WILDERNESS

BLACKTAIL CRK TR

Cyn Cr.

SHELL MTN

95

94

Blacktail Lake

DAVIS CREEK TR

Davis Creek

WEST BOULDER TR

West Fork Boulder

101

SOUTH FORK DEEP CREEK TR

MT DELANO

Deep Creek Divide

LION MTN

Basin Creek

WEST BOULDER

Deep Creek South Fork Rd

South Fork Deep Cr.

SHELL

To Elephanthead
Mountain and North
Fork Deep Creek

**BLACKTAIL CREEK
TRAIL**

Blacktail Cr.

Canyon Creek

TRAIL

DAVIS CREEK

ABSAROKA–BEARTOOTH
WILDERNESS

To Deep Creek Divide
and Paradise Valley

95.
Davis Creek Trail
to Blacktail Creek
WEST BOULDER VALLEY

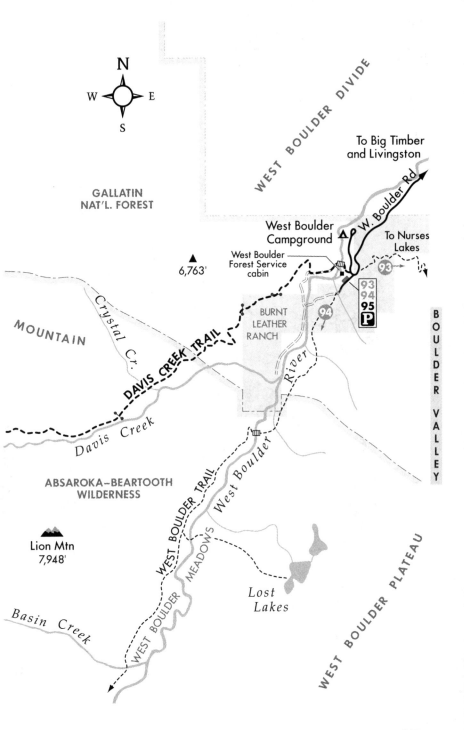

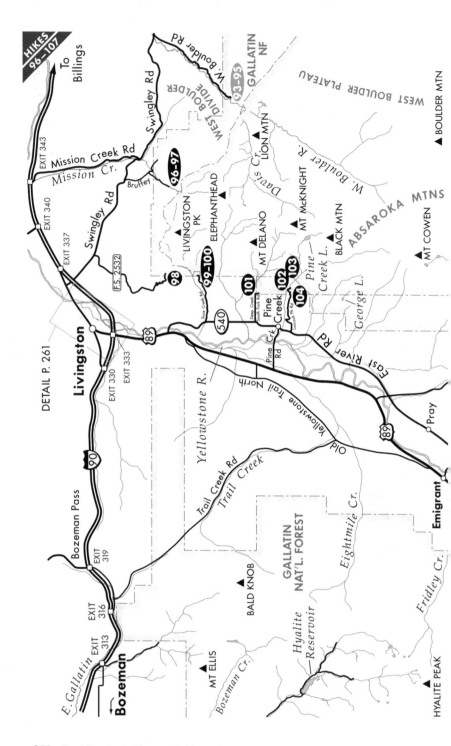

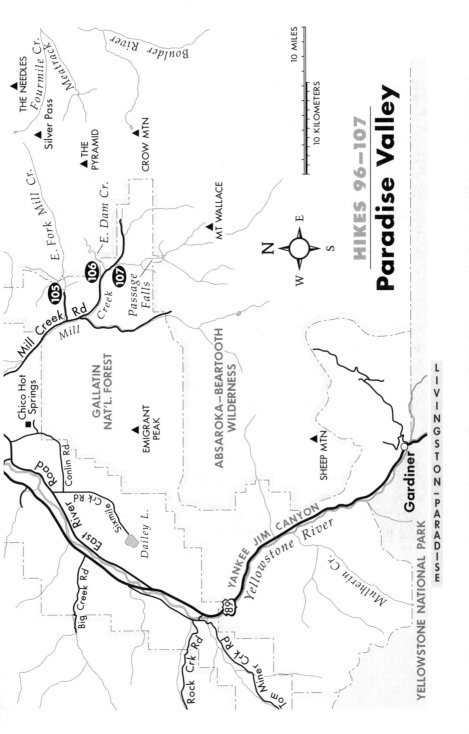

THE NEEDLES

Fourmile Cr.

Meatrack

Silver Pass

Boulder River

▲ THE PYRAMID

CROW MTN

E. Fork Mill Cr.

E. Dam Cr.

▲ MT WALLACE

N

W ——○—— E

S

10 MILES

10 KILOMETERS

Mill Creek Rd

105

106

107

Mill Creek

Passage Falls

Chico Hot Springs

GALLATIN NAT'L. FOREST

ABSAROKA–BEARTOOTH WILDERNESS

EMIGRANT PEAK

Conlin Rd

Road

East River

Sixmile Crk Rd

Dailey L.

Big Creek Rd

SHEEP MTN

YANKEE JIM CANYON

Yellowstone River

89

Rock Crk Rd

Tom Miner Crk Rd

Mulherin Cr.

Gardiner

YELLOWSTONE NATIONAL PARK

LIVINGSTON–PARADISE

Paradise Valley

HIKES 96–107

Paradise Valley is known as the Valley of the Yellowstone River. The river flows through the valley from the north end of Yellowstone National Park to Livingston. It is a wide, scenic valley bordered on the east by the steep, craggy Absaroka Range and on the west by the Gallatin Range.

Highway 89 follows the course of the river through the broad valley, connecting Livingston with Gardiner and Yellowstone Park. Livingston sits at the head of the verdant valley in the north. The town of Gardiner is located at the other end of the valley by the northern entrance to Yellowstone Park. It is the only approach into the park that is open all year.

These hikes are located on the east side of Paradise Valley in the 930,584-acre Absaroka-Beartooth Wilderness, the second largest wilderness area in Montana. The Absaroka Range and the Beartooth Range run through the wilderness. The area is known for heavily wooded slopes and high ridge-top meadows. The Absarokas and the Beartooths stretch southward into Yellowstone, forming an integral part of the park's ecosystem.

The hikes begin from the major trailheads on the east side of the Yellowstone River along the wilderness boundary. The trails travel through steep, forested valleys amongst the craggy peaks of the Absaroka Range. The trails continue over the plateaus and peaks into the Boulder Valley, the next drainage to the east. Mill Creek (Hikes 105–107) is a major corridor that extends deep into the Absaroka-Beartooth Wilderness.

For many more miles of backcountry hiking, the hikes from Paradise Valley access a vast network of trails in the Absaroka-Beartooth Wilderness, the Gallatins, and Yellowstone Park.

N
E
W
S

1/2 MILE
1 KILOMETER

To I-90 via
Exit 337

To
Billings

GARNIER AVE ST

CHESTNUT

89
10

BENNETT ST

O ST
N ST
M ST
L ST
K ST
I ST
H ST
G ST
F ST
E ST
D ST
C ST
B ST

SUMMIT ST
MONTANA ST
GALLATIN ST
K ST
PARK ST
CALLENDAR ST

RESERVOIR ST

C ST
MAIN ST
2ND ST
3RD ST
YELLOW ST.

LEWIS ST
CLARK ST
GEYSER ST

VIEW VISTA RD

Yellowstone River

FRONT ST
CHINOOK ST

5TH ST
6TH ST
7TH ST
8TH ST
9TH ST

9TH ST
10TH ST
11TH ST
12TH ST
13TH ST
14TH ST

STAR RD

GLOBE ST

CRAWFORD AVE
CAMBRIDGE
CLARENCE

LIVINGSTON-PARADISE

I-90

To I-90 via
Exit 330

10

89

EXIT
333

ranger
station

POINTS of INTEREST
❶ CHAMBER of COMMERCE
❷ DOWNTOWN AREA
❸ PARK COUNTY MUSEUM
❹ LIVINGSTON MEM. HOSPITAL
❺ MILES PARK
❻ SACAJAWEA PARK
❼ MARS PARK
❽ GREEN ACRES PARK
❾ PARK CTY. FAIRGROUNDS

90

To
Bozeman

Billman Creek

89

To Gardiner
and Yellowstone
Nat'l. Park

Livingston

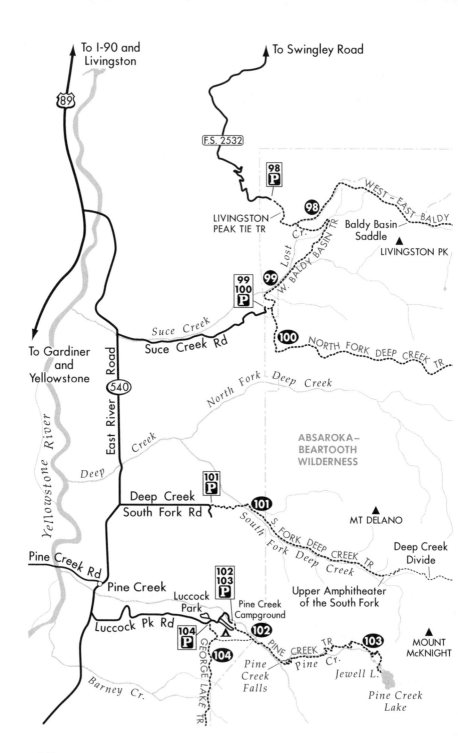

To I-90 and
Livingston

To Swingley Road

89

F.S. 2532

98
P

98

WEST–EAST BALDY

LIVINGSTON
PEAK TIE TR

Lost Cr.

Baldy Basin
Saddle

LIVINGSTON PK

99
100
P

99

W. BALDY BASIN TR

100

NORTH FORK DEEP CREEK TR

Suce Creek

Suce Creek Rd

To Gardiner
and
Yellowstone

East River Road

540

North Fork Deep Creek

Yellowstone River

Deep Creek

ABSAROKA–
BEARTOOTH
WILDERNESS

101
P

Deep Creek
South Fork Rd

101

S. FORK DEEP CREEK TR

MT DELANO

South Fork Deep Creek

Deep Creek
Divide

Pine Creek Rd

Pine Creek

Luccock
Park

102
103
P

Pine Creek
Campground

Upper Amphitheater
of the South Fork

Luccock Pk Rd

104
P

102

PINE CREEK TR

103

MOUNT
McKNIGHT

GEORGE LAKE TR

104

Pine
Creek
Falls

Pine Cr.

Pine Cr.

Jewell L.

Pine Creek
Lake

Barney Cr.

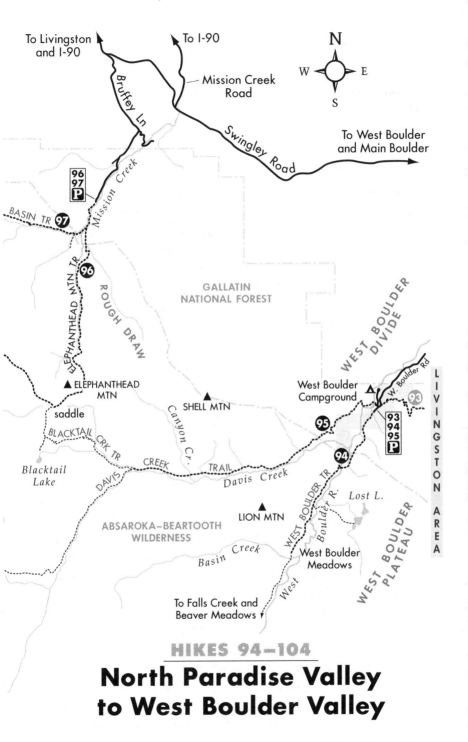

To Livingston
and I-90

To I-90

Mission Creek
Road

Bruffey Ln

N

W ✦ E

S

Swingley Road

To West Boulder
and Main Boulder

96
97
P

BASIN TR 97

Mission Creek

ELEPHANTHEAD MTN TR

96

ROUGH DRAW

GALLATIN
NATIONAL FOREST

WEST BOULDER DIVIDE

West Boulder
Campground

W. Boulder Rd

93

▲ ELEPHANTHEAD
MTN

SHELL MTN

95

93
94
95
P

LIVINGSTON AREA

saddle

BLACKTAIL CRK TR

Canyon Cr.

CREEK

TRAIL

94

Blacktail
Lake

DAVIS

Davis Creek

WEST BOULDER TR

Boulder R.

Lost L.

WEST BOULDER PLATEAU

ABSAROKA–BEARTOOTH
WILDERNESS

▲ LION MTN

Basin Creek

West Boulder
Meadows

West

Boulder

To Falls Creek and
Beaver Meadows

HIKES 94–104
North Paradise Valley
to West Boulder Valley

96. Elephanthead Mountain Trail
LIVINGSTON AREA

Hiking distance: 7.5 miles round trip
Hiking time: 4.5 hours
Elevation gain: 3,200 feet
Maps: U.S.G.S. Livingston Peak
Beartooth Publishing: Absaroka Beartooth Wilderness

Summary of hike: Elephanthead Mountain, in the Absaroka-Beartooth Wilderness, rises along the northern edge of the Absaroka Range on the outskirts of Livingston. The sheer limestone cliffs at the southern head of the mountain are dramatic. There are several accesses to Elephanthead Mountain. This trail strenuously climbs along the eastern base of the mountain beneath the limestone walls. It follows the watercourse of Mission Creek from the mouth of the canyon to a saddle past its headwaters. (Mission Creek was the infamous location where John Bozeman was killed by the Blackfoot Indians.) En route, the trail passes through dense forest, grassy streamside meadows, and expansive alpine tundra with scenic panoramas in every direction. From the 8,900-foot ridge at the head of the canyon are views into Canyon Creek Canyon, Blacktail Creek Canyon, and across three layers of ridges and plateaus in the Boulder River Canyon. The views are worth the steep climb.

Driving directions: From I-90, there are three exits into the town of Livingston—Exit 330, Exit 333, and Exit 337. From Exit 333, drive 3.9 miles northeast on Park Street (Highway 89) through downtown Livingston to Swingley Road on the right. From Exit 337, on the east edge of Livingston, drive 1.3 miles west towards downtown to Swingley Road on the left.

Turn south on Swingley Road, and continue 7 miles to signed Bruffey Lane on the right. Turn right and go 1.7 miles to the 63 Ranch entrance on the right. Turn right, entering the private ranch land on a forest service easement. (Stay strictly on the road, as the land is private.) Drive 0.6 miles to a signed road fork just before reaching the ranch house. Veer left on the narrow road for one mile—following the national forest access sign—to

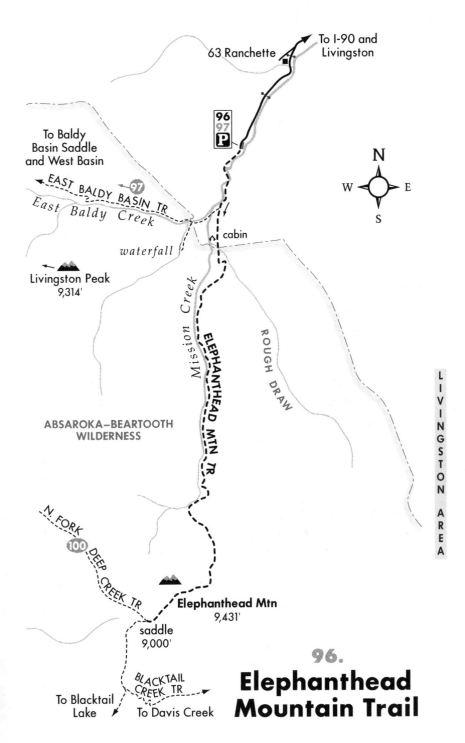

To I-90 and
Livingston

63 Ranchette

To Baldy
Basin Saddle
and West Basin

EAST BALDY BASIN TR

East Baldy Creek

waterfall

cabin

Livingston Peak
9,314'

Mission Creek

ELEPHANTHEAD MTN TR

ROUGH DRAW

ABSAROKA–BEARTOOTH
WILDERNESS

N. FORK DEEP CREEK TR

Elephanthead Mtn
9,431'

saddle
9,000'

BLACKTAIL CREEK TR

To Blacktail
Lake

To Davis Creek

N
W · E
S

LIVINGSTON AREA

96.
Elephanthead
Mountain Trail

the trailhead parking area at the end of the road. En route, pass through forest service gates at 0.1 mile and 0.4 miles.

Hiking directions: Walk past the trailhead kiosk, and head south into the forest. Follow the west side of Mission Creek on a gentle uphill grade. At 0.3 miles, rock-hop over Mission Creek to a Y-fork marked with a cairn. The right fork crosses Mission Creek and climbs up East Baldy Basin (Hike 97). Stay on the Elephanthead Mountain Trail, and pass an old cabin. Enter the Absaroka–Beartooth Wilderness at 0.9 miles, and cross Rough Draw Creek. Weave up the lush drainage, with periodic views of Livingston Peak to the west, Shell Mountain to the east, and Elephanthead Mountain to the south. Traverse the east wall of Mission Creek Canyon high above the creek. Pass through the burn area from the Rough Draw Fire and a sloping, wildflower-filled meadow with skeleton trees. In August, this stretch is abundant with thimbleberries, huckleberries, elderberries, and raspberries. Cross a small tributary stream and a talus field. Zigzag up the hillside, following the cascading creek. The view down canyon spans across Shields Valley to the Crazy Mountains. Enter a pine forest and keep ascending the canyon to a grassy knoll surrounded by mountains. Meander through a tree-rimmed meadow with large granite outcrops. Climb up the open tundra landscape, following cairns to the 9,040-foot saddle at the head of the canyon and the vertical rock cliffs. This is our turn-around spot.

To extend the hike, bear right and follow the edge of the steep cliffs and dolomite boulders, with awesome views of the world-class topography. Skirt the southern rock-face of Elephanthead Mountain, and traverse the steep slope on a downhill grade. When the trail fades, cairns mark the route. Ascend the hill to a 9,000-foot grassy saddle, and descend to a signed junction. The left fork heads 0.9 miles downhill to Blacktail Lake, a 4-acre lake surrounded by timber. To the east, the trail connects to the Davis Creek Trail and the West Boulder drainage (Hike 95). The North Fork Deep Creek Trail (Hike 100) goes to the right (east) and follows the rim of the creek-fed canyon 5.5 miles to Paradise Valley. ■

97. East Baldy Basin Trail
from the Elephanthead Mountain Trailhead
LIVINGSTON AREA

Hiking distance: 7 miles round trip
Hiking time: 4 hours
Elevation gain: 2,550 feet
Maps: U.S.G.S. Livingston Peak
      Beartooth Publishing: Absaroka Beartooth Wilderness

Summary of hike: Baldy Basin is a narrow stream-fed canyon along the northern base of Livingston Peak in the Absaroka Range. At the head of the basin is Baldy Basin Saddle, lying a thousand feet below Livingston Peak at an elevation of 8,300 feet. The alpine saddle divides West Baldy Basin from East Baldy Basin. Hikes 97 and 98 climb up to the saddle from opposite directions. This hike begins at the eastern trailhead from the Elephanthead Mountain Trail in the Mission Creek drainage. The trail follows Mission Creek a short distance, then veers west into East Baldy Basin, entering the Absaroka-Beartooth Wilderness. The hike passes a waterfall and weaves through wildflower-covered meadows, steadily climbing towards the saddle. From the summit are sweeping vistas of Livingston Peak, Elephanthead Mountain, Shell Mountain, and the West Boulder Divide.

Driving directions: From I-90, there are three exits into the town of Livingston—Exit 330, Exit 333, and Exit 337. From Exit 333, drive 3.9 miles northeast on Park Street (Highway 89) through downtown Livingston to Swingley Road on the right. From Exit 337, on the east edge of Livingston, drive 1.3 miles west towards downtown to Swingley Road on the left.

    Turn south on Swingley Road, and continue 7 miles to signed Bruffey Lane on the right. Turn right and go 1.7 miles to the 63 Ranch entrance on the right. Turn right, entering the private ranch land on a forest service easement. (Stay strictly on the road, as the land is private.) Drive 0.6 miles to a signed road fork just before reaching the ranch house. Veer left on the narrow road for one mile—following the national forest access sign—to the trailhead parking area at the end of the road. En route, pass through forest service gates at 0.1 mile and 0.4 miles.

Hiking directions: Walk past the trailhead kiosk, and head south into the forest on the Elephanthead Mountain Trail. Follow the west side of Mission Creek on a gentle uphill grade. At 0.3 miles, rock-hop over Mission Creek to a Y-fork marked with a cairn. The left fork, straight ahead, continues up to the head of the canyon and the southern base of Elephanthead Mountain (Hike 96). Veer right on the East Baldy Basin Trail, and rock-hop back over Mission Creek to the Absaroka-Beartooth Wilderness and a trail split at East Baldy Creek. Detour left on an unnamed path, and follow a tributary stream 0.2 miles to a beautiful 100-foot cascading waterfall.

Return to the junction and cross East Baldy Creek. Follow the north edge of the creek for nearly a quarter mile, then ascend the hillside, climbing high above the creek. The trail is fairly easy to follow, but may be overgrown with vegetation. Pass through a small flower-filled meadow, and climb up two switchbacks. Continue west, weaving across the hillside on the north flank of the canyon. Cross through another meadow, with a view of Livingston Peak, and return to the forest. Pass a couple of 3-foot cairns, and cross East Baldy Creek two times near its headwaters. Steeply climb to a 4-foot cairn on the edge of a boulder field and a view of the saddle that separates the East and West Baldy drainages. Walk through a log fence and make the final steep ascent, passing three tall cairns to the Baldy Basin Saddle at 8,300 feet, just below Livingston Peak. This is our turn-around spot.

To extend the hike, the West Baldy Basin Trail continues downhill along West Baldy Creek. The trail follows the north rim of Lost Creek Canyon to the Livingston Peak Trailhead to the west (Hike 98) and the Suce Creek Trailhead in Paradise Valley to the south (Hike 99). ▪

98. West Baldy Basin Trail
from the Livingston Peak Trailhead
LIVINGSTON AREA

Hiking distance: 6.4 miles round trip
Hiking time: 3.5 hours
Elevation gain: 2,100 feet
Maps: U.S.G.S. Brisbin and Livingston Peak
      Beartooth Publishing: Absaroka Beartooth Wilderness

Summary of hike: Baldy Basin is a narrow stream-fed canyon along the northern base of Livingston Peak in the Absaroka Range. At the head of the basin is Baldy Basin Saddle, lying a thousand feet below Livingston Peak at an elevation of 8,300 feet. The alpine saddle divides West Baldy Basin from East Baldy Basin. Hikes 97 and 98 climb up to the saddle from opposite directions. This hike begins from the western end at the upper Livingston Peak Trailhead in Paradise Valley. The trail enters the Absaroka-Beartooth Wilderness (via the Livingston Peak Tie Trail), overlooking Lost Creek Canyon, Suce Creek Canyon, Paradise Valley, and the Gallatin Range. The steep path traverses weather-carved cliffs, passes through lush meadows, and tops out on Baldy Basin Saddle. The sweeping vistas include Livingston Peak, Elephanthead Mountain, Shell Mountain, and the West Boulder Divide.

Driving directions: From I-90, there are three exits into the town of Livingston—Exit 330, Exit 333, and Exit 337. From Exit 333, drive 3.9 miles northeast on Park Street (Highway 89) through downtown Livingston to Swingley Road on the right. From Exit 337, on the east edge of Livingston, drive 1.3 miles west towards downtown to Swingley Road on the left.

Turn south on Swingley Road, and continue 2.3 miles to the signed Forest Service Road 2532 on the right. Turn right on the dirt road, and go 0.7 miles to a fork. Veer left, staying on Forest Service Road 2532. Drive 6.6 miles, winding up the mountain road to the signed Livingston Peak Trailhead at the end of the road.

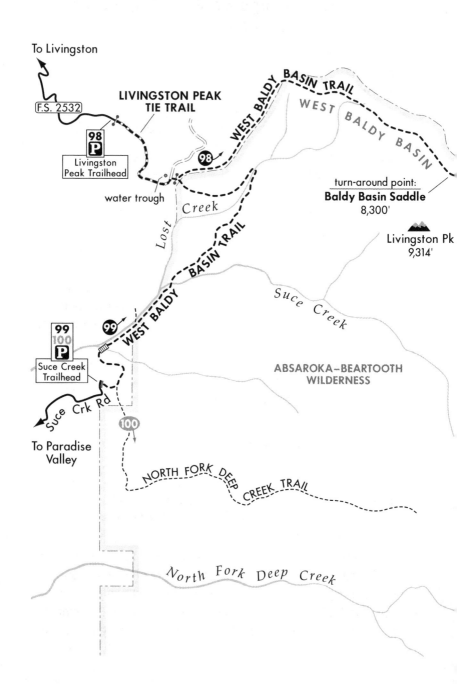

To Livingston

F.S. 2532

LIVINGSTON PEAK TIE TRAIL

WEST BALDY BASIN TRAIL

WEST BALDY BASIN

98
P
Livingston
Peak Trailhead

98

water trough

Lost Creek

turn-around point:
Baldy Basin Saddle
8,300'

Livingston Pk
9,314'

WEST BALDY BASIN TRAIL

Suce Creek

99
100
P
Suce Creek
Trailhead

99

WEST BALDY

ABSAROKA–BEARTOOTH
WILDERNESS

Suce Crk Rd

100

To Paradise
Valley

NORTH FORK DEEP CREEK TRAIL

North Fork Deep Creek

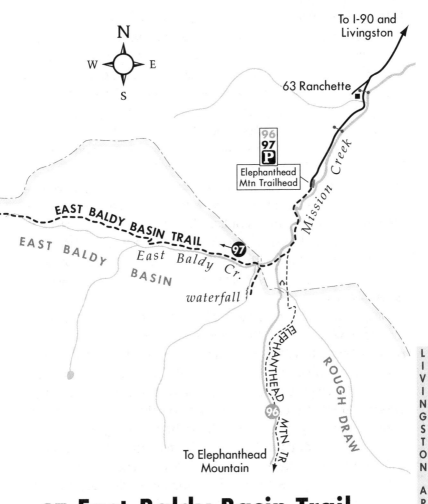

97. **East Baldy Basin Trail**
from Elephanthead Mountain Trailhead

98. **West Baldy Basin Trail**
from Livingston Peak Trailhead

99. **West Baldy Basin Trail**
from Suce Creek Trailhead
PARADISE VALLEY

Hiking directions: Walk past the trail gate on the Livingston Peak Tie Trail, a 2-track dirt road. Follow the road through the open pine forest. Make a wide U-bend to the left, with a straight-on view of pyramid-shaped Livingston Peak. At the far end of the bend is a horse watering trough and a trail sign at a half mile. Bear right on the footpath and go 80 yards to a gate, located at a junction with the West Baldy Basin Trail and the Absaroka-Beartooth Wilderness on a ridge overlooking Suce Creek Canyon. The right fork—Hike 99—descends 3 miles to the Suce Creek Trailhead in Paradise Valley. Bear left on the West Baldy Basin Trail, skirting the outside edge of the wilderness. Climb at a moderate grade to the north rim of Lost Creek Canyon. The trail levels out and follows the lip of the forested canyon. Livingston Peak looms close by, along with vistas across Lost Creek Canyon, Suce Creek Canyon, and far-reaching views of Paradise Valley and the Gallatin Range.

Drop down and cross a tributary stream in a flower-filled meadow. Walk through the tree-rimmed meadow on the north flank of Livingston Peak. Begin a steep ascent through the open forest. Cross a saddle into West Baldy Basin, and traverse the basin cliffs. Climb to the head of the basin beneath the craggy, weather-sculpted cliffs. Cross and parallel the rock-strewn drainage at a very steep grade. Cross the stream again, and climb to the 8,300-foot Baldy Basin Saddle, marked with two cairns.

To extend the hike, the East Baldy Basin Trail continues downhill, parallel to East Baldy Creek to the Elephanthead Mountain trailhead (Hike 97). ▪

99. West Baldy Basin Trail from the Suce Creek Trailhead
PARADISE VALLEY

Hiking distance: 6 miles round trip
Hiking time: 3 hours
Elevation gain: 900 feet
Maps: U.S.G.S. Brisbon and Livingston Peak
  Beartooth Publishing: Absaroka Beartooth Wilderness

Summary of hike: Baldy Basin is a narrow stream-fed canyon along the northern base of Livingston Peak in the Absaroka Range. At the head of the basin is Baldy Basin Saddle, lying a thousand feet below Livingston Peak at an elevation of 8,300 feet. The alpine saddle divides West Baldy Basin from East Baldy Basin.

Baldy Basin Saddle is accessed from three trailheads. Hikes 97 and 98 climb up to the saddle from opposite directions in the Baldy Basin Canyon. The third route up to the saddle—this hike—begins from the Suce Creek Trailhead in Paradise Valley. The hike follows the beginning of the West Baldy Basin Trail for 3 miles to the upper trailhead. The trail parallels and crosses both Suce Creek and Lost Creek in the Absaroka-Beartooth Wilderness. En route are beautiful views of the Gallatin Range and Paradise Valley. After the junction to the upper trailhead, the hike may be continued 2.7 miles up to the Baldy Basin Saddle (Hike 98).

Driving directions: From Livingston at the I-90 and Highway 89 junction (Exit 333), drive 3.1 miles south on Highway 89 to East River Road (Highway 540). Turn left and drive 2.7 miles to Suce Creek Road on the left. Turn left and continue 3 miles—following the trailhead signs—to the Suce Creek Trailhead at the end of the road. Park in the spaces on the right.

Hiking directions: Pass the trailhead kiosk, and veer to the right up the meadow. Enter the shade of the forest to a posted junction at a quarter mile. The North Fork Deep Creek Trail—Hike 100—heads south and leads to Elephanthead Mountain. For this hike, continue straight on the left fork on the West Baldy Basin Trail. Descend into a large meadow with a picture-perfect view of the Gallatin Mountains. Cross a single-log bridge over a tributary of Suce Creek. Veer right and parallel Suce Creek upstream to a trail split at the creek. Stay on the main (right) fork and ascend the slope. Pass through a meadow, returning to Suce Creek. At just over one mile, wade across the creek or use downfall logs. Gently gain elevation through the forest to Lost Creek. Parallel Lost Creek 0.3 miles and cross over it. Switchback to the left and traverse the north slope of the canyon, with views down Suce Creek Canyon. At 3 miles, the trail levels out at a posted junction on a ridge with sweeping vistas.

The Livingston Peak Tie Trail descends to the left for a half mile to the Livingston Peak Trailhead (Hike 98). Continue with Hike 98 to extend the hike on the West Baldy Basin Trail to the saddle on the divide between West and East Baldy Basins. ▪

100. North Fork Deep Creek Trail to Elephanthead Mountain
PARADISE VALLEY

Hiking distance: 11 miles round trip
Hiking time: 6 hours
Elevation gain: 3,400 feet
Maps: U.S.G.S. Brisbon and Livingston Peak
  Beartooth Publishing: Absaroka Beartooth Wilderness

Summary of hike: The North Fork Deep Creek Trail begins from the Suce Creek Trailhead in Paradise Valley. The trail follows the north rim of the forested, creek-fed canyon to the head of Elephanthead Mountain and its dramatic rock cliffs at the edge of the open tundra. The strenuous route never comes near the creek, but it leads to spectacular backcountry. The trail heads into the Absaroka-Beartooth Wilderness through mixed forests and flower-laden meadows, traveling eastward to overlooks of the weather-sculpted rock formations, the surrounding mountain peaks, and the expansive valleys. Just south of Elephanthead Mountain is Blacktail Lake, with a connecting trail to Davis Creek and the West Boulder drainage.

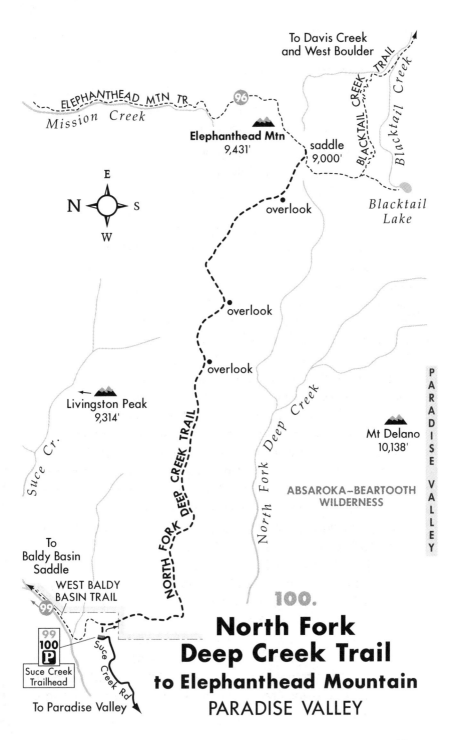

To Davis Creek
and West Boulder

ELEPHANTHEAD MTN TR

Mission Creek

96

BLACKTAIL CREEK TRAIL

Blacktail Creek

Elephanthead Mtn
9,431'

saddle
9,000'

overlook

Blacktail Lake

N — E — S — W

overlook

overlook

NORTH FORK DEEP CREEK TRAIL

Livingston Peak
9,314'

Suce Cr.

North Fork Deep Creek

Mt Delano
10,138'

P
A
R
A
D
I
S
E

V
A
L
L
E
Y

**ABSAROKA–BEARTOOTH
WILDERNESS**

To
Baldy Basin
Saddle

**WEST BALDY
BASIN TRAIL**

99

99
100
P
Suce Creek
Trailhead

Suce Creek Rd

To Paradise Valley

100.

North Fork
Deep Creek Trail
to Elephanthead Mountain
PARADISE VALLEY

Driving directions: From Livingston at the I-90 and Highway 89 junction (Exit 333), drive 3.1 miles south on Highway 89 to East River Road (Highway 540). Turn left and drive 2.7 miles to Suce Creek Road on the left. Turn left and continue 3 miles—following the trailhead signs—to the Suce Creek Trailhead at the end of the road. Park in the spaces on the right.

Hiking directions: Pass the trailhead kiosk, and veer to the right up the meadow. Enter the forest to a posted junction at a quarter mile. The West Baldy Basin Trail continues straight (Hike 99). Take the right fork on the North Fork Deep Creek Trail and head south. Enter the Absaroka-Beartooth Wilderness, and climb to the north rim of the forested North Fork Deep Creek Canyon at one mile. Curve left and follow the ridge east, steadily climbing through a lodgepole pine forest. Stroll through the dense forest as the steep grade temporarily eases up. Continue up to a tree-obscured overlook into the Blacktail Creek drainage at 2.5 miles. Descend through a meadow while enjoying a grand view of Elephanthead Mountain and its tilted rock cliffs. Continue downhill through a mix of forest and meadows, then climb again to an overlook beneath jagged, weather-sculpted formations. The views extend to a cirque of mountain peaks, from Mount Delano on the south horizon to Lyon Mountain in the West Boulder drainage.

Cross a trickling branch of the North Fork Deep Creek in a meadow. Follow the easy rolling terrain to another overlook of Elephanthead Mountain. Drop down and cross the open, tree-dotted expanse. Make the final ascent and top the ridge to the open tundra and a posted junction. The right fork leads 0.9 miles down to Blacktail Lake, a 4-acre lake surrounded by timber. The left fork climbs 100 yards to the 9,000-foot saddle overlooking the rock face of Elephanthead Mountain, Canyon Creek Canyon, Blacktail Creek Canyon, and three layers of ridges and plateaus in the Boulder Canyon drainage. This is our turn-around spot.

To extend the hike, follow the cairns across the head of Blacktail Creek Canyon. Traverse the rocky north canyon wall, steadily climbing to the southern base of Elephanthead Mountain to the top of Mission Creek Canyon (Hike 96), located a half mile from the saddle. ∎

101. South Fork Deep Creek Trail
PARADISE VALLEY

Hiking distance: 8 miles round trip to cirque
10 miles round trip to Deep Creek Divide
Hiking time: 4 to 6 hours
Elevation gain: 2,150 (to cirque)
3,570 feet (to divide)
Maps: U.S.G.S. Brisbin and Livingston Peak
Beartooth Publishing: Absaroka Beartooth Wilderness

Summary of hike: The South Fork Deep Creek Trail follows a narrow, stream-fed canyon to the Deep Creek Divide, a pass between Paradise Valley and the West Boulder drainage. This remote, backcountry hike in the Absaroka-Beartooth Wilderness leads through the deep canyon between Mount Delano and Mount McKnight. After dropping down to the canyon floor, the path crosses and follows the South Fork Deep Creek to the Amphitheater of the South Fork, a spectacular mountain cirque. Beyond the cirque, the trail climbs up the steep valley wall to the Deep Creek Divide, where you are rewarded with spectacular views from high above Deep Creek.

Driving directions: From Livingston at the I-90 and Highway 89 junction (Exit 333), drive 3.1 miles south on Highway 89 to East River Road (Highway 540). Turn left and drive 5.5 miles south to Deep Creek South Fork Road on the left. Turn left and continue 1.6 miles to the signed trailhead. Park in the spaces on the left.

Hiking directions: From the trailhead are sweeping views across Paradise Valley and the Yellowstone River to the Gallatin Range. After enjoying the views, go through the trailhead gate and head east up the grassy slope. Pass through another gate at 0.3 miles and continue ascending, gaining 500 feet to the ridge and treeline. Cross the ridge and drop down to the South Fork Deep Creek at one mile. Walk upstream a short distance to the log bridge. Cross over the cascading creek, and head up the lush canyon above the creek. Rock-hop over a feeder stream, and steadily gain elevation at a moderate grade. Climb through an open lodgepole pine forest a hundred feet above the creek. Gently descend and enter the Absaroka-Beartooth Wilderness. Return to and follow the tumbling whitewater of the South Fork Deep Creek at the southwest foot of Mount Delano. Climb the north wall of the forested canyon, and cross a tributary stream formed on the upper slope of the mountain. Cross a couple of seasonal drainages beneath the massive, vertical rock wall. Stroll through a 7,000-foot flat below craggy rock formations. At 4 miles, enter the Upper Amphitheater of the South Fork, a cirque of mountains that includes Mount McKnight towering more than 2,000 feet above the trail. The South Fork Deep Creek veers south, while the trail continues east. This is a good turn-around spot.

To extend the hike to the 9,112-foot Deep Creek Divide, which is visible to the east, enter the forest again. Head up the mountain, leaving the South Fork Deep Creek. Zigzag up the steep path, gaining 1,450 feet over the next 1.2 miles. The trail levels out near the saddle. From the saddle are sweeping vistas down into the Davis Creek drainage and across the West Boulder Valley and beyond. The Davis Creek Trail (Hike 95) descends and follows Davis Creek 8.7 miles to the West Boulder trailheads. ▪

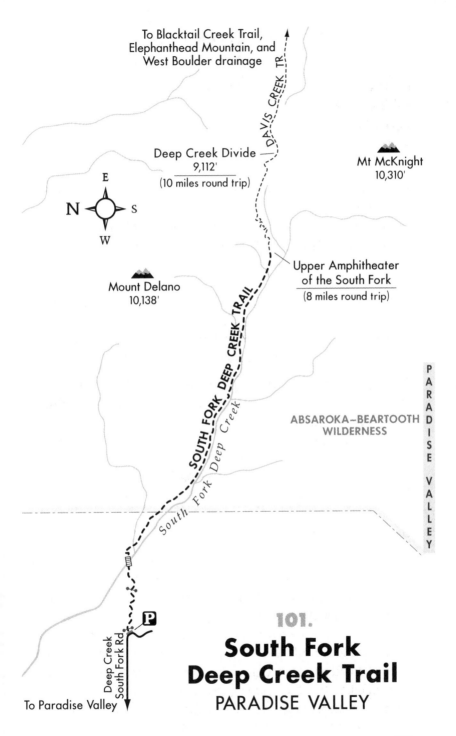

To Blacktail Creek Trail,
Elephanthead Mountain, and
West Boulder drainage

DAVIS CREEK TR.

Deep Creek Divide
9,112'
(10 miles round trip)

Mt McKnight
10,310'

N E S W

Upper Amphitheater
of the South Fork
(8 miles round trip)

Mount Delano
10,138'

SOUTH FORK DEEP CREEK TRAIL

South Fork Deep Creek

ABSAROKA–BEARTOOTH
WILDERNESS

PARADISE VALLEY

P

Deep Creek
South Fork Rd

To Paradise Valley

101.
South Fork
Deep Creek Trail
PARADISE VALLEY

102. Pine Creek Falls

PARADISE VALLEY

Hiking distance: 2.2 miles round trip
Hiking time: 1 hour
Elevation gain: 350 feet
Maps: U.S.G.S. Dexter Point
Beartooth Publishing: Absaroka Beartooth Wilderness

Summary of hike: Pine Creek Falls is a tall and narrow, double-tier cataract that fans out as it plunges over a large rock outcrop. The headwaters of Pine Creek form at Black Mountain in the Absaroka-Beartooth Wilderness. The creek fills Pine Creek Lake as it cascades 3,000 feet down the east wall of Paradise Valley to the valley floor. The Pine Creek Trail is a 5-mile-long trail that climbs 3,100 feet to Pine Creek Lake (Hike 103). This hike follows the first mile of the trail along the cascading creek to the magnificent falls. The path meanders through a spruce, fir, aspen, and maple forest en route to the base of the falls.

Driving directions: From Livingston at the I-90 and Highway 89 junction, drive 9.6 miles south on Highway 89 to Pine Creek Road on the left, between mile markers 43 and 44. Turn left and continue 2.4 miles (crossing over the Yellowstone River) to East River Road. Turn right and drive 0.7 miles to Luccock Park Road on the left. A sign is posted for the Pine Creek Campground. Turn left (east) on Luccock Park Road, and wind 3.1 miles up the foothills to the trailhead parking area at road's end (0.6 miles past the George Lake turnoff).

Hiking directions: Take the posted trail from the far end of the parking area. Immediately enter a deep, lush forest to a junction. Stay to the right on the Pine Creek Trail. At a quarter mile, pass a junction to the George Lake Trail (Hike 104) on the right. Cross a bridge over Pine Creek at 0.5 miles, and enter the Absaroka-Beartooth Wilderness. Continue along the north side of the cascading creek to a second bridge over Pine Creek at just over 1.1 mile. From the bridge is a dramatic view of towering Pine Creek Falls. Thirty yards beyond the bridge is a side shoot of the waterfall. Several unmaintained trails access the upper chute of the falls.

To hike farther, the trail continues to Pine Creek Lake, 4 miles ahead and 3,000 feet up—Hike 103. The pristine alpine lake sits in a glacial cirque high above Paradise Valley. ∎

103. Pine Creek Lake
PARADISE VALLEY

Hiking distance: 10 miles round trip
Hiking time: 6 hours
Elevation gain: 3,400 feet
Maps: U.S.G.S. Dexter Point and Mount Cowen
Rocky Mountain: Surveys Mt. Cowen Area

Summary of hike: Pine Creek Lake is a pristine alpine lake in a huge, 9,032-foot basin high above Paradise Valley. The 31-acre lake sits in the glacial cirque on the north slope of Black Mountain, towering 900 feet above the lake in the Absaroka-Beartooth Wilderness. The strenuous but well-defined trail climbs past a series of spectacular waterfalls (including Pine Creek Falls) and a couple of smaller lakes to Pine Creek Lake. En route are vistas across Paradise Valley to the Gallatin Range.

Driving directions: From Livingston at the I-90 and Highway 89 junction, drive 9.6 miles south on Highway 89 to Pine Creek Road on the left, between mile markers 43 and 44. Turn left and continue 2.4 miles (crossing over the Yellowstone River) to East River Road. Turn right and drive 0.7 miles to Luccock Park Road on the left. A sign is posted for the Pine Creek Campground. Turn left (east) on Luccock Park Road, and wind 3.1 miles up the foothills to the trailhead parking area at road's end (0.6 miles past the George Lake turnoff).

Hiking directions: Take the posted trail from the far end of the parking area. Immediately enter a deep, lush forest to a junction. Stay to the right on the Pine Creek Trail. At a quarter mile, pass a junction to the George Lake Trail (Hike 104) on the right. Cross a bridge over Pine Creek at 0.5 miles, and enter the

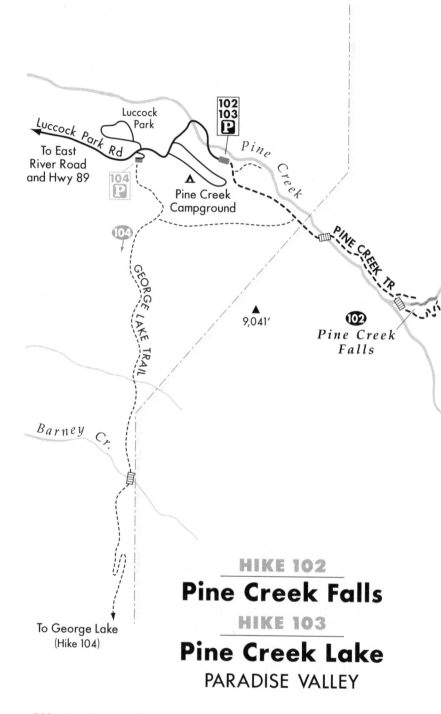

Luccock Park

102
103
P

Luccock Park Rd

To East
River Road
and Hwy 89

104
P

Pine Creek

104

Pine Creek
Campground

GEORGE LAKE TRAIL

PINE CREEK TR

▲
9,041'

102
*Pine Creek
Falls*

Barney Cr.

To George Lake
(Hike 104)

HIKE 102
Pine Creek Falls
HIKE 103
Pine Creek Lake
PARADISE VALLEY

N

W ⊕ E

S

Mount
McKnight
10,310'

PINE CREEK TRAIL

waterfall

103

waterfall *Jewell L.*

**ABSAROKA–BEARTOOTH
WILDERNESS**

103
*Pine Creek
Lake*

S. Fork Pine Cr.

P
A
R
A
D
I
S
E

V
A
L
L
E
Y

Black Mtn
10,941'

Absaroka-Beartooth Wilderness. Continue along the north side of the cascading creek to a second bridge over Pine Creek at just over 1.1 mile. From the bridge is a dramatic view of towering Pine Creek Falls. Thirty yards beyond the bridge is a side shoot of the waterfall. Several unmaintained trails access the upper chute of the falls.

Continue on the main trail past the bridge, and cross downfall logs over the south channel of the creek. Zigzag up the hillside to a view down canyon of Paradise Valley. A side path on the left leads 30 yards to the brink of the falls at the narrow rock chute. The main trail follows the cascading creek, steadily climbing past huge granite boulders. The rock-embedded path leads to the creek at just under 2 miles, with a view of a 200-foot waterfall upstream.

Carefully cross the creek on downfall logs and rocks to the north side of Pine Creek. Curve left, away from the creek. Loop around the mountainside, crossing a northern tributary of the creek. Climb more switchbacks beneath the jagged spires on the north canyon wall. Return to Pine Creek and a waterfall. Follow the cascading whitewater past a series of falls. Curve away from the slope, and zigzag up the rocky slope through a scree field. Skirt the edge of a vertical rock wall beneath the crowns of Mount McKnight and Black Mountain. Top the slope and enter a forested cirque with another 200-foot waterfall. Descend to the creek and follow it upstream. A side path on the right leads to a campsite by a small lake and a full view of the waterfall.

Veer left and climb five switchbacks to another view of the falls and the lake below the rock-walled bowl. At the top of the rock face, the trail overlooks Jewel Lake and the cascade feeding the tarn. Descend to the end of Jewel Lake. Follow the west shore and cross the outlet creek 20 yards upstream from the falls. Bear left and continue past the lake, climbing out of the bowl. Pass two waterfalls filling a pool just above Jewel Lake. Above the falls, the trail reaches broad slabs of granite rock that line the north shore of gorgeous Pine Creek Lake. Another waterfall feeds the south end of the lake. After enjoying the views and well-earned rest, return along the same route. ■

104. George Lake
PARADISE VALLEY

Hiking distance: 11 miles round trip
Hiking time: 6 hours
Elevation gain: 2,500 feet
Maps: U.S.G.S. Dexter Point
Beartooth Publishing: Absaroka Beartooth Wilderness

Summary of hike: George Lake (also known as Shorthill Lake) is a high-alpine lake that sits in a depression on the lower west slope of Black Mountain. The tree-lined lake has a rocky shoreline and a towering rock wall to the east that rises 1,600 feet above the lake. The trail traverses the western slope of the Absaroka Range just outside of the Absaroka–Beartooth Wilderness, with vast views overlooking Paradise Valley, the Yellowstone River, and the east face of the Gallatin Range. En route, the trail crosses Barney Creek and Cascade Creek.

Driving directions: From Livingston at the I-90 and Highway 89 junction, drive 9.6 miles south on Highway 89 to Pine Creek Road on the left, between mile markers 43 and 44. Turn left and continue 2.4 miles (crossing over the Yellowstone River) to East River Road. Turn right and drive 0.7 miles to Luccock Park Road on the left. A sign is posted for the Pine Creek Campground. Turn left (east) and wind 2.5 miles up the foothills to the posted George Lake Trailhead on the right. Veer right on the gravel road 0.15 miles to the parking area.

Pine Creek Road is 12.3 miles north of Emigrant and 42 miles north of Gardiner.

Hiking directions: Walk up the grassy slope beneath the majestic peaks of Mount McKnight and Black Mountain. Weave through the pine forest to a posted junction at a half mile. The left fork connects with the Pine Creek Trail (Hikes 102—103). Bear right up the mountain slope as views open of Paradise Valley, the Gallatin Range, and the Yellowstone River. Cross a trickling stream in a small grotto with ferns and moss-covered rocks at just under 2 miles. Traverse the hillside along the mountain contours, and cross a small log bridge over Barney Creek at 2.5 miles. Zigzag over a talus slope, with sweeping vistas of the valley, and cross a bridge over a fern-filled drainage at 3 miles.

Descend 0.6 miles into the vast Cascade Creek canyon on a series of nine rock-strewn switchbacks. At the creek, walk a short distance downstream, and rock-hop or cross downfall logs over Cascade Creek. Wind through the riparian vegetation, and ascend the south canyon slope. Leave the drainage, continuing through a lodgepole pine forest. Begin a steep half-mile climb that levels out near George Lake. The faint path is marked with a few cairns as it descends to the north shore of the lake. After enjoying a well-earned rest, return along the same path. ▪

Luccock Park Rd
To East River Road and Hwy 89
Luccock Park
102 103 P
P
Pine Creek Campground
102 103

PINE CREEK TRAIL
to Pine Creek Falls and Pine Creek Lake

GEORGE LAKE TRAIL

ABSAROKA-BEARTOOTH WILDERNESS

Barney Cr.

N
W　　E
S

Cascade Cr.

104.
George Lake
PARADISE VALLEY

George Lake

105. East Fork Mill Creek
PARADISE VALLEY

Hiking distance: 3 to 24 (overnight) miles round trip
Hiking time: 1.5 to 14 hours
Elevation gain: 300 to 3,900 feet
Maps: U.S.G.S. Knowles Peak and The Pyramid
Rocky Mountain Surveys: Mt. Cowen Area
Beartooth Publishing: Absaroka Beartooth Wilderness

Summary of hike: The East Fork of Mill Creek forms near Silver Pass, tumbling down from the upper reaches of Boulder Mountain at the Paradise Valley–Boulder River divide. The East Fork Mill Creek Trail stretches 12 miles eastward to Silver Pass, located on the ridge between Boulder Mountain and The Pyramid. The trail continuously follows the creek in the Absaroka-Beartooth Wilderness, steadily passing through flower-filled meadows and limestone cliffs. Atop the divide, the trail connects with the Fourmile Creek Trail and descends to the Boulder River (Hike 90). At the lower end of the trail is a connection with the Elbow Lake Trail, the main access route to 11,212-foot Mount Cowen, the highest peak in the Absaroka Range. This hike follows the lower end of the East Fork Mill Creek Trail along the watercourse and forested canyon floor. You may turn around at any point along the creekside trail.

Driving directions: From Livingston at the I-90 and Highway 89 junction, drive 15.7 miles south on Highway 89 to Mill Creek Road on the left, between mile markers 37 and 38. Turn left (southeast) and continue 9.2 miles to the posted East Fork Mill Creek Road. Turn left and follow the creek 1.5 miles upstream to the posted trailhead parking area on the right.

Mill Creek Road is 6.2 miles north of Emigrant and 36 miles north of Gardiner.

Hiking directions: From the east end of the parking area, enter the dense pine forest on the posted trail. Follow the south side of the creek, skirting the Snowy Range Ranch. Traverse the hillside and loop around a small drainage to a posted trail junction at a quarter mile. The Highland Trail veers right on the east flank of Knowles Peak, connecting with the Anderson Ridge Trail and Mill Creek. Stay left, looping through a quiet side canyon and crossing a small feeder stream. Return to the main canyon, with a view of bald Arrow Peak. Continue east on the cliffside path. Zigzag up four switchbacks and enter the Absaroka-Beartooth Wilderness. Drop down and cross a wooden bridge over East Fork Mill Creek to a posted junction with the Elbow Lake Trail. The left fork follows Upper Sage Creek to Elbow Lake for 6 miles, located at the southern foot of Mount Cowen. Stay to the right on the East Fork Mill Creek Trail, following the north side of the creek. The trail steadily gains elevation for 12 miles en route to Silver Pass. Choose your own turn-around spot. ▓

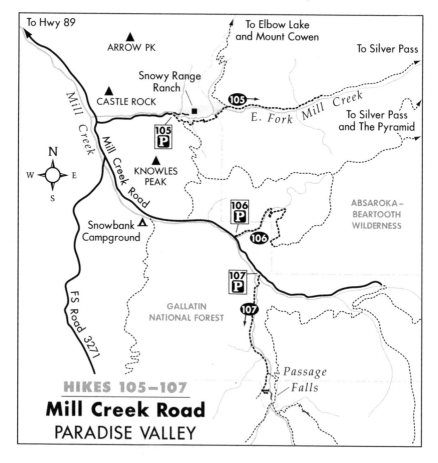

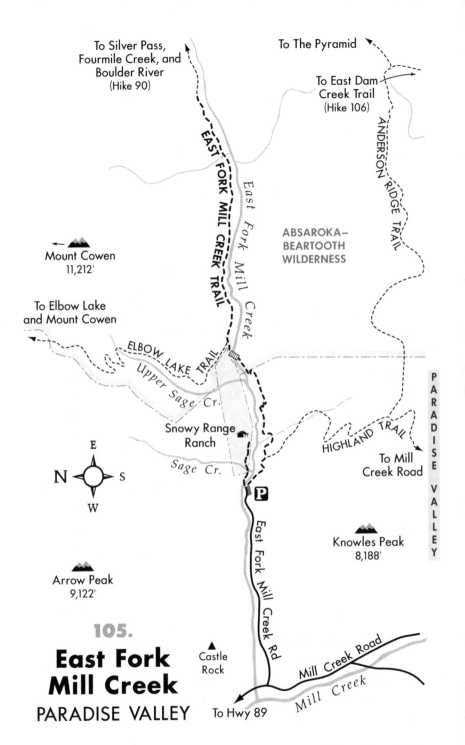

To Silver Pass,
Fourmile Creek, and
Boulder River
(Hike 90)

To The Pyramid

To East Dam
Creek Trail
(Hike 106)

EAST FORK MILL CREEK TRAIL

East Fork Mill Creek

ANDERSON RIDGE TRAIL

ABSAROKA–
BEARTOOTH
WILDERNESS

Mount Cowen
11,212'

To Elbow Lake
and Mount Cowen

ELBOW LAKE TRAIL

Upper Sage Cr.

Snowy Range
Ranch

Sage Cr.

HIGHLAND TRAIL

To Mill
Creek Road

P A R A D I S E   V A L L E Y

N
E
S
W

P

East Fork Mill Creek Rd

Knowles Peak
8,188'

Arrow Peak
9,122'

105.
East Fork
Mill Creek
PARADISE VALLEY

Castle
Rock

Mill Creek Road

Mill Creek

To Hwy 89

106. East Dam Creek Trail
PARADISE VALLEY

Hiking distance: 3 miles to 9 miles round trip (for a loop)
Hiking time: 1.5 to 6 hours
Elevation gain: 900 to 2,500 feet
Maps: U.S.G.S. Knowles Peak and The Pyramid
Rocky Mountain Surveys: Mt. Cowen Area
Beartooth Publishing: Absaroka Beartooth Wilderness

Summary of hike: East Dam Creek is a small tributary of Mill Creek. The creek trickles through a narrow side canyon between Mill Creek and The Pyramid. It is also a horsepacking route and cross-country ski trail. This hike follows the lower creekside portion of the trail to open meadows and overlooks. The trail makes connections with the Anderson Ridge Trail, East Fork Mill Creek, and the Moose Park Trail along the western base of The Pyramid.

Driving directions: From Livingston at the I-90 and Highway 89 junction, drive 15.7 miles south on Highway 89 to Mill Creek Road on the left, between mile markers 37 and 38. Turn left (southeast) and continue 13.3 miles to the signed East Dam Creek Trailhead turnoff. Turn left and drive 100 yards to the trailhead and parking area on the right.

Mill Creek Road is 6.2 miles north of Emigrant and 36 miles north of Gardiner.

Hiking directions: Head east into the forest on a steady but easy incline. Follow the north side of East Dam Creek in the narrow canyon, passing talus slopes and small meadows. Meander through the riparian habitat with moss-covered rocks, crossing the trickling stream four times. Enter the Absaroka-Beartooth Wilderness. Continue through a lush meadow rimmed with conifers and backed by forested mountains and jagged rocky cliffs. Cross over the creek and loop around the upper end of the meadow at one mile. Traverse the hillside and curve left on a horseshoe bend. Climb to the south wall of the East Dam Creek drainage, overlooking the meadow and the canyon below.

Continue into a large mountain cirque and curve right, skirting the base of the upper mountains. Leave the East Dam Creek canyon, heading south. Curve along the contours of the mountain while steadily gaining elevation. Choose your own turn-around spot.

To extend the hike, the trail continues 3 more miles to the Anderson Ridge Trail, gaining an additional 1,600 feet. The Anderson Ridge Trail loops westward, joining with the Highland Trail for a 9-mile loop. To the east, the trail heads up to The Pyramid. ▪

To Moose Park Trail and The Pyramid

East Dam Cr.

ANDERSON RIDGE TRAIL

ABSAROKA– BEARTOOTH WILDERNESS

optional 9-mile loop hike

EAST DAM CREEK TR

P

To East Fork Mill Creek Trail (Hike 105)

Montanapolis Springs

Mill Creek Road

HIGHLAND TR

E

N — S

W

106.
East Dam Creek
PARADISE VALLEY

To Hwy 89

107. Passage Falls
PARADISE VALLEY

Hiking distance: 4.2 miles round trip
Hiking time: 2.5 hours
Elevation gain: 480 feet
Maps: U.S.G.S. Knowles Peak, The Pyramid, Mount Wallace
U.S.F.S. Gallatin National Forest: East Half
Beartooth Publishing: Absaroka Beartooth Wilderness

Summary of hike: Passage Falls is a massive, powerful waterfall that leaps over moss-covered rocks and plunges straight down to the narrow, rocky canyon floor. The waterfall is located in the Mill Creek watershed beneath Mount Wallace, just outside the Absaroka-Beartooth Wilderness in the Gallatin National Forest. The trail parallels Passage Creek on the Wallace Creek Trail. The falls is located just below the confluence of Wallace Creek and Passage Creek.

Driving directions: From Livingston at the I-90 and Highway 89 junction, drive 15.7 miles south on Highway 89 to Mill Creek Road on the left, between mile markers 37 and 38. Turn left (southeast) and drive 14 miles up Mill Creek Road to the Wallace Creek trailhead parking area on the right.

Mill Creek Road is 6.2 miles north of Emigrant and 36 miles north of Gardiner.

Hiking directions: The trail begins at the bridge by the confluence of Mill Creek and Passage Creek. Once over Mill Creek, continue south to another bridge crossing over Passage Creek. At one mile, cross a stream by a small waterfall and cascade. After a second stream crossing, the forested trail emerges into a small meadow, then ducks back into the forest canopy. At 1.6 miles the path forks just before a bridge on the left. Take the right branch to Passage Falls. Climb up the short, steep hill to a slope. From the slope are views overlooking a large meadow on private land. Take the trail to the left, and descend the eight switchbacks to Passage Falls. After enjoying the falls, return along the same route.

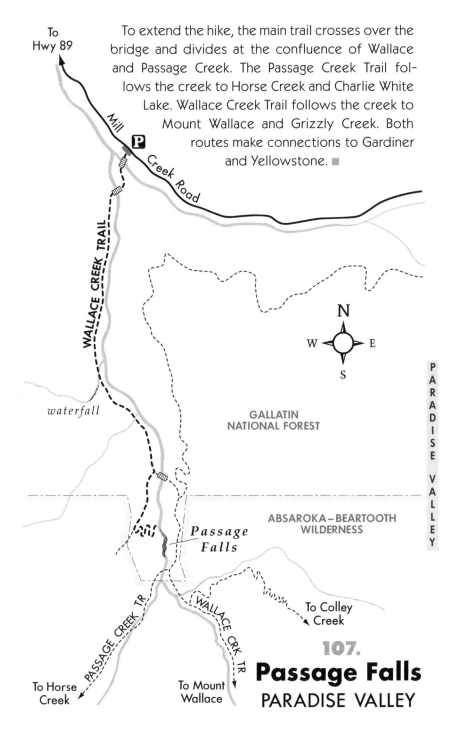

To extend the hike, the main trail crosses over the bridge and divides at the confluence of Wallace and Passage Creek. The Passage Creek Trail follows the creek to Horse Creek and Charlie White Lake. Wallace Creek Trail follows the creek to Mount Wallace and Grizzly Creek. Both routes make connections to Gardiner and Yellowstone. ◼

To Hwy 89

Mill Creek Road

P

WALLACE CREEK TRAIL

waterfall

GALLATIN NATIONAL FOREST

N
W · E
S

PARADISE VALLEY

ABSAROKA–BEARTOOTH WILDERNESS

Passage Falls

PASSAGE CREEK TR.

WALLACE CRK. TR.

To Colley Creek

To Horse Creek

To Mount Wallace

107.
Passage Falls
PARADISE VALLEY

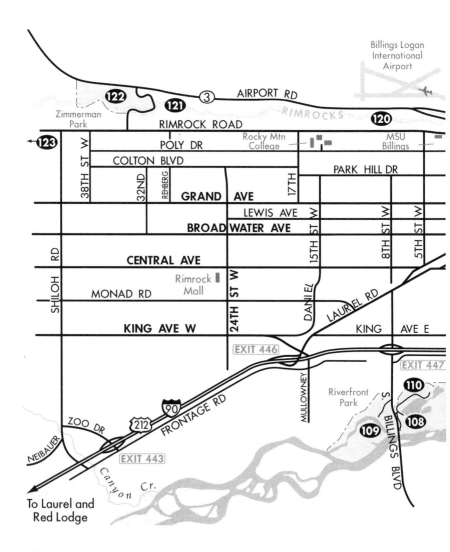

To Roundup

312

PEMBERTON LANE

117

Lake Elmo

GOVERNORS BLVD

LAKE ELMO RD

MARY ST

HAWTHORNE LN

BITTERROOT DR

BARRETT

87

BENCH BLVD

WICKS LANE

MAIN ST

YELLOWSTONE RIVER RD

Billings Heights

SENATORS

ALKALI CREEK RD

118

HILLTOP

Pow Wow Park

Alkali Cr.

114–116

Two Moon Park

AIRPORT RD

318

119

Swords Park

EXIT 452

OLD HARDIN RD

90

N 27TH ST

N 30TH ST

N 32ND ST

6TH AVE N

4TH AVE N

1ST AVE N

To Forsyth, Miles City, and Wall Drug

DIVISION

DOWNTOWN

Coulson Park

Lockwood

I 90

Four Dances Natural Area

MONTANA AVE

1ST AVE

S 27TH ST

212

112

STATE AVE

WASHINGTON

SUGAR

EXIT 450

Mystic Park

COBURN RD

B I L L I N G S

S FRONTAGE RD

111

Yellowstone River

Old Washington Bridge

Pictograph Cave State Park

113

HIKES 108–123
Billings

108. Lake Josephine—Beaver Pond Loop

RIVERFRONT PARK

BILLINGS

Hiking distance: 1.2-mile loop
Hiking time: 40 minutes
Elevation gain: Level
Maps: U.S.G.S. Yegen
Riverfront Park/Schoenthal Island Area trail map

Summary of hike: Historic Riverfront Park encompasses 347 acres along the Yellowstone River at the south end of Billings. The park, bordering the north edge of the river, is a popular site for hiking, jogging, biking, birding, canoeing, kayaking, fishing, and picnicking. Within the forested park, meandering streams connect two ponds and Lake Josephine. The 24-acre lake was named for a steamboat that reached Billings in 1875, the farthest point upstream that any boat had reached from the mouth of the Yellowstone River. This hike circles Lake Josephine through a lush riparian habitat with poplar and cottonwood groves surrounded by grassy meadows. Dogs are allowed in the park.

Driving directions: From I-90 in Billings, exit on South Billings Boulevard (Exit 447). Head 0.6 miles south to Riverfront Park on the left. Turn left into Riverfront Park, and drive straight ahead to Lake Josephine. Turn right and continue 0.1 mile to the parking lot on the right at the end of the road.

Hiking directions: From the west end of Lake Josephine, head south on the old asphalt road 100 yards to a road fork. The right fork leads a half mile to Wendell's Bridge and Norm Schoenthal Island (Hike 109). Stay to the left through groves of cottonwood and Russian olive trees. At a quarter mile, a side path on the right curves west, away from Lake Josephine. (The side path meanders through the forest to the banks of the Yellowstone River and connects with the trail to Schoenthal Island.) For this hike, remain on the main trail along the south side of Lake Josephine. Curve away from the lake, and follow the wetlands around the south edge of Beaver Pond. Just beyond

the pond, cross a footbridge over the connector stream between Lake Josephine and Cochran Pond. Follow the path along
the north edge of the lake, parallel to Riverfront Park Road, and
complete the loop. ◼

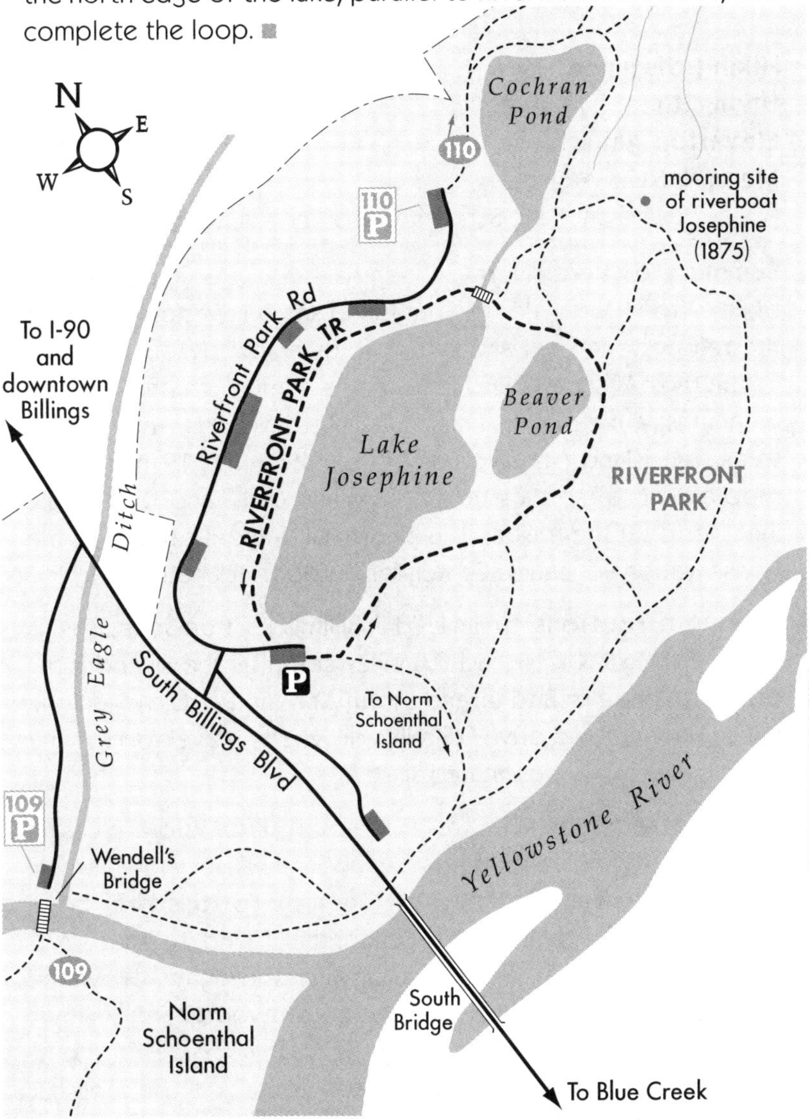

N E
W S

*Cochran
Pond*

110

mooring site
of riverboat
Josephine
(1875)

110
P

Riverfront Park Rd

RIVERFRONT PARK TR

*Beaver
Pond*

To I-90
and
downtown
Billings

*Lake
Josephine*

**RIVERFRONT
PARK**

Ditch

P

To Norm
Schoenthal
Island

Grey Eagle

South Billings Blvd

Yellowstone River

109
P

Wendell's
Bridge

109

Norm
Schoenthal
Island

South
Bridge

To Blue Creek

B
I
L
L
I
N
G
S

108. Riverfront Park:
Lake Josephine—Beaver Pond Loop
BILLINGS

109. Norm Schoenthal Island
RIVERFRONT PARK
BILLINGS

Hiking distance: 1.9-mile loop
Hiking time: 1 hour
Elevation gain: Level
Maps: U.S.G.S. Yegen
Riverfront Park/Schoenthal Island Area trail map

Summary of hike: Norm Schoenthal Island is on the west end of Riverfront Park in Billings. The island sits on the north edge of the Yellowstone River and is formed by an oxbow side channel of the river. Wendell's Bridge accesses the lush sanctuary, filled with grassy meadows, stands of cottonwoods, and willow trees. The island has two level loop trails—the 1.9-mile outer loop around the perimeter of the island and a shorter 1.2-mile inner loop. At the trailhead, just north of Wendell's Bridge, is the Conservation Education Center for outdoor education.

Driving directions: From I-90 in Billings, exit on South Billings Boulevard (Exit 447). Head 0.5 miles south to the signed turn-off for Wendell's Bridge and Norm Schoenthal Island on the right. Turn right and drive 0.3 miles down the gravel road to the bridge. Park in the designated spaces.

Hiking directions: The trail on the left, just before crossing Wendell's Bridge, follows the Yellowstone River downstream a half mile to Lake Josephine (Hike 108). For this hike, cross Wendell's Bridge onto Norm Schoenthal Island to the Island Loop Trail and kiosk. Begin the loop to the right. Follow the north channel of the river through cottonwoods and willows to a Y-fork. The birdhouses along the trail are part of the out-door education programs. The left fork is the 0.2-mile Crosscut Trail for a shorter 1.2-mile loop. Stay to the right on the Island Loop Trail along the island's northwest edge. At the west tip of the island is a bench overlooking the fork between the river and the north branch. After enjoying the river views, head east, following the Yellowstone River downstream. Pass the Crosscut

Trail on the left. Continue through the tree-covered grassland, completing the loop at Wendell's Bridge. ■

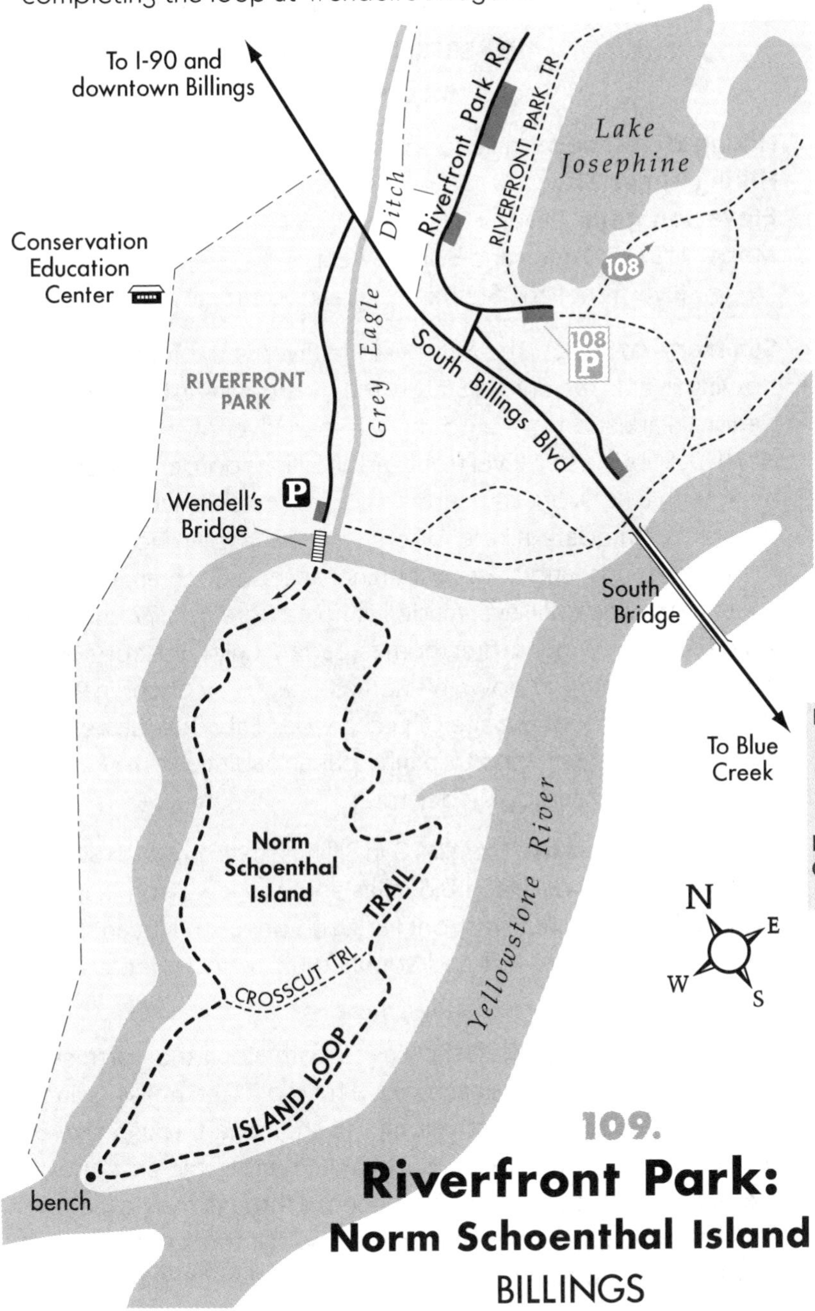

To I-90 and
downtown Billings

Riverfront Park Rd

RIVERFRONT PARK TR

*Lake
Josephine*

Conservation
Education
Center

108

108
P

Grey Eagle Ditch

South Billings Blvd

RIVERFRONT
PARK

Wendell's
Bridge

P

South
Bridge

To Blue
Creek

B
I
L
L
I
N
G
S

Yellowstone River

**Norm
Schoenthal
Island**

TRAIL

CROSSCUT TRL.

ISLAND LOOP

N
E
W
S

bench

109.
Riverfront Park:
Norm Schoenthal Island
BILLINGS

110. Riverfront Park Trail
Cochran Pond—Old Washington Bridge Site Loop
RIVERFRONT PARK
BILLINGS

Hiking distance: 2-mile loop
Hiking time: 1 hour
Elevation gain: Level
Maps: U.S.G.S. Yegen and Billings West
Riverfront Park/Schoenthal Island Area trail map

Summary of hike: The Yellowstone River is the longest free-flowing river in the United States. The river begins in Yellowstone National Park and flows into the Missouri River at the Montana-North Dakota border. Riverfront Park in Billings borders the scenic river, with a network of nearly 7 miles of established trails. The trails accommodate hikers, bikers, and equestrian riders along the river, ponds, and Lake Josephine. Joseph Cochran, the first white settler near Billings, made his home here in 1877 and was Yellowstone County's first homesteader. Chief Joseph's Nez Perce Indians burned down his home, located by Cochran Pond. He rebuilt a home at the site of present day Lake Josephine. This hike circles Cochran Pond through riparian habitats with pockets of cottonwood and box elder trees.

Driving directions: From I-90 in Billings, exit on South Billings Boulevard (Exit 447). Head 0.6 miles south to Riverfront Park on the left. Turn left into Riverfront Park, and drive straight ahead to Lake Josephine. Turn left and continue 0.7 miles to the parking lot at the end of the road.

Hiking directions: Take the paved path along the north side of Cochran Pond. Halfway across is a trail split. The trails rejoin to the east. Take the footpath along the shoreline through groves of cottonwoods to a Y-fork. Stay to the right to the east end of the pond, then veer to the left. Meander through the dense forest along the north edge of a waterway. The three paths merge at the end of the paved path. At the east end of the pavement is a Y-fork. Begin the middle loop on the left fork, hiking clockwise under a canopy of box elder trees and lush riparian vegetation. Pass several connector paths to the Yellowstone River, our return route. The trail ends at the trailhead off of Frontage Road by the Grey Eagle Ditch.

Take the right fork south along the water canal on the old road. Pass the park's eastern trails on the left, labeled with the nature preserve sign. The road ends at the site of the Old Washington Bridge. (Hike 111). Return up the road 50 yards to the north edge of the river. Bear left on the footpath, and follow the bank of the river upstream under towering cottonwoods. Return to the end of the paved path, completing the loop. Follow the left path along the south edge of Cochran Pond. At the trail split, veer right to the connector stream between Lake Josephine and Cochran Pond. Bear right on the paved park road, returning to the parking area. ▦

111. Old Washington Bridge Site
RIVERFRONT PARK
BILLINGS

Hiking distance: 0.6-mile loop
Hiking time: 20 minutes
Elevation gain: Level
Maps: U.S.G.S. Yegen
Riverfront Park/Schoenthal Island Area trail map

Summary of hike: Until a few years ago, the old Washington Bridge spanned the east end of Riverfront Park in Billings. The iron bridge extended across the Yellowstone River from the south end of Washington Street. The bridge was originally built in 1894, then replaced in the 1950s. It was constructed across the river at the old Cummings Ferry Crossing by Washington Street to a 33-acre island in the river. Washington Street now dead-ends on the north side of Interstate 90. Citing safety reasons, the bridge was removed in 2005. This hike strolls along Grey Eagle Ditch, weaves through a verdant shaded forest with tree-filtered sunlight, and meanders along the Yellowstone River. This short but scenic trail can be combined with Hike 110 for a longer walk.

Driving directions: From I-90 in Billings, exit on South Billings Boulevard (Exit 447). Head south and quickly turn left on South Frontage Road. Drive 1.3 miles to the gravel road on the right. Turn right and park in the pullout on the right.

Hiking directions: Walk to the trail gate at the end of the road. Follow the wide gravel road along the west edge of Grey Eagle Ditch, an irrigation channel diverted from an inlet by Schoenthal Island. Pass the Riverfront Park Trail (Hike 110) on the right. One hundred yards ahead is a posted trail on the left. Begin the loop and bear left through the gated access. Stroll through the forest on the south side of the water canal. The canal curves away to the left, and the path crosses a grassy meadow under towering old-growth cottonwoods. Near the Yellowstone River is a looping side path on the left. Both routes rejoin at the river's edge and head upstream to where the Washington Bridge once spanned the river. Return to the old paved road and bear right, passing the Riverfront Park Trail on the left. Complete the loop a short distance ahead. ▪

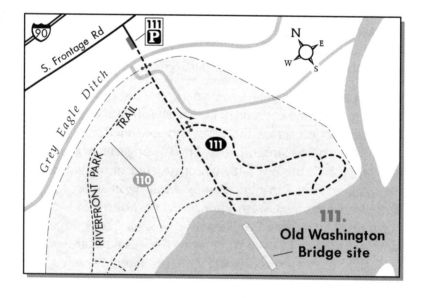

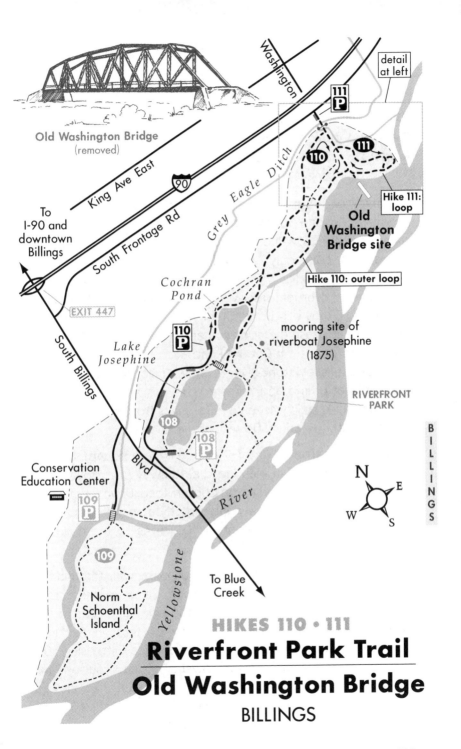

Old Washington Bridge
(removed)

Washington

King Ave East

I-90

To
I-90 and
downtown
Billings

South Frontage Rd

Grey Eagle Ditch

EXIT 447

111 P

detail
at left

110

111

Hike 111:
loop

**Old
Washington
Bridge
site**

Hike 110: outer loop

*Cochran
Pond*

110 P

*Lake
Josephine*

mooring site of
riverboat Josephine
(1875)

RIVERFRONT
PARK

South Billings

108

108 P

River

B
I
L
L
I
N
G
S

Conservation
Education Center

109 P

Blvd

N
W   E
S

109

Yellowstone

**Norm
Schoenthal
Island**

To Blue
Creek

HIKES 110 • 111
Riverfront Park Trail
Old Washington Bridge
BILLINGS

112. Four Dances Natural Area
BILLINGS

Hiking distance: 2.5 miles round trip
Hiking time: 1.5 hours
Elevation gain: 550 feet
Maps: U.S.G.S. Billings East
       Four Dances Natural Area: Bureau of Land Mgmnt. map

Summary of hike: Four Dances Natural Area is a 765-acre undeveloped park located on the east edge of Billings. It is named for the Crow Indian leader known as Four Dances. The natural area, commonly referred to as Sacrifice Cliff, was the site of a Crow Indian village. According to legend, when returning Indian warriors discovered their village was decimated by smallpox, they blindfolded their horses and rode them over the cliff to appease the gods and end the epidemic. The walk-in park stretches from Coburn Road atop the east rims to the banks of the Yellowstone River, with two miles of shoreline. This hike explores prairie land, forested canyons, and riparian riverside habitat. Amazing vistas span for miles from the bluffs atop Sacrifice Cliff, towering 500 feet above the river.

Driving directions: From I-90 on the east side of Billings, exit on Lockwood (Exit 452). Head east, away from downtown Billings, and quickly turn right on Coburn Road. Drive 1.4 miles to the signed entrance on the right, directly across from Canyon Trail Road. Turn right and continue 0.2 miles to the trailhead parking lot on the right.

Hiking directions: From the trailhead kiosk, walk through the gate and head west on the rocky road. Climb up and across the rolling hill to a posted trail split. The right fork leads to the Yellowstone River access. For now, bear left through the sage-covered hill to the rim of 3,640-foot Sacrifice Cliff, rising 500 feet above the Yellowstone River, Mystic Park, and Coulson Park. The vistas stretch across Billings and the Yellowstone Valley to the Beartooth Mountains. To the right, a footpath leads 40 yards north on a narrow finger of land. Back at the overlook, a trail follows the edge of Sacrifice Cliff to the north. As the cliffs curve right, the trail fades and several faint paths meander through the hills, passing eroded sandstone formations. Return to the main trail and descend back to the junction. Take the Yellowstone River Access Trail north below the ridge. Gradually descend through junipers, cedar, and ponderosa pines. Curve left to a canyon with massive sandstone cliffs with caves. Steeply drop down into the canyon, zigzagging to the valley floor. Weave through the forested river valley and grassy meadows. Cross a wash to the east banks of the river directly across from Coulson Park. After exploring the river, return along your own route. ■

To downtown Billings

1st Ave North

Lockwood

EXIT 452

90

To Two
Moon Park

114

To Laurel

COULSON PARK

Yellowstone River

CANYON

FOUR DANCES
NATURAL AREA

Coburn Road

B
I
L
L
I
N
G
S

YELLOWSTONE
RIVER
—ACCESS TRAIL

N

W   E

S

P

Canyon Trail
Road

SACRIFICE CLIFF

overlook

To Pictograph
Cave State Park

112. **Four Dances**
Natural Area
BILLINGS

113. Pictograph Cave State Park
BILLINGS

Hiking distance: 0.3-mile loop
Hiking time: 30 minutes
Elevation gain: 100 feet
Maps: U.S.G.S. Soda Springs Northwest
Pictograph Caves Trail Map

Summary of hike: Pictograph Cave State Park is a 23-acre national historic landmark located 6 miles south of Billings. Nestled at the base of south-facing sandstone cliffs in Bitter Creek Valley, the archaeological treasure is a prehistoric habitation site dating back 10,000 years. Three large caves are tucked into a semi-circle of eroding cliffs with overhanging rocks. The caves served as a shelter for the ancient people who left their mark with over 30,000 pottery, tool, jewelry, and weapon artifacts. More than 100 pictographs have been found on the cave walls. The painted images were used to record spiritual topics and meaningful events, including animal images, human-like figures, and shield-bearing warriors. Some of the fading images date back 2,000 years. A paved path with interpretive plaques loops around the base of the cliffs to Ghost Cave, Middle Cave, and Pictograph Cave. Interpretive signs explain the archaeological studies and significance of the inhabitation and natural features. Near the trailhead is a picnic area with box elder, Russian olive, and cottonwood groves.

Driving directions: From I-90 on the east side of Billings, exit on Lockwood (Exit 452). Head east, away from downtown Billings, and quickly turn right on Coburn Road. Drive 5 miles to the trailhead parking area on the left.

Hiking directions: Pick up the guide at the trailhead, and follow the interpretive trail to the right. Head up the hill to a junction. Detour to the right 60 yards to Pictograph Cave, the largest of the three caves. Notice the gourd-shaped cliff swallow nests attached to the rock wall above the cave.

Return to the main trail and curve around the cirque of rock walls and outcroppings to Middle Cave, a shallow cave. The V-shaped notch in the sandstone rock above the cave was formed from thousands of years of rainwater. Continue under the roof of Ghost Cave, used as a living and working area for making tools. The cave has concretions—round boulders attached to the cave walls. As the sandstone around the boulders wears away, the concretions tumble to the ground. The faint red lines on the cave wall represent the pre-excavation level of the floor. Descend and complete the loop. ■

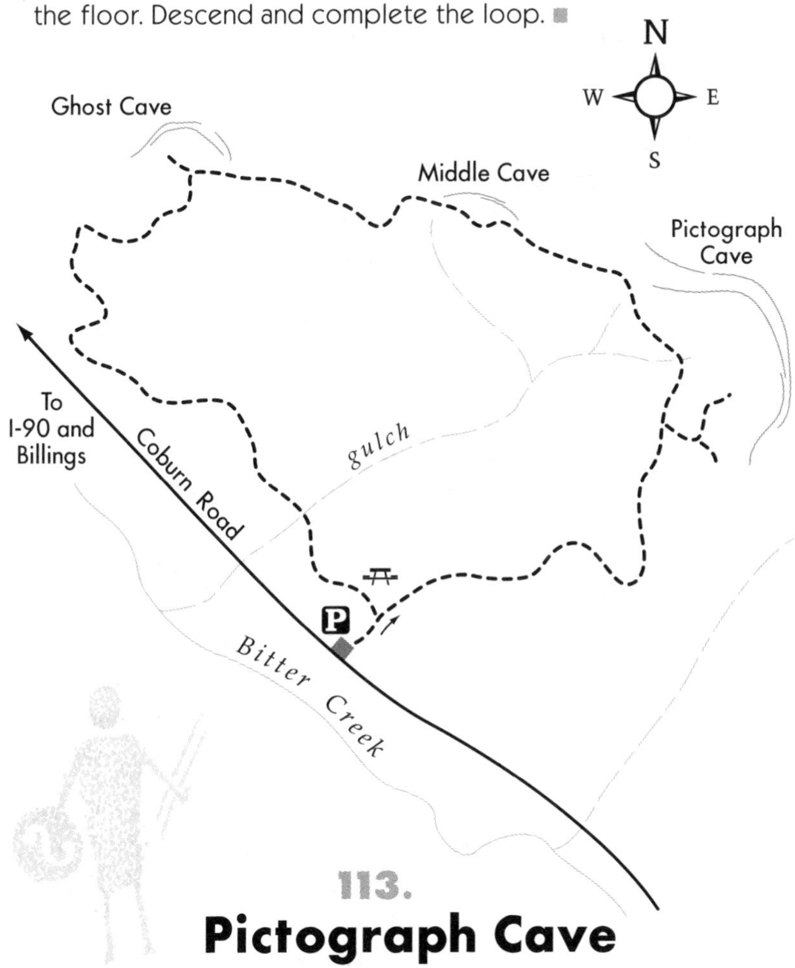

N

W ←◇→ E

S

Ghost Cave

Middle Cave

Pictograph Cave

To I-90 and Billings

Coburn Road

gulch

Bitter Creek

P

113.

Pictograph Cave
State Park
BILLINGS

114. Dutcher Trail: Heritage Trail System
TWO MOON PARK to COULSON PARK
BILLINGS

Hiking distance: 6 miles round trip
Hiking time: 3 hours
Elevation gain: 100 feet
Maps: U.S.G.S. Billings East

Summary of hike: The Heritage Trail is comprised of a network of walking and biking paths linking the greater Billings area with the Yellowstone River, the Rimrocks, county and city parks, and open spaces. The Dutcher Trail is a segment of the Heritage Trail along the Yellowstone River. It was named for Jim Dutcher, who originally developed the trails in Riverfront Park. This hike follows the scenic Dutcher Trail from Two Moon Park atop the rims, then travels down the sandstone shelves to Coulson Park on the banks of the Yellowstone River. This stretch is also called the Metra Trail (due to its close proximity to Metra Park) and the Coulson Trail (from East River Bridge to Coulson Park).

Driving directions: TWO MOON PARK TRAILHEAD (hiking south): From Main Street in Billings Heights, drive 0.6 miles east on Hilltop Road to the gravel parking area on left. Turn left and park. (Hilltop Road becomes Yellowstone River Road en route.)

COULSON PARK TRAILHEAD (hiking north): From the southeast end of South 27th Street, one block east of I-90, turn left on Garden Avenue. Drive 0.1 mile to Belkamp Avenue and turn left. Drive one block to Charlene Street and turn right. Continue one mile into Coulson Park at the west bank of the Yellowstone.

Hiking directions: FROM TWO MOON PARK: To the right (north), the paved Kiwanis Trail heads 1.6 miles through a greenbelt, terminating at Mary Street. En route the path crosses Wicks Lane at 0.6 miles and Barrett Road at 1.1 miles. For this hike, take the left (south) fork, and walk through the Yellowstone River Road tunnel. Emerge on the clifftop rim of Two Moon Park. Follow the elevated edge of the forested park, and cross the park entrance

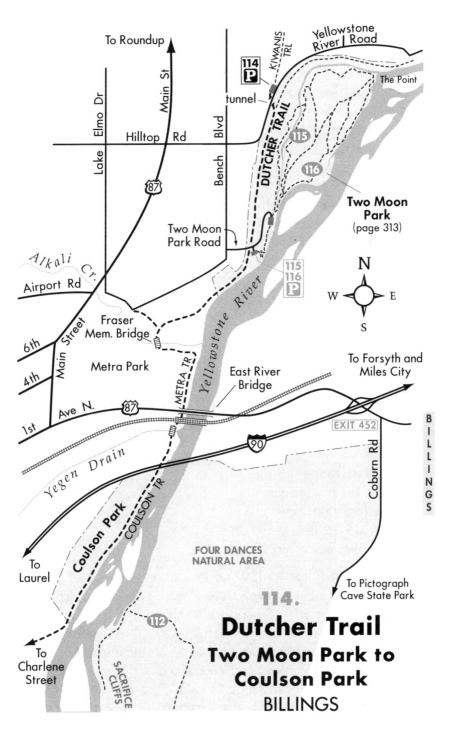

To Roundup

Elmo Dr

Lake

Main St

KIWANIS TRL

Yellowstone River Road

114 P

tunnel

Hilltop Rd

Bench Blvd

DUTCHER TRAIL

The Point

115

116

Two Moon Park
(page 313)

Alkali Cr.

Airport Rd

Two Moon Park Road

115 116 P

N
W   E
S

Fraser Mem. Bridge

Main Street

6th

4th

Metra Park

METRA TR

Yellowstone River

East River Bridge

To Forsyth and Miles City

1st

Ave N.

87

EXIT 452

I-90

Coburn Rd

B I L L I N G S

Yegen Drain

Coulson Park

COULSON TR

FOUR DANCES NATURAL AREA

To Laurel

To Pictograph Cave State Park

112

To Charlene Street

SACRIFICE CLIFFS

114.

Dutcher Trail
Two Moon Park to Coulson Park
BILLINGS

road. Descend to views of the Yellowstone River and Sacrifice Cliff (Hike 112). Pass a picnic shelter and a connector path from Bench Boulevard. Loop around the back (east) side of Metra Park, and pass another trailhead from the south end of Lake Elmo Drive. Cross the Fraser Memorial Bridge over Alkali Creek, and descend from the rims along the south edge of the creek to its confluence with the Yellowstone River. Curve right, following the river upstream. Cross a road and in quick succession, go under East River Bridge (Highway 87), the railroad bridge, and a bridge over Yegen Drain. Continue south along the river. Walk under the I-90 bridge spanning the river. Enter the north end of tree-lined Coulson Park beneath the vertical Sacrifice Cliff across the river. The paved path follows the banks of the Yellowstone River 0.6 miles, then curves away from the river to the Coulson Park trailhead.

To extend the hike, the path continues 1.5 miles, parallel to Charlene Street, and weaves back to the Yellowstone River in Mystic Park. ∎

115. Rocke Jeune—Dull Knife Loop
TWO MOON PARK NATURAL AREA
BILLINGS

Hiking distance: 1.5-mile loop
Hiking time: 45 minutes
Elevation gain: Level
Maps: U.S.G.S. Billings East
      Two Moon Park Trail Map

Summary of hike: Two Moon Park encompasses 150 acres on the banks of the Yellowstone River on the southeast side of Billings Heights. The park was named for one of the key Cheyenne Indian chiefs at the Battle of the Little Bighorn. It sits in a natural riparian area beneath 80-foot sandstone cliffs. The popular hiking and biking paths are also dog-friendly. This loop hike follows the Rocke Jeune Trail along the Yellowstone River. The path weaves through lush groves of cottonwood, box elder, willows, and Russian olive trees, passing small sandy beaches. The return route on the Dull Knife Trail meanders through grassland meadows with scattered cottonwoods.

Driving directions: From Main Street in Billings Heights, turn east on Hilltop Road. Drive 0.3 miles to Bench Boulevard and turn right. Continue 0.4 miles to Two Moon Park Road and turn left. Drive 0.4 miles, descending on a gravel road to the banks of the Yellowstone River and the trailhead parking lot.

Hiking directions: From the trailhead kiosk, at the north end of the parking lot, are two trails. The Weeping Wall Trail (Hike 116) bears left. Walk straight ahead on the Rocke Jeune Trail to the banks of the Yellowstone River. Head downstream to a junction. Begin the loop on the right fork, staying close to the river. Meander through meadows, groves of cottonwood, Russian olive trees, and beaver-chewed tree stumps. At 0.8 miles, the trail ends at The Point, where the eroding Weeping Wall cliffs meet the river. To the left, The Weeping Wall Trail follows a stream along the base of the cliffs (Hike 116). For this hike return along the same route 40 yards to a Y-fork. Take the Dull Knife Trail to the right. Weave through grassland meadows dotted with cottonwoods to a trail split. The left branch returns to the riverfront path. Stay on the Dull Knife Trail to the right, completing the loop at the Rocke Jeune Trail. ▪

116. Weeping Wall—Mallard Loop
TWO MOON PARK NATURAL AREA
BILLINGS

Hiking distance: 1.8-mile loop
Hiking time: 50 minutes
Elevation gain: Level
Maps: U.S.G.S. Billings East
       Two Moon Park Trail Map

Summary of hike: The Weeping Wall is an 80-foot vertical sandstone wall towering above the trail system in secluded Two

Moon Park. Groundwater drains year-round from the Heights above the rock wall and seeps through the sedimentary cliffs, feeding trees, bushes, and lush green moss. The water collects into a stream at the base of the wall and flows into the Yellowstone River. This hike weaves through open grassy meadows, dense wetland thickets, footbridges over clear-water streams, and canopied tunnels of trees en route to the weeping riverfront wall. The return on the Mallard Loop strolls across gently rolling meadows dotted with cottonwoods.

Driving directions: From Main Street in Billings Heights, turn east on Hilltop Road. Drive 0.3 miles to Bench Boulevard and turn right. Continue 0.4 miles to Two Moon Park Road and turn left. Drive 0.4 miles, descending on a gravel road to the banks of the Yellowstone River and trailhead parking lot.

Hiking directions: From the trailhead kiosk, at the north end of the parking lot, are two trails. The Rocke Jeune Trail (Hike 115) heads east (straight ahead) to the Yellowstone River. Bear left and cross a wood bridge on the Weeping Wall Trail. Stroll through the riparian woodland. Weave through the wetlands with towering cottonwoods, crossing a series of five bridges over small drainages. At 0.4 miles, walk through a grassy meadow and descend through more wetlands and small streams. Pass the junction with the Mallard Loop Trail on the right, our return route. Continue north along the west edge of the meadow towards the 80-foot Weeping Wall cliffs. Enter a shady canopy at a Y-fork with the Fox Trot Trail. Curve left and follow the south edge of the stream along the base of the cliffs. The trail ends at The Point, where the stream and eroding cliffs meet the Yellowstone River. The Rocke Jeune Trail follows the river upstream to the trailhead (Hike 115).

This hike returns along the same route to the Y-fork with the Mallard Loop Trail. Veer left on the Mallard Loop Trail, and head through the gently rolling meadow with scattered cottonwoods. The trail merges with the Dull Knife Trail, then again with the Rocke Jeune Trail. Continue south, back to the trailhead. ▪

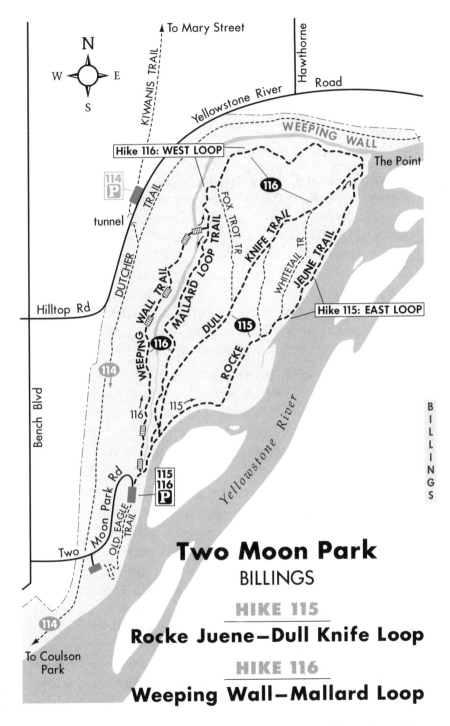

Two Moon Park
BILLINGS

Rocke Juene–Dull Knife Loop

Weeping Wall–Mallard Loop

117. Lake Elmo State Park
BILLINGS

Hiking distance: 1.3-mile loop
Hiking time: 40 minutes
Elevation gain: Level
Maps: U.S.G.S. Billings East
      Lake Elmo State Park map

Summary of hike: Billings Heights is a geological benchland that rises above the Yellowstone River Valley. Lake Elmo State Park, located at the north end of Billings Heights, encompasses 123 acres. The centerpiece of the park is the beautiful 64-acre manmade lake built in 1906. Water is diverted from the Yellowstone River west of Laurel and travels 30 miles through canals to the Heights, feeding the lake. The recreational park offers sandy beaches for swimming, picnicking, fishing, paddleboating, wind surfing, canoeing, and sailboating. An interpretive nature trail with lakeside benches circles the 1.3-mile shoreline.

Driving directions: From Main Street in Billings Heights, turn west on Pemberton Lane, located just south of Highway 87, where it heads off to Roundup. Drive 0.8 miles on Pemberton Lane to the Lake Elmo State Park entrance on the left. (Pemberton Lane becomes Rolling Hills Drive en route.) Turn left into the park. Turn right, just after the entrance station, and park in the lot on the north end of the lake.

Hiking directions: From the trailhead kiosk, head down the west side of the lake, passing a covered lakefront picnic area. The main trail weaves through the meadow dotted with cottonwoods, while a footpath follows the shoreline. Both routes rejoin at the shoreline less than a quarter mile ahead by an osprey interpretive sign. Just beyond the sign, the Nature Trail, a narrow footpath, meanders through the wetlands and rejoins the main trail. Curve around the south end of the lake to another trailhead by the regional headquarters of the Montana Department of Fish, Wildlife and Parks. Follow the lake by an eroded 8-foot sandstone ledge to Rogers Pier, a fishing pier. At the north end of the building, take the gravel path along the contours of the lake to Lake Elmo Drive. Follow the road 100 yards, and pick up the trail again by the kiosk on the left. Take the paved path along the northeast side of Lake Elmo, passing picnic grounds, parking areas, and a sandy beach. At the north end of the beach, a footpath follows the edge of the lake, completing the loop. ■

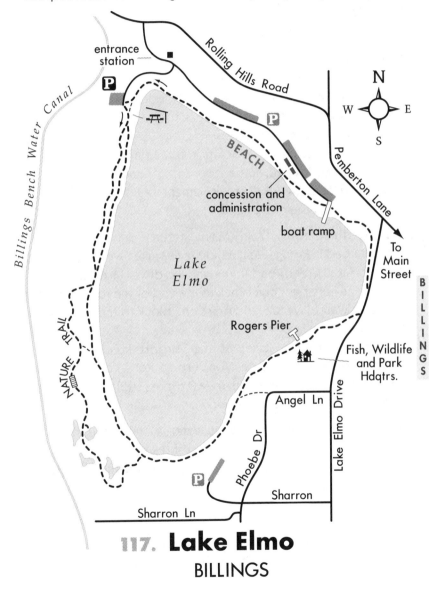

117. Lake Elmo
BILLINGS

118. Pow Wow Park
ALKALI CREEK NATURAL AREA
BILLINGS

Hiking distance: 1.6 miles round trip
Hiking time: 1 hour
Elevation gain: 60 feet
Maps: U.S.G.S. Billings East and Billings West

Summary of hike: The Alkali Creek Natural Area is a 54-acre open space and wetland known as Pow Wow Park. The city park sits in Alkali Creek Valley in the Heights, bordered by the eroding rims on the north and Alkali Creek to the south. The park has steep gorges, caves, natural springs, ponds with beaver dams, and swampy areas. Access points into the park are at the south end of Judicial Avenue, at the west end of Quiet Water Avenue, and at a trailhead by Alkali Creek Elementary School off of Alkali Creek Road. Dogs are allowed.

Driving directions: From Main Street (Highway 87) and Airport Road in Billings Heights, drive 0.2 miles west on Airport Road to Alkali Creek Road. Turn right and drive 0.6 miles to Black Pine Street. Turn right one block to the end of the road. Turn left on Quiet Water Avenue, and drive one block to the trailhead at the end of the road.

From North 27th Street at the Airport Road/Highway 3 junction, drive 2.7 miles east on Airport Road to Alkali Creek Road on the left. Turn left and drive 0.6 miles to Black Pine Street. Continue with the directions above.

Hiking directions: From Quiet Water Avenue: Take the posted trail 100 yards to a Y-fork. Both routes rejoin ahead, where the park bends to the north. For now, climb the hill on the right fork to the base of the eroding rims and huge sandstone boulders. Continue 100 yards to a trail split, where starlings can be spotted in the cracks along the cliffs. The left fork descends to the trailhead across Alkali Creek on the south side of Alkali Creek Elementary School. Stay right on the upper path to a third junction. Again stay right and cross a drainage at the foot of the cliffs. The path soon ends on a cul-de-sac at the end of Judicial Avenue. Return to the third (last) junction and descend to the right. Cross a feeder stream of Alkali Creek. Cross the meadow on the lower route, completing the loop. ■

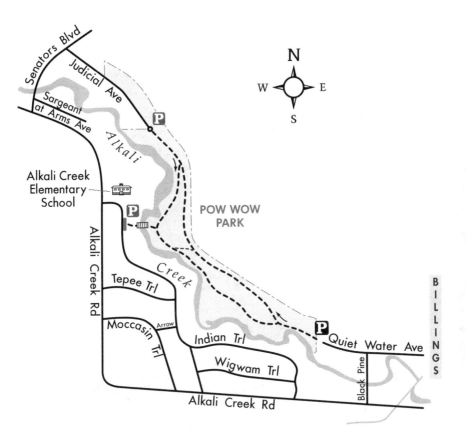

118.
Pow Wow Park
Alkali Creek Natural Area
BILLINGS

119. Swords Park

Black Otter Trail to Yellowstone Kelly's Grave and Boot Hill Cemetery

BILLINGS

Hiking distance: 6.5 miles round trip
Hiking time: 3.5 hours
Elevation gain: 300 feet
Maps: U.S.G.S. Billings West and Billings East

Summary of hike: Swords Park is a long, narrow undeveloped park perched atop the distinctive Rimrocks. The park is located north of downtown and adjacent to the airport. The Black Otter Trail, named for a Crow Indian chief buried atop the cliffs, snakes along the elevated sandstone skyline overlooking the Yellowstone Valley. Yellowstone Kelly's grave sits on Kelly Mountain within the park. He was a scout, guide, explorer, and trapper who was instrumental in the exploration of the

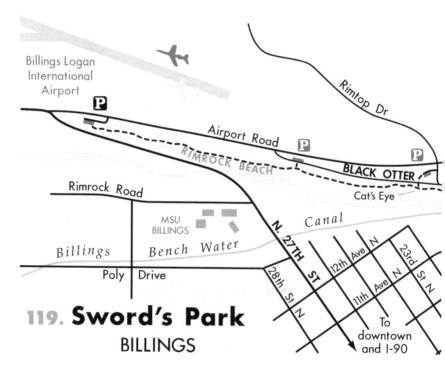

119. **Sword's Park**
BILLINGS

Yellowstone River in the 1870s and 1880s. Skeleton Cliff (also in Swords Park) is a tree-dotted knoll overlooking East Billings and Coulson Park. Across from Skeleton Cliff is a maze of dirt paths winding through the rolling hills above Airport Road and Alkali Creek Valley. Near the east end of the park is the historic Boot Hill Cemetery, dating back to the 1880s. This hike follows the edge of the rims, climbs Kelly Mountain and Skeleton Cliff, then descends to Boot Hill Cemetery.

Driving directions: Swords Park is located along Airport Road (Highway 318) between North 27th Street and Main Street. From the north end of North 27th Street, drive 0.2 miles to the parking lot on the right.

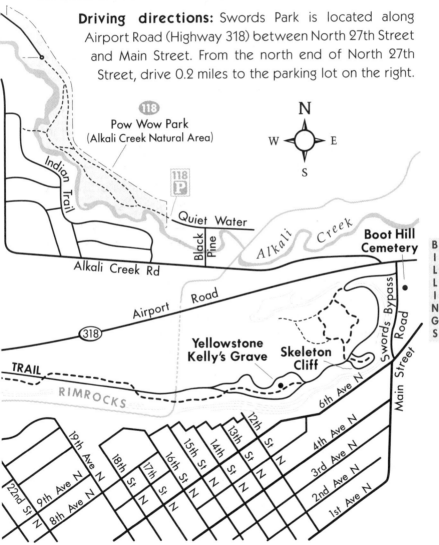

Turn right and park. A second parking lot is at the beginning of Black Otter Trail, located at 0.9 miles from 27th Street. Turn right onto Black Otter Trail, and park in the pullouts along the sides of the paved road.

From Main Street (Highway 87) in Billings Heights, drive 2.0 miles west on Airport Road to Black Otter Trail on the left, or 2.7 miles to the west parking lot.

Hiking directions: FROM WEST PARKING AREA: Head east on the serpentine multi-use path. Weave along the rims 300 feet above Montana State University, and walk parallel to North 27th Street as it descends. To the right, a slab rock path follows the edge of the rims. At one mile, just past an area known as Rimrock Beach, is the beginning of the Black Otter Trail, a road that follows the length of the park. All three parallel routes continue along the sandstone shelf and soon give way to rounded weather-sculpted mounds. At 1.4 miles, in an area called Cat's Eye, is a paved parking area off of Airport Road, directly across from Rimtop Drive. The trail soon crosses over to the north side of Black Otter Trail and crosses back again at 1.9 miles by the rising rock cliffs, just before the power poles. Far below at the base of the rims, the Billings Bench Water Canal curves north through a tunnel in the 3,400-foot cliffs.

At the beginning of the looping one-way road split, climb the dirt path on the left, a utility road up Kelly Mountain. Meander across the rolling hills and knolls between the two roads. Pass Yellowstone Kelly's Grave to where the one-way roads merge at 2.4 miles. Follow the road downhill 200 yards to another road split at the base of Skeleton Cliff. To the right, the road loops around the cliff. A short, steep path climbs to the knoll and overlook of the Yellowstone River, Sacrifice Cliff, Boot Hill Cemetery, and East Billings. To the north across Black Otter Trail is a network of trails that weave through the rolling hills to the lower trailhead on a horseshoe bend, just south of Airport Road. From the lower trailhead, follow Black Otter Trail to the intersection with Swords Bypass Road, just shy of Airport Road. Across the road to the right is Boot Hill Cemetery, west of Main Street. ▪

120. Zimmerman Trail from the East End
BILLINGS

Hiking distance: 2.8 miles round trip
Hiking time: 1.5 hours
Elevation gain: 100 feet
Maps: U.S.G.S. Billings West

Summary of hike: The Rimrocks, weather-sculpted sedimentary cliffs, are the signature landmark of Billings. From the dramatic 300-foot eroding cliffs are exceptional views across Billings and the Yellowstone Valley to the Beartooth Mountains. The Zimmerman Trail footpath follows the dramatic sandstone bluffs across the north end of the city along Highway 3, from North 27th Street to Zimmerman Trail Road. Hikers, bikers, climbers, and dog-walkers use the trail. This hike begins from the east end of the trail and follows the rock shelf through pine-studded bluffs, passing magnificent rock formations. (Hike 121 begins from the opposite/west end of the trail.)

Driving directions: From the north end of North 27th Street at the Airport Road/Highway 3 junction, drive 0.2 miles west on Highway 3 to the long parking area on the left.

Hiking directions: Numerous footpaths descend from the parking area atop the rim to the rock shelf trail. Bear right on the flat rock shelf and sand path. Head west through ponderosa pines, weather-sculpted rock formations, and endless vistas across Billings from 400 feet above the valley floor. At times a couple of parallel paths wind along the contours of the cliffs on different levels, high above Rocky Mountain College. At 1 mile, pass a brick pumping station above the trail, where a gravel access road leads up to Highway 3. At 1.3 miles, the path climbs up a sandstone formation. Weave along the rock shelf above a network of dirt paths. Curve left atop a vertical rock wall, skirting the perimeter of cliff-top homes. This is the turn-around spot.

The trail continues 1.6 miles along the edge of the cliffs to Zimmerman Trail Road. To hike farther—or for a one-way shuttle hike—continue with the next hike. ■

BILLINGS

121. Zimmerman Trail
from the West End at Zimmerman Park
BILLINGS

Hiking distance: 3.6 miles round trip
Hiking time: 1.5 hours
Elevation gain: 50 feet
Maps: U.S.G.S. Billings West

Summary of hike: Billings lies in a valley lined by dramatic sandstone formations known as the Rimrocks. They were formed from thick deposits of sand that accumulated as barrier islands along the coast of an ancient inland sea. The landmark frames the north and east sides of the city. The Zimmerman Trail skirts the edge of the eroding sedimentary bluffs along the north side of Billings. Throughout the hike are amazing views of the city, river valley, and surrounding mountain ranges. This hike begins from the west end of the Zimmerman Trail. The footpath follows the weather-sculpted cliffs east through scattered pine groves. (Hike 120 begins from the opposite/east end of the trail.)

Driving directions: The Zimmerman Trail footpath follows the rims parallel to Highway 3, between North 27th Street and

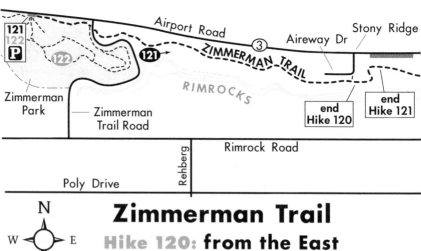

Zimmerman Trail Road. From the north end of North 27th Street at the Airport Road/Highway 3 junction, drive 3.4 miles west on Highway 3 to the posted Zimmerman Park parking area on the left (south) side of the road. It is located a quarter mile west of Zimmerman Trail Road.

Hiking directions: Take the trail east along Highway 3 to Zimmerman Trail Road. Walk down Zimmerman Trail Road 30 yards to the footpath on the east (left) side of the road. Descend to the floor of the forested draw. Follow the draw, passing sandstone boulders to the flat, slick-rock shelf beneath the caves in the sedimentary cliffs. Traverse the cliffs 400 feet above the city. Weave along the contours of the eroding rock wall below the rim. Pass through 100 yards of private land on an easement. Skirt the outside edge of homes, staying on the cliff's edge. Pass a connector path leading to Aireway Drive at Stony Ridge Road. After the last home, make a sweeping S-curve to a sandstone formation and the west end of a long parking area on Highway 3. A network of dirt paths lie below the formation. This is the turn-around spot.

The trail continues another 1.6 miles along the edge of the cliffs to North 27th Street. To hike farther—or for a one-way shuttle hike—continue with Hike 120. ▪

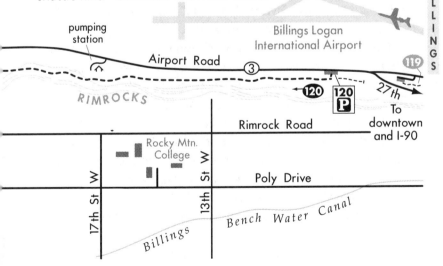

122. Zimmerman (Wilshire) Park
BILLINGS

Hiking distance: 1—4 miles round trip
Hiking time: 30 minutes—2 hours
Elevation gain: 100 feet
Maps: U.S.G.S. Billings West

Summary of hike: Zimmerman Park (also known as Wilshire Park) is a natural area that sits atop the rims just west of Zimmerman Trail Road and Highway 3. Billings service clubs purchased the parkland from the Zimmermans in 1938. It is a popular spot for hiking, mountain biking, jogging, dog walking, and rock climbing. The trails vary from easy cliff-side trails to steep slickrock slopes. The sweeping vistas across Yellowstone Valley take in five mountain ranges—the Bighorns, Pryors, Beartooths, Crazies, and the Snowies.

Driving directions: The Zimmerman Park entrance is on the south side of Highway 3, a quarter mile west of Zimmerman Trail Road. From the north end of North 27th Street at the Airport Road/Highway 3 junction, drive 3.4 miles west on Highway 3 to the posted Zimmerman Park on the left.

Hiking directions: Five trails fan out from the trailhead. The right trail follows the upper edge of the mesa 0.3 miles to the west, crossing rolling hills to the park boundary. The middle three trails head southward to the rims. For a loop, take the left fork and head east across the flat, open meadow for 0.2 miles to Zimmerman Trail Road. Curve to the right, parallel to Zimmerman Trail Road, which quickly descends from the rims. Just beyond a fenceline, veer left on a footpath through pine groves. Stay atop the plateau, following the edge of the sandstone cliffs above Zimmerman Canyon. Side paths on the left lead to additional parallel trails, traversing the cliffs at varying elevation levels. Curve around to the south-facing cliffs, with vistas across Yellowstone Valley to the Pryor and Beartooth Mountains. A mosaic of inter-connecting paths weave across the rimtop plateau and along the contours of the cliffs. The various cliff-edge trails follow flat, rock shelves and sandy paths, passing huge sandstone boulders. Explore along your own route. All of the trails connect back to the trailhead. ▪

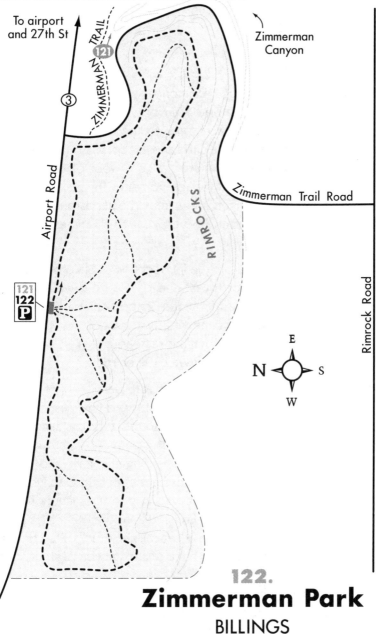

To airport
and 27th St

Zimmerman
Canyon

ZIMMERMAN TRAIL

121

3

Airport Road

RIMROCKS

Zimmerman Trail Road

Rimrock Road

121
122
P

E

N ◆ S

W

122.
Zimmerman Park
BILLINGS

123. Phipps Diamond X Ranch Park
BILLINGS

Hiking distance: 3 miles round trip
Hiking time: 1.5 hours
Elevation gain: 450 feet
Maps: U.S.G.S. Rimrock

Summary of hike: Phipps Diamond X Ranch Park sits in an undeveloped section of Echo Canyon west of Billings. Curtis Phipps donated the 355-acre park to the city of Billings. The park has dramatic sandstone cliffs and exceptional views across the Yellowstone Valley from atop a 3,800-foot plateau. It is a popular hiking, biking, and frisbee golf site. The trail begins at the mouth of Echo Canyon and climbs the sandstone cliffs to the plateau. Trails meander atop the rims to an endless display of vistas.

Driving directions: From the intersection of Shiloh Road and Rimrock Road on the northwest end of Billings, drive 4.3 miles west on Rimrock Road to the posted Phipps Park parking lot on the left. It is located past the Yellowstone Country Club, immediately after crossing under the railroad overpass. (Rimrock Road becomes Molt Road/Highway 302 en route.)

Hiking directions: Take the wide path past the metal gate, parallel to the railroad tracks. Head toward the east side of crescent-shaped Echo Canyon. Near the eroding sandstone cliffs, a path veers off to the left. This path curves around the base of the 3,810-foot formation along the east and south slopes. Stay on the main trail into the mouth of the canyon. At the back end of the north-facing bowl is another junction. The left fork traverses the lower cliffs and joins the other side path on the east flank, 40 feet above the railroad tracks. Stay on the main path, bending along the back of the canyon past massive boulders, overhanging rocks, and cave-pocked cliffs. Cross the rolling grassland, and ascend the cliffs on the west side of the bowl to the 3,800-foot plateau and a trail fork. The right fork is the return route for the west loop.

For now, stay to the left, passing a second junction 60 yards ahead. Again stay left, curving around the top of Echo Canyon and overlooking Yellowstone Valley, Billings, the Pryors, and the Beartooth Mountains. Cross the exposed ridge to a Y-fork. Begin the loop on the left path, hiking clockwise. On the northeast end of the mesa are several parallel paths on various levels. A few steep paths descend the cliffs back to the canyon floor. The footpaths curve around the east edge of the cliffs and follow the rim, completing the loop. Return to the second junction and bear left. Head west on the old road, and cross the pine-dotted meadow one mile to the fenced boundary. Bend sharply right and follow the fenced property line on a footpath, high above a rifle range. Follow the contours of the west rim, passing numerous faint paths that cross the plateau. Pass the head of a few canyons, completing the loop on the main trail. Return into Echo Canyon and the trailhead on the left. ■

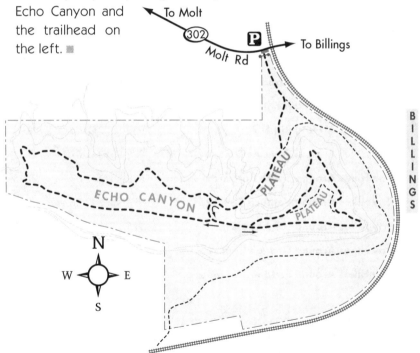

B
I
L
L
I
N
G
S

123. **Phipps Diamond X Ranch**
BILLINGS

DAY HIKE BOOKS

These books may be purchased at your local bookstore or outdoor shop. Or, order them directly from the distributor:

National Book Network

800-462-6420

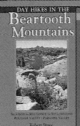

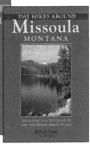

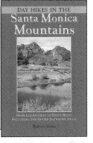

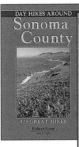

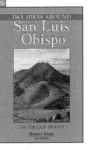

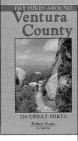
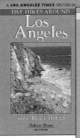

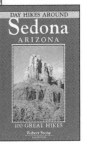

Day Hikes In Yellowstone National Park

Yellowstone National Park is a magnificent area with beautiful, dramatic scenery and incredible hydrothermal features. Within its 2.2-millions acres lies some of the earth's greatest natural treasures.

Day Hikes In Yellowstone National Park includes a thorough cross-section of 82 hikes throughout the park. Now in its fourth edition, the guide includes all of the park's most popular hikes as well as a wide assortment of secluded backcountry trails. Highlights include thundering waterfalls, unusual thermal features, expansive meadows, alpine lakes, the Grand Canyon of the Yellowstone, geysers, hot springs, and 360-degree vistas of the park.

184 pages • 82 hikes • 4th Edition 2005 • ISBN 978-1-57342-048-8

Day Hikes Around Bozeman, Montana

Bozeman, Montana is an amiable mountain community steeped in history and surrounded by stunning landscape. The city lies between the Gallatin and Yellowstone River valleys amidst several mountain ranges that run through the Continental Divide. The fantastic scenery combined with national forests, wilderness areas, and an outdoor-oriented community make the hiking in this area superb.

Day Hikes Around Bozeman, Montana has won awards from both the Northwest Outdoor Writers Association and the Rocky Mountain Outdoor Writers and Photographers. This guide book includes 110 of the best day hikes in a straight-forward, hassle-free guide aimed to get you on the trails. *Outside Bozeman Magazine* affirms, "This is a must-have book. Period."

320 pages • 110 hikes • 4th Edition 2011 • ISBN 978-1-57342-063-1

INDEX

ADRIENNE METTER

About the Author

Since 1991, Robert Stone has been writer, photographer, and publisher of Day Hike Books. He is a Los Angeles Times Best Selling Author and an award-winning journalist of Rocky Mountain Outdoor Writers and Photographers, the Outdoor Writers Association of California, the Northwest Outdoor Writers Association, the Outdoor Writers Association of America, and the Bay Area Travel Writers.

Robert has hiked every trail in the Day Hike Book series. With 20 hiking guides in the series, many in their fourth and fifth editions, he has hiked thousands of miles of trails throughout the western United States. When Robert is not hiking, he researches, writes, and maps the hikes before returning to the trails. He spends summers in the Rocky Mountains of Montana and winters on the California Central Coast.